"Lynne Epstein has written a searing account of a year long Internet relationship which was emotionally devastating. In her search for love, she stumbles upon a man who, in the world of cyberspace, appears charming but turns out to be a deceiver. What a wonderful wake up call to all those who seek love via the Internet. For as many successes, there *are* Internet nightmares. Here is one such nightmare."

Tony Villecco
Singer/Performer/Artist
www.TonyVillecco.com
Author *Silent Stars Speak*
Performed at Don't Tell Momma and Rose's Turn, New York City

/ Subtle Deception

A woman's struggle to let go of an Internet relationship

LYNNE C. EPSTEIN

Bloomington, IN   Milton Keynes, UK
authorHOUSE

To Brandi, Thank you for coming. Enjoy! Lynne C Epstein

AuthorHouse™
1663 Liberty Drive, Suite 200
Bloomington, IN 47403
www.authorhouse.com
Phone: 1-800-839-8640

AuthorHouse™ UK Ltd.
500 Avebury Boulevard
Central Milton Keynes, MK9 2BE
www.authorhouse.co.uk
Phone: 08001974150

©2007 Lynne C. Epstein. All rights reserved.

No part of this book may be reproduced, stored in a retrieval system, or transmitted by any means without the written permission of the author.

First published by AuthorHouse 4/30/2007

ISBN: 978-1-4259-7959-1 (e)
ISBN: 978-1-4259-7958-4 (sc)

Library of Congress Control Number: 2006910505

Printed in the United States of America
Bloomington, Indiana

This book is printed on acid-free paper.

Even though this is a true story, the name "Lance" is fictitious, as are all characters connected to him, either friends or family.

Most of the characters connected to me are real names, and I have obtained permission to use them.

Note to reader: Lance's e-mails are exactly as he wrote them. I did not change the grammar, capitalizations or punctuation.

Lynne C. Epstein

ACKNOWLEDGEMENTS

There is no way a book can be written without the encouragement, suggestions, and insight of others. With pleasure, I express my gratitude to the following people:

I thank Mr. William F. Mitchell, Jr., author of "The More You Know; Getting the Evidence and Support You Need to Investigate a Troubled Relationship" and *Adultery: Facing Its Reality (Mitchell Reports Investigations)* for taking time to critique the first thirty chapters of my book. His suggestions and insight were very helpful.

I also thank my close friend, Tony Villecco, author of "Silent Stars Speak" for not only critiquing my work, but for advising and supporting me through my one-year journey with Lance.

Others who have taken time to read, reread and edit my work are Naomi VanHart, Marjorie Mason, Pat Mithelavage, and Nancy Baldwin. To them, I will be forever grateful.

My sister, Lea Tartanian, was an instrumental force in this project, always suggesting, encouraging, and finding time to read over my work and offer constructive criticism and helpful feedback.

I also thank my friend, Brenda Rhodes, for spending an entire weekend reviewing my final manuscript for grammatical and spelling errors.

Lastly, I want to thank my husband, Larry Epstein, for his support and encouragement and my stepson, Nolan Epstein, for helping me with the technical part of this project.

Without all of you, this book would not have been written.

DEDICATION

I dedicate this book to my sister, Lea, and her husband, Dave, for being there for me through thick and thin.

Without you, I would have given up long ago.

CONTENTS

Introduction		xiii
Preface		xv
Chapter 1	Love at AOL	1
Chapter 2	Getting to Know Lance Online and on the Telephone	4
Chapter 3	My History	7
Chapter 4	Flag Number One; The Solomon Letter	10
Chapter 5	Putting my Rose-Colored Glasses Back On	14
Chapter 6	The Relationship Progresses	18
Chapter 7	Meeting Lance in Person	21
Chapter 8	The First Cool-down	25
Chapter 9	Blow Up on New Year's Eve	31
Chapter 10	Trying to Patch Things Up	36
Chapter 11	Lance's Wife	42
Chapter 12	The Emotional Rollercoaster Continues	44
Chapter 13	January 20 in New York City	47
Chapter 14	Ending the Relationship	50
Chapter 15	Blame-shift	55
Chapter 16	Asking for Forgiveness	59
Chapter 17	Communicating and Understanding Each Other	61
Chapter 18	Two Wonderful Invitations	65
Chapter 19	Deep Conversations	68
Chapter 20	Lance's Ministry at the Nursing Home	72
Chapter 21	Second Meeting in New York City	74
Chapter 22	The Relationship Blossoms	77
Chapter 23	Seeing Lance in New Jersey	81
Chapter 24	"In Love"	86

Chapter 25	Wife and Church Issues	89
Chapter 26	Preparing for the Wedding in Roslyn	94
Chapter 27	The Condolence Call in Long Island	98
Chapter 28	The Wedding in Roslyn, New York	104
Chapter 29	Back to Reality	111
Chapter 30	Getting the Relationship Back on Track	117
Chapter 31	Taking the Relationship to the Highest Level	124
Chapter 32	Overnight Change	129
Chapter 33	Flip-flop of Emotions	134
Chapter 34	Easter Sunday	139
Chapter 35	The Bar Mitzvah	143
Chapter 36	Painful Departure	150
Chapter 37	Torturous Reflections	153
Chapter 38	Emotional Denial	156
Chapter 39	The Mixed Signals Continue	158
Chapter 40	Getting My Hopes Up Again	162
Chapter 41	Lance's Visit to New York State	166
Chapter 42	A Secret Revealed	172
Chapter 43	Vacation Plans	178
Chapter 44	Lance's Problems on the Job	182
Chapter 45	Vacation in Lancaster with Lance	184
Chapter 46	Dark Zone	191
Chapter 47	Lance Gets Fired	196
Chapter 48	Trip to Cooperstown	198
Chapter 49	Nightmare Visit in New Jersey	204
Chapter 50	September 11, 2001	210
Chapter 51	Empty Conversations	218
Chapter 52	The Breakup	223
Chapter 53	Cruel Kindness	229
Chapter 54	Struggling to Let Go	236
Chapter 55	Empowerment and Enlightenment	243
Epilogue		251

INTRODUCTION

    I wrote this book to let other women know how vulnerable we can be when we truly love someone. Precious days, sometimes years, of our lives are wasted if we linger and allow a relationship to drag on when we sense, in our hearts, there is no longer any substance or depth to it.

    We hang on. We hope something will change, even when the sparks are no longer there on his end. We long to rekindle what once was, but never again will be.

    If only one person manifests the courage to end a destructive, fruitless relationship as a result of reading this book, the time, energy, and passion with which I have written will have been worth it.

PREFACE

The table is set with exquisite china and silverware atop a white-linen tablecloth, with matching napkins. A centerpiece of yellow, red, and pink carnations, with two lit candles on either side, creates a wonderfully romantic atmosphere.

The man of my dreams is sipping white zinfandel out of a frosted glass. He savors every bite of the meal I have lovingly prepared for him: hot Italian bread, linguine with homemade marinara sauce, and a crisp, garden salad with balsamic vinaigrette dressing. A fresh-baked apple pie prepared from scratch and a fresh cup of coffee cap off this meal.

But where am I in this scenario?

I am offering him a feast, and he is giving me crumbs in return.

This describes my relationship with Lance.

This book is not about Lance. It is about me. As I take the reader on my year-long journey with Lance, he or she will wonder why I stayed in the relationship. Today I see clearly what I did not want to see when I was dating this man.

Here is my story…

CHAPTER 1

Love at AOL

Thursday, August 17, 2000

His face is handsome. His hair is dark brown and wavy. His ad reads, "Honesty Prevails." I have browsed hundreds of personal ads, yet I cannot take my eyes off this man's photo.

I like his statement regarding honesty. He says, "Sometimes being honest doesn't get you what you want. But when you learn the value of honesty, it really doesn't matter if you don't get what you want, because you end up with something better."

This man's entire identity is honesty. The more I read, the more interested I become. This man is so much like me!

He describes himself as "spiritual, but not religious." I am not religious but have a strong faith in God.

He works out five days a week in the gym to stay physically fit. I am an aerobics instructor and very much into fitness.

He does not smoke, he drinks occasionally, and has a stable job. He loves fine dining, the movies, and cats. Being a cat-lover seals the deal for me. I have two cats who are "family" to me. I also love fine dining and the movies.

He believes in being deeply in love and has a tremendous desire to experience that to the fullest with "one special woman." When he finds that special woman, he will be "totally devoted and committed."

He will not string anyone on, as he believes it is extremely cruel and unfair. He writes:

I am genuine and straightforward (no BS). I am also sensitive, passionate, kind, thoughtful, caring, and compassionate."

This man has been told he has "special gifts of wisdom and understanding human beings." He loves to talk and teach, he is a good listener, and he loves to learn about things that have meaning in life.

Suddenly my mind snaps back to reality. What am I thinking? I am not going to answer a personal ad.

Before logging off, I notice he lives near Princeton, New Jersey. I live in upstate New York, about three and a half hours away.

Two weeks later, I am spending the day in Atlantic City with my close friend, Tony. I cannot stop thinking about this nice-looking man. I need a photo to send to him. I ask Tony to take my picture.

Saturday, September 30, 2000

My photo looks great! I am wearing a multicolored jacket and sunglasses. My blonde, shoulder-length hair is blowing in the breeze, with the boardwalk in the background. I have decided to answer this handsome man's ad!

I write a short note to his screen name, since I do not know his actual name:

> *Hi there. I saw your ad while I was browsing the personals on Love on AOL. I have never responded to a personal ad before, but I liked what you had to say. You seem like a person with character. It is very rare these days to find someone like you.*
>
> *I am from New York State. I am not sure if I am looking for a serious relationship, but I would like to correspond with you. I teach aerobics, and I love cats. I travel to New Jersey quite often. I hope to hear back from you. Sincerely, Lynne*

I attach my photo to the e-mail. Hesitating for a moment, I hit the "send" button. I am nervous. I have never done anything like this before.

Later that evening, I check my e-mail. He has answered it!

His name is Lance. He loves my photo. He writes:

> *Hello Lynne,*
> *What are you teasing me? For one thing you are gorgeous, exactly the type of woman that appeals to me physically, (slim, blonde, natu-*

rally beautiful, great smile, teeth and nails), and for another you seem to value the same things I do. Then you tell me you are from New York State and are not sure if you are looking for a serious relationship?

I am so flattered such an attractive young looking woman with a seemingly great head on her shoulders would contact me thinking I am special! I have always thought and hoped I was, but few women have ever seen it. Only why do you have to live so far away?

He wants to meet me.

When things like this happen, I believe they happen for a reason and we must seize the moment or it could slip away so I come back to you in hopes that this will NOT slip away and we can at least meet. Until then, I must say, you have made my day! Lance

My heart is pounding! I have not been interested in anyone since my divorce in January, 1999. Lance appears to be the man of my dreams! I cannot believe I met him through a personal ad!

Little do I know I have begun a journey of subtle deception that will continue for a year.

CHAPTER 2

Getting to Know Lance Online and on the Telephone

Sunday, October 1, 2000

I am so excited Lance has written to me! I answer his letter the next day.

Wow, what a nice surprise to hear from you. Thank you for all the complimentary things you said to me.

I tell him more about myself. I love God and the Bible, but I am not religious. I am divorced and not seeing anyone. I love blonde jokes and smiley faces. I am a college graduate and have been recently certified as an aerobics instructor.

I end my letter by telling him if he rents the movie, *City of Angels* he will learn more about me. I add an Internet "smiley," which is a colon and a right parenthesis. This becomes a trademark in all of our future correspondence.

Tuesday, October 3, 2000

It has been over forty-eight hours and no response from Lance. Why am I concerned about hearing from a man I did not know existed a week ago? I hope to hear back from him soon. I tell myself to get a grip.

Lance e-mails me this afternoon. He is in Philadelphia at an employees meeting and was able to access a computer and check his e-mail.

He finds me attractive and interesting. He would like to get to know me better. He also loves smiley faces and knows some blonde jokes. He gives me his telephone number at work and asks me to call him. He wants to hear my voice.

He is going to rent the movie *City of Angels*. He wants to know all about me. He signs the letter, "Truly, Lance," and adds the Internet smiley.

Thursday, October 5, 2000

I call Lance at work as he requested. I love his voice. Our conversation is brief, and he e-mails me later telling me he enjoyed talking with me.

Lance and I continue e-mailing each other for the next few days. It is exciting to check my e-mails and see titles like "Mysterious Lynne," "Amazing Lynne," and "Fantastic Sparkling Lynne." He has rented *City of Angels* and will watch it tonight.

I tell him to let me know what line in the movie jumps out at him. I am thrilled he is renting the film to find out more about me. I hope he will notice the line where Seth tells Maggie that one kiss from her is worth more than an eternity of never having experienced it.

Lance e-mails me after watching the movie. He notices the exact same line in the movie as I did. Is this a sign? My heart is racing. Seeing the movie has enhanced his desire to know more about me.

As Lance and I continue our communication he informs me he is still living with his wife. He will be moving out in another week. She wants him to leave. Apparently I had overlooked his ad, which stated he was "separated."

He has been married seventeen years. He loves his wife, but is not "in love" with her. His love for her is similar to the love of a sister or a friend.

I tell myself his being married does not matter, since I am not looking for a serious relationship. My mind is clouded, and I am not being honest with myself. The truth is, I long to be with someone special.

Of all the contacts he has made in the past two months, I exceed them all in what he thinks he would want in a woman whom he would consider having a serious long term relationship with.

I know he has a personal ad on AOL and is probably corresponding with several women. I feel a little jealous, but I remind myself he is *honest* and likes me the best.

We make plans to meet in New York City on November 11. I will take a bus from Binghamton, NY, and he will take a train from Newark, New Jersey.

Lynne C. Epstein

He writes:

> *All I want to do is spend ONE day with you, to look into your eyes and see your smile and to touch and kiss your hand and hug you. I want to have a holy fun time with you, and just see what might be.*
>
> *Lynne, there is indeed a soulish and physical and spiritual connection here between you and me that you MUST be aware of, because I certainly am, and I do not want to make light of it, but instead, face it head on, that's all. I want a clearer vision of what God has in mind for our future and I believe meeting you in person will make that vision clearer.*

For the first time in years, I feel like a teenager. Am I in love?

CHAPTER 3

My History

My mother, Ruythe, and my dad, Oscar, are alcoholics. They love my sister, Lea, and myself, but are unable to care for us. Oscar's parents adopt us on our birthday at age four.

Oscar and Ruythe divorce and are living separately in New York City. Lea and I live in upstate New York with our adoptive grandparents, Florence and Jay. My dad, Oscar, visits us two or three times a year. I love Oscar. He is tall and handsome, with reddish hair. I am proud to have him as my dad.

I am twelve years old. Oscar comes for a weekend visit. It is the month of June.

On Saturday morning, I barge into the bathroom without knocking on the door. Oscar is using the toilet. He is embarrassed, mortified, and furious! He screams at me, "You brat! Don't you know enough to knock?" He then yells at Florence, "These girls are spoiled rotten and inconsiderate brats!"

Cowering and ashamed, I feel awful. Oscar hates me and is mad at me! "I'm sorry Oscar," I gulp. He doesn't answer. He goes back to New York City the next day, leaving me with a feeling of guilt and loneliness that will follow me for several years in my relationships with men.

Two weeks later, Oscar dies suddenly at age thirty-five. I am a child left with the memory of disapproval, rejection, abandonment, and unforgiveness from a man I loved and cherished. This begins a pattern of believing I am unworthy of a man's love and affection.

Seven years later, I graduate from the State University of New York, at Delhi, and begin working at IBM in White Plains, New York. A coworker introduces me to her brother. A year later, he becomes my first husband. I marry him, knowing I have had deeper feelings for other men, but I want to be married and have a family.

I quit IBM and become a wife, homemaker, mother, and churchgoer. I love the family life and living in the country on a farm. I ignore the fact my husband is an alcoholic.

All of this falls apart when I discover he has fallen in love with another woman. After thirteen years of marriage, he wants a divorce.

I move out of the house. A few months later, my children move in with their dad. They miss their school and their friends. They are sad, bitter, and heartbroken. This is a terrible time for them and for me.

I feel guilty for the breakup of my marriage. I also have to return to work. I brush up on my secretarial skills and take a civil service test. A few weeks later, I am hired as secretary to the principal at a nearby school.

Unfortunately, my pattern is to have a man. This has always been my priority.

A year later, a woman from my church introduces me to her son. He is also an alcoholic. She hopes I can help him understand the Bible. This man becomes my second husband. His needs come first, not mine. They are beer, cigarettes, a wife, lover, friend, and confidant. This man truly loves me, but his relationship with alcohol is his priority. I put one hundred percent into this marriage. I will never leave him. I cling to a chemical in a body for companionship, and hope for eight years he will get better. His two attempts at a rehab fail, and he takes his own life in April of 1993. He is the only man I have truly loved.

Grief-stricken and alone, I am charmed by a man at a singles dance nine months later. I marry him within six months. He is also a drinker. One week after taking my marriage vows, I realize that I have made *another* mistake. This man is not compatible with me at all! I had ignored the flags during our short courtship. He is verbally abusive and irresponsible. The only thing we have in common is an orgasm. Sex becomes my drug to drown out my sorrows. I want to be touched and loved. All we do is have sex and argue. Then we argue and have sex. This marriage is my worst nightmare.

We live together nine months and he walks out on me. I again feel rejected. However, this time I'm relieved. It takes me four years to legally end this destructive relationship.

During this four-year period I am transferred to another facility at my employment, and I meet Tony. He is my supervisor, and he becomes a wonderful friend and stabilizing force in my life. Tony is gay, and very much out of the closet. We have a *Will and Grace* friendship and are always supportive of one another.

I develop my creativity by taking theatre courses, dance classes, and becoming a certified aerobics instructor. I become content with who I am. My life is full. However, a part of me has a desire for a happy, stable relationship with the right man. I do not want to make another mistake.

I am impressed that Lance does not smoke, as did all three of my husbands, and according to him, he is not a drinker. He likes a glass of wine at dinner, like me. My last two husbands made less money than me, and I was the main breadwinner. Lance has a stable job and a good income. He is the first man I have met whose earning power is greater than mine.

I have not learned to maintain the proper balance of communication in order to have a healthy relationship. I will discover I try too hard to please my man. Also, I never want to offend him.

I do not know the difference between assertiveness and aggressiveness. I am going to make Lance the happiest man on earth. As usual, his needs matter more than mine. This is my pattern, and I am not yet aware of it.

CHAPTER 4

Flag Number One: The Solomon Letter

Sunday, October 15, 2000

Lance and I have been e-mailing each other for two weeks. Today he writes:

> I feel a real closeness with you in a very short period of time, and I am glad, because you bring a healthy approach to life with your spirituality and positive attitude and your great sense of humor. But I want a clearer vision of what God has in mind for our future and I believe meeting you in person will make that vision clearer.

Lance has said several times he is anxious to meet me. I look forward to meeting him in New York City on November 11.

Friday, October 20, 2000

I have not heard from Lance for three days. This is strange, since we have been e-mailing each other two or three times a day since the first week of October.

Checking from work, I am happy to finally see an e-mail from him. The title is "Who Am I and Who Will I become?"

It is a two-page narrative written in essay form. This puzzles me.

He writes:

> *I am Lance [last name], uniquely created by God. There is no one like me that was or is or will ever be born or created again. I and Jesus are one, yet we are still totally separate beings.*

Lance and I have discussed our spiritual beliefs. Why is he telling me this now?

He goes on to say there are two men in the Bible he bears certain characteristics of: David the Psalmist; and David's son, Solomon.

He describes David and compares himself to him:

> *God has blessed me abundantly by bestowing upon me the gift of a psalmist. I, like David am a worship leader, music minister and have been anointed to usher in the presence of God through my singing, my guitar playing and with the music He has given me.*

Why is Lance writing this? Is he bragging?

He then compares himself to Solomon, the other Bible character:

> *God has blessed me abundantly by bestowing upon me the gifts of wisdom, insight and teaching but unfortunately there are also certain characteristics in Solomon which are NOT Godly. Solomon had many wives and mistresses, VERY many.*

Lance then states he realizes he could be the same as Solomon by "having multiples." He continues:

> *It is not hard for me to see the beauty in many different women, and to experience with each of them the great things they have to offer a man. But the problem is, that in doing so, I will end up like Solomon…*

He concludes:

> *I can choose now, to play around some more and having lots of fun by sharing my love and wisdom with many women. But in doing so, I will be doing the most unwise thing to myself and probably also to the women, and the most unloving thing to God.*

Lance then poses the question:

> *So what will I choose and what will I become?*
> *I will make the CHOICE to dedicate myself to one special woman, and one woman only. In doing that, I will have peace and fulfillment myself, and I will bring peace and fulfillment to one very special woman. By doing that, I will be choosing God.*

Now I understand! Lance is writing to inform me he has chosen me to be that "one special woman!" He has chosen me above all other women with whom he has been corresponding! Why else would he send me this long narrative?

I then read the last paragraph:

> *My dear friend Lynne, I have found that woman I want to pursue. She lives 15 minutes away from me. She is an accountant like me, and like you, saw my ad and pursued me. She is very mellow and has no real baggage. I can't say enough great things about her except we met once and have talked quite a bit and until I know where I stand with her, I am not going to meet any other woman,* **which includes you.** *[bold is author's]. I want to continue, however, as we have in our e-mail communication with possibly a phone call here or there. But rather than complicate matters or throw temptation into my face, I want to hold off meeting you in person. I'll keep you posted. Lance* [smiley added]

Lance adds the Internet smiley after his name. I cannot believe it.

I am stunned and furious! My heart is pounding. Who does this man think he is? I feel betrayed, hurt, and stupid! How could I have been so blind?

I meet Tony for a break. He notices I am upset.

I tell him about Lance and show him the letter. Tony laughs out loud after reading the last paragraph. He thinks the letter is ridiculous, and he tells me to forget it and to forget Lance! This man is not worth my time or emotional energy.

I am surprised at how upset I am over a man I have never met.

Tony is right. I will not respond to Lance's e-mail. I have learned a hard lesson.

Subtle Deception

This is where it should have stopped; right here. This should have been the end. I have not learned how to disengage myself from a man I am interested in. A vulnerable person is one who continues to make wrong choices. I am vulnerable. Will I ever learn my lesson? Will I ever be healthy and stable in a relationship with a man? When will it stop?

My desire to be loved exceeds my common sense.

CHAPTER 5

Putting my Rose-Colored Glasses Back On

Friday, October 20, 2000

After Lance's ridiculous e-mail, I am convinced our "relationship" is over.

My head is on straight. I am not heartbroken. It was senseless for me to get caught up emotionally with a man on the Internet no less. He is a ladies man. I don't need him.

In fact, after re-reading his "Solomon letter" I say to Tony, "You know what? I think this was sent to other women besides me. Lance changed the names at the beginning and the end and sent all of us the same e-mail."

Tony agrees. Lance had indicated in the past that there were "other women" he was corresponding with. This man thinks he is God's gift to the female population.

That evening, Lance sends me an instant message. I log off immediately, which is the same as hanging up on someone. Now he will get the point.

Monday, October 23, 2000

Lance e-mails me.

> Lynne, what happened? I instant messaged you and you didn't respond, and I also sent you that heavy e-mail and I haven't heard from you. Are you mad or upset with me? Are you okay? Let me know.
> Lance [smiley added]

He adds an inappropriate Internet smiley to this message.
I respond with a short note.

> *I agree your e-mail was heavy, in fact, I believed it was sent only to me, until I got to the last paragraph and realized that it was a newsletter sent to all of your female correspondents. I did not respond, because there is nothing more for me to say to you. I am glad you have made your choice and that she has no baggage, either.*

Three hours later Lance is back on the scene again:

> *Oh Lynne, you misunderstood what I had to say. I feel like crying... REALLY! How can you say there is no reason for us to communicate any further? I have NOT made any life or long term decisions, REALLY!*

Lance admits the Solomon letter was sent to other women, not just me.

> *What I was saying to you and the other female recipients of that e-mail is that I had made the choice that this particular woman is the one I would PURSUE right NOW. I just came to the realization I might complicate things by carrying on face to face communication with any other woman and I might end up doing 'a Solomon' and "falling away from God".*

This guy is a piece of work.

> *I want "in love" Lynne and I want physical soulish, spiritual and practical. If it doesn't happen with this woman then I will pursue other women until I find that ONE special person. I don't see any reason why you and I can't go on just as we have, only without the immediate face to face meeting we were planning. Please...okay? Always truly, Lance*

As I am writing this, I am appalled I would even continue to communicate with this man. He is so full of himself, but I have my blinders on.

Lance could have kept in touch with me without writing the Solomon letter. It was not necessary. All it did was elevate him as a supposedly irresistible man who all of us (women) were so honored to have in our lives.

Wednesday, October 25, 2000

Tony and I have a good laugh when Lance writes:

> *Well the lady I wanted to pursue is not pursuable at this point. I was wrong about her not having baggage. I will go back to seeing women on a casual basis.*
>
> *So what does that mean? It means I want to plan on meeting you again as we spoke about, before the year is over, maybe around the holidays. Please, I really want to. Lance* [smiley added]

Another Internet smiley caps off this note. Unbelievable! I do not respond to his letter.

Thursday, October 26, 2000

Lance sends me an e-mail titled "Please Talk to me, Lynne"

> *Please don't shut me out. I don't understand this. You can call me at work. Please talk to me.*

He sends me his phone number at work. This is because he has a wife at home. It takes me months to realize I have no business corresponding with a married man. I fool myself into believing it is all right, since he is planning to move out in the next few days.

I send him a short response. I tell him I want no part of the chaos he is creating for himself and his "many women," meaning he is like Solomon and has to have several girlfriends.

The back-and-forth dialogue continues between us in several e-mails. If that were today, I would know better. There are enough flags to decorate the United Nations. What am I thinking? Why even respond?

Lance is clever. He convinces me that we can be friends. He is good at blame-shifting and reminds me *I* was the one who said I was not looking for a serious relationship from day one; so why should *I* be so concerned?

Saturday, October 28, 2000

Today is my birthday. I write him a short note. I say:

> *It's my birthday so be nice, okay? I guess we can be friends.*

I think to myself, no harm in being friends.
Lance is pleased. He writes back:

> *Happy Birthday day to you! Oh Lynnie thank you, thank you, thank you.*
> *(kiss kiss, hug hug). Have a wonderful birthday!*

Lance has several other women to talk to, including me. Lance needs this to feed his insecurities. I am a football field away from knowing this.

He writes back:

> *By the time I feel strong about any one woman; I trust I will have my heart's priorities in order. There will be absolutely NO need for my potential lifetime partner to be concerned about that, if we can come to an agreement as to whom I could continue to correspond with on a 'friendship only' basis.*

Lance is telling he cannot be with just one woman. It is not an option for him. If he ever meets his "one and only," he will still have a "need" to correspond with other women, and his "lifetime partner" will have to agree to this.

Again, at this point, I should have known better than to communicate with this man. It is not possible for Lance to commit to one woman.

CHAPTER 6

The Relationship Progresses

November, 2000

The e-mails and the phone calls continue. Lance shares with me some of his escapades with other women he has met online. He is constantly on the Internet, browsing the personals. He has several ads out on several websites. In addition to that, he is answering ads that other women have put out.

My emotions are in check, and I am amused at this man who thinks he is a real Casanova.

Lance is no longer living with his wife, Karen. He has moved to another apartment in the same complex as she. A man from his from church, Roy, is Lance's roommate. Roy is single, a Christian, and does not approve of Lance leaving his wife. However, he needs a place to stay and is Lance's friend.

Lance feels terrible that his wife is hurt. He writes:

> *The fact that my wife wants nothing to do with me hurts a lot because I still love her like family. I know she does too with me, but her wounds are too fresh now, so she says things like: "I don't care if I ever see you again in my life" and that makes me feel terrible. Well I have made her feel terrible plenty so I guess I will have to bear it and hopefully in time she will soften.*

At this time, I am not objective, because I want to see Lance as a decent human being. I am mistaking his egotism for compassion.

It is sad he does not love her. He certainly has feelings for me, though. I can tell from his e-mails. They are lengthy and personal. I am getting to know him better and liking him more and more.

He writes:

> *I truly look forward to seeing you at least once in person before or around the holidays. From there we will take it one very slow step at a time* [smiley added].

A few days later he writes:

> *I never want to say anything unkind or insulting to you. I always want to remain humble and transparent before you and I hope you will feel at some point you can do the same with me.*
>
> *Right now, I feel I couldn't find anyone I could like or want to fall in love with more than you. Anyway, I don't know where I am on your list, but you have been number one now on my list for over three weeks....and THAT is a record* [smiley added]!

How nice, I think! I am "number one" on his "list!"

Lance and I continue to get closer in our telephone conversations. We share things about our families with one another. I mail Lance a couple more photos of myself. He thinks I am gorgeous and look around thirty years old, even though I am a grandmother.

The November 11 trip had been canceled after the "Solomon letter" farce. I start thinking it would be nice to meet him.

Thursday, November 30, 2000

Lance informs me he will be in New York City the second week of December for a training session relating to his job.

Spontaneously, I come up with an idea. I send him an e-mail titled "I Love Adventure." I suggest I travel by bus to New York City for the day to visit my cousin during the week Lance is at his training session. I can then meet him for dinner around 5:30 p.m., after he gets out of his meeting. Knowing my bus would be leaving at 7:00 p.m. would create a comfortable situation for us our first meeting.

Lance loves my idea! We make a plan to meet in the city on Wednesday, December 13.

Lynne C. Epstein

Wednesday, December 6, 2000

Lance is counting the days until we meet. He can't wait. He is calling me Lynniekins, Sparky, and other fond names. I am calling him Lancekins and Lancecat. Today he writes:

Seven days and less than 12 hours to go until my eyes will set themselves on you face to face for the first time!

Lance's e-mails are lengthy, communicative and intimate. He is putting a lot of time and energy into our relationship. He ends another e-mail with:

I BELIEVE IN YOU LYNNIE. I believe in you Sparky! I believe in you! [Two smileys added]

Tuesday, December 12, 2000

Lance sends me an e-mail titled "Less Than Twenty-three Hours Away." He will buy dinner instead of our going "Dutch" as I had suggested. He wants our first meeting to be romantic and special.

I want nothing less than beautiful for you on our first meeting. I want this to be special.

We will meet at Chez Louie, a French restaurant across the street from Radio City Music Hall.

CHAPTER 7

Meeting Lance in Person

Wednesday, December 13, 2000

I am up at 5:00 a.m. My heart is pounding. I board the bus to New York City at 7:00 a.m. The bus drops me off in front of a McDonald's on Sixth Avenue at 10:30 a.m. My cousin is unable to meet me, so I spend the day Christmas shopping.

It is cold in the city this day. I continually duck into the stores to get warm. Twice I stop for a hot cup of Starbuck's coffee. I occasionally see Santa walking the streets, ringing a bell. The holiday atmosphere is exhilarating, as is the anticipation and excitement of meeting Lance for the first time. I feel like a teenager!

The air is brisk, and the city has a festive spirit. Sprinkles of snow fall occasionally. I enjoy the decorations and the sounds of Christmas music as I hurry along Sixth Avenue. I call Tony on my cell phone. I want to feel like a "real New Yorker" by walking down the street, talking on the phone.

At 4:30 p.m., I stop at the Hilton Hotel, two blocks uptown from Radio City, to warm up. I find a lounge, comb my hair, put on fresh lipstick, and brush my teeth. My heart is racing.

I spray myself with "Rain" Cologne. I want to smell enticing.

My cell phone rings at 5:00 p.m. Lance is only two blocks away! He is standing in front of Chez Louie, right across from Radio City Music Hall. I tell him I am on my way.

I dash out of the hotel and crash into a pedestrian. I say to the bewildered man, "I am on the way to meet a man, how do I look?"

"Great," he mutters with a puzzled look on his face.

Not noticing the cold, I run down the street. It is dark out, and the city is aglow with Christmas lights, music, and decorations. I dart in and out of the crowds of people at the crosswalks. I am almost to Radio City.

I stand behind a large group of people in front of Radio City as I prepare to cross Fiftieth Street. The Chez Louie Restaurant is only a few yards away. There he is! I recognize him right away, even though he does not look like his photo. He is looking in my direction. I wave, and he waves back.

I cross the street, and he walks towards me. He is wearing glasses and has on a green jacket. He is only five feet, seven inches. I like that. I am attracted to shorter men.

We hug and we say hello. Our eyes meet, and we smile at each other. I am surprised he does not look like his picture, but I am not disappointed. I later learn he had "doctored" up his photo on the Internet and changed his hair to make it look longer.

We enter the Chez Louie Restaurant. We are told there is a special party going on that night, and they are not open to the public. I suggest the Algonquin Inn, which is six blocks away on Forty-fourth Street.

The cold does not concern me as I take Lance's arm and we head down Sixth Avenue, amid the hustle and bustle of the holidays in this wonderful city. This is a very romantic moment for me. The festive spirit of New York adds to the magic.

The Algonquin Hotel is old and quaint. Its oak walls and rustic atmosphere provide a romantic setting for our first dinner together.

We are seated, and Lance orders a bottle of wine. There are three waiters continually at his beck and call. Lance reads the menu, orders for me, and is a true gentleman. He is playful, witty, and he laughs a lot. I like him. I am also impressed at his expertise with the wine list and his etiquette for fine dining.

He shows me photos of his family, himself as a child, and his cat. I also show him photos of my family. I have my camera and Lance asks the waiter to take a picture of us together.

The meal and the hour with Lance are wonderful. Everything flows perfectly. During our time together, he leans toward me and kisses me a few times. What a great kisser he is!

As we leave the inn, we pet the famous Algonquin cat the hotel is notorious for housing. We head back up Sixth Avenue to my bus, which is leaving at 7:00 p.m. Lance waits with his arm around me. I ask a passenger to take another picture of us together.

Lance gives me a hug, and I board the bus. He will go to the Cyber Café on Broadway and send me an e-mail to read when I arrive home. He waits by the bus near my window and waves as it pulls away.

As the bus drives out of the city, I look across the river and see the lights of Manhattan. The Empire State Building is aglow with holiday red and green. What a wonderful romantic memory of my first meeting with Lance! I think of the movie *An Affair to Remember* with Cary Grant and Deborah Kerr, and I feel the magic of young love.

I lean back in my seat and close my eyes. I am in heaven.

I dream about Lance's arms around me during the bus ride back. As soon as I get home, I log on to my computer. Lance has e-mailed me as promised. He titles it "I don't know what to say... this second" with, of course, the smiley.

His e-mail is two pages long. He talks about the movie *City of Angels*, which I had asked him to watch the first week we met. The two central characters, Seth and Maggie, fall in love. Seth, an angel, is willing to give up his immortality for Maggie. Lance writes:

> *If I am going to be Seth and you are going to be Maggie we must develop something TOGETHER face to face that goes beyond e-mails and phone conversations.*
>
> *You know, I didn't want to really say goodbye tonight and just couldn't leave you until you were out of my sight, yet it was getting awkward for me just standing there not being able to talk to you.*
>
> *I try very hard to be honest and open minded about myself and express my feelings very easily and openly so that a woman that I think I might eventually **be in love with** will really know me and really know my heart and the way I think, but more so the way I CHOOSE to think.*
>
> *Well now I would like to try and find a way to spend some time with you during this holiday season. I am on vacation from Wednesday next week through Tuesday, January 3. I WILL travel four hours alone in my car to see you.*

Lance ends his e-mail with:

Lynne C. Epstein

> *MY precious beautiful Lynnie, how I do like your soul. Sleep sweet, I will. Lance* [smiley added]

I think about Lance wanting to visit me over the holidays. I will suggest he visit me later after the New Year. Meanwhile, I am sure we will find ways to meet again and get to know each other better.

I go to sleep dreaming about my meeting with Lance. I look forward to a wonderful future with him.

CHAPTER 8

The First Cool-down

Friday, December 15, 2000

It is two days after my first meeting with Lance. Lance's e-mails have been lengthy, personal and intimate. I especially look forward to his evening e-mails. Today he writes to tell me this is his last day of training. He will be returning to New Jersey tomorrow.

Later that afternoon, Lance e-mails me.

> *This will probably be my last e-mail for the day…oh how will I survive?*

I am a little surprised. Lance has been e-mailing me every evening for weeks.

Saturday, December 16, 2000

The hard drive goes on my computer, and I am unable to use it. How am I going to be able to correspond with Lance? I can't call him. I don't call men. Lance has always telephoned me. If he doesn't receive my e-mails, I'm afraid he'll forget me. My unhealthy and unrealistic pattern continues.

At least I will be able to check my e-mails at work, but will have to forgo hearing from him at night.

Saturday, December 23, 2000

Lance's e-mails are pleasant; however, they are not as personal as before. He writes me about a family he knows needs "advice and reconciliation." He believes *he* is "the one God can use to bring restoration to the family." He chats about some holiday videos he plans to rent. This is all very nice. Yet, I wonder, what about *us?* Have you nothing to say about *us?*

Perhaps I should write something personal to him.

Sunday, December 24, 2000 - Christmas Eve

I cannot stop thinking about Lance. I stop by at my sister's and ask to use her computer. I send Lance an e-mail. I write:

> *I have an idea. How about we meet in New York City on Saturday, January 20? We can walk around Central Park, hold hands, have lunch, look at each other, and talk.*

I add the Internet smiley to my e-mail. Lance enjoys our smileys. I want to recapture the magic we had the first night we met. It will be wonderful and romantic!

Lance lives near Princeton, New Jersey. He can easily take a train to the city which, is a little over an hour trip. It is not a problem for me to travel over three hours by bus to see him. I am sure he will love this suggestion and respond right away!

Monday, December 25, 2000 - Christmas Day

I am invited to my sister's house for Christmas dinner. I am going crazy not having my computer. I miss Lance's e-mails.

I check my inbox on my sister's computer. Lance has answered my letter from yesterday. However, there is no mention or response to my suggestion that we meet in New York City on January 20.

How could he have missed that part of my e-mail, I wonder?

I feel as if I have swallowed a rock.

Tuesday, December 26, 2000

Lance telephones me. I tell him to check the e-mail that I sent him on Christmas Eve. He apparently overlooked the January 20 invitation. Is he not *reading* my e-mails? I know he got it, because he did respond and comment on other parts of it.

Friday, December 29, 2000

I am still without a hard drive on my computer. I go to the local library to check my e-mails from Lance.

He has reread my e-mail from Christmas Eve with the suggestion we meet in New York City on January 20. He is sorry about missing that paragraph. He writes:

> *I am sorry about missing that paragraph about January 20. Please forgive me. I did pick up a stronger insistence to reread it, almost uncharacteristic of you, so I DID feel compelled to read it again. And boy, I am glad I did. I too was pretty insistent about thinking I hadn't missed anything, so again, I am glad I just TRUSTED YOU and the way you are, to recognize something was definitely not adding up.*

Even though Lance acknowledges he missed my suggestion, he still does not respond to it. Does he not want to meet me on January 20?

He is very empathetic about all that I am going through with my computer. He also has a perfume that he wants me to wear, "L'aire de Temps," by Ninni Ricci which is a special fragrance to him. I am the *first* (and only) woman he has asked to wear this fragrance since his wife.

How could he have missed my suggestion to meet me on January 20? Is he just skimming my e-mails? I am reading, absorbing, and rereading his. If it were me, I would not have missed something that important. Also, the January 20 suggestion was in a paragraph by itself. I feel disheartened.

Later that evening the technician comes to my home and installs my hard drive. I am finally up and running. I have my AOL back!

I immediately check my e-mail to see if Lance has written to me. He has sent me a holiday card, but nothing else. I send him a thank you note for the card. I get a short reply saying he is glad I liked the card.

I am totally perplexed. I have been without a computer for over a week. I am back online, and Lance has not e-mailed me.

Saturday, December 30, 2000

I get Lance's usual Saturday-morning phone call. He talks about himself, his past use of pot, and his childhood. He does not mention anything about my latest correspondence with him. His call-waiting comes on, so he tells me to have a nice day and hangs up.

Twelve hours later, I check my e-mail. Lance has not written to me all day, except a very short note right after calling me, telling me he is sorry he hung up so fast and that the call-waiting was a wrong number. It is unusual not to hear from him the rest of the day. I am used to several lengthy, intimate, daily e-mails. At 10:00 p.m., I send him a short e-mail. I title it, "Please Hear What I Am Not Saying." I write:

> *I am a little puzzled. I have been back online for over twenty-four hours, and I have not had a real message from you since I got back online. Is everything okay? I think I heard more from you when I didn't have a computer. Thank you for your honesty.*

I send Lance the e-mail, and I hear back from him immediately. He is online. He has probably been online all day. He never even e-mailed me or thought about it. Knowing that he has been online all day makes me angry. His e-mail makes me angrier. He writes:

> *Hello Lynnie, I decided to call you this morning rather than e-mail you so we could talk. I honestly prefer the phone, and if you notice, I am doing a lot more phone with you lately than e-mail, because I generally DO prefer phone, I know I have said that to you before. I just figured I would call you tomorrow unless you wrote ME a longer e-mail today.*

No, I had not noticed he had been "doing" the phone more with me than e-mail, nor had I remembered him telling me that before. He must have me mixed up with someone else.

His next line infuriates me:

> *Are you suddenly feeling a tad insecure about our relationship? Besides this lack of e-mail today, has anything else I have done or not done been causing you to think or have feelings of insecurity? Could this be what you are NOT saying? I am not sure what to say now.*

I stayed in napped for two hours today. I watched 'The Matrix' with Roy for two hours, communicated with some other people on my computer today (both sexes), and talked to Mandy briefly on the phone. I don't think there is anything wrong between you and I, do you? Why is my not e-mailing you for about 13 hours mean something could be wrong?

I think we are fine. I am not upset or disappointed with you in any way. I was even telling one of my online women friends today about you and how I believe that I could and might one day fall in love with you and maybe one day marry you. I also sent her your picture.

Why do you feel something might be wrong? What has actually happened in your mind to make you feel a tad insecure here? Your turn to be honest.

Talk to you tomorrow morning. Oh, and by the way, I may have to do music at the Nursing home tomorrow, so my morning call may be quick.

I hope YOU are okay Lynnie. Everything is fine with me [Smiley].
Lance [Three smileys]

What is wrong with this picture? Lance has not been consistent in his interaction with me. He has suddenly stopped the affectionate and caring e-mails. I am unable to understand why he is acting passive and complacent after indicating to me how much he cared about me after our evening in New York City. I feel that my question to him was a valid one and not an insecure one.

I am furious at this e-mail. His tone is cocky and patronizing. Also, he openly admits that he is online all the time, and with other women. He had told me about Mandy, who he had met online and seen once, but that was *before* our meeting in New York. Why would he be calling Mandy now?

My caring for Lance is exclusive, and I am not online with other men all day.

Lance is again making himself out to be the one with all the right answers and telling me I am insecure because I can't understand why he is intimate with me one day and cool the next. I am getting mixed signals from him. I do not understand why he has suddenly stopped e-mailing me.

I want to be loved. I have so much to offer the right man, and I thought Lance was the one for me.

Why can't I see he is a womanizer and wants me to be one of his string of women? I don't want to see it. If this were today, I would not have sent him that e-mail. I would have enough confidence in who I am and not be worried about when I would hear from him or see him.

I still do not know my worth and am focusing on him rather than taking care of myself. This is my pattern.

CHAPTER 9

Blow Up on New Year's Eve

Sunday, December 31, 2000

I awaken early, still furious at Lance's e-mail from last night. How could he be so cocky? How dare he accuse me of being insecure!

If I am to be honest with myself, the real reason I am angry is because in my heart I know Lance is not thinking about me the way I am thinking about him. He is going about his business, thinking of everything and everyone except me. I, on the other hand, am thinking mainly about him while my other interests are secondary. I am not using my head in this situation. I am vulnerable and thinking with my heart.

I answer Lance's patronizing e-mail. I simply state I missed hearing from him, so had decided to write. I tell him I don't think he is reading my e-mails, and I feel disheartened that he did not notice my suggestion we meet on January 20. In addition, I am not happy to be told I am insecure.

Right after sending him my response, I receive an e-mail from Lance commenting on several things that I had written to him over the past few days. He sends it at the same time that I am sending my e-mail to him. Our e-mails must have crossed.

He has reread my recent e-mails and is now being attentive to them. He says:

January 20 is a date!

It is too late. My e-mail has been sent, and Lance is not happy. He is angry and writes back that this situation has gotten way out of hand. He picks apart my e-mail, paragraph by paragraph.

As usual, I want to patch things up. I tell him I had canceled my bus reservations for January 20, because he had not given me an answer. I tell him all is well, and I do not want to argue. I want everything to be okay. Lance will e-mail me later and plans to call me at midnight, as it is New Year's Eve.

I go out for the day, and I visit some friends early in the evening. I am home by 9:00 p.m. I am looking forward to Lance's call at midnight. It will be a pleasant way to start off the year 2001. I check my e-mail, since Lance had said he would write to me later. I open a note from him written about an hour ago.

He is still talking about my e-mail from last night! He wants to discuss it when he calls me later this evening.

He asks me if I am afraid of losing him. He tells me he was not a good writer of letters before I came into his life. This has me puzzled, since he has sent me very long e-mails in the past. I write back:

> I don't think there is anything more to discuss. We have said it all. Please don't make a big deal out of the phone call tonight. Happy New Year is fine.
>
> How could I be afraid of losing you? I never thought I had you. Losing someone implies a committed relationship and we don't have that. If I felt I was losing you I would say so right now.
>
> I asked you not to get defensive, and you have. Please don't blow this up.
>
> I am looking forward to your call at midnight. It will be a nice way to start the New Year.

I turn off my computer and watch television. It is 10:00 p.m.

Midnight, January 1, 2001

The phone does not ring. There is no call from Lance. I am a little puzzled. Perhaps he fell asleep.

I will learn in the months to come this is how Lance gains control and power. He enjoys the head games and the back–and-forth interaction that belittles and upsets his significant other. Lance has to be right. He thinks he is a wise wizard and has all the answers. Lance likes his women to be weak, and he is not happy if he is crossed or if someone disagrees with him.

I can't sleep. Something is not right. Around 2:00 a.m., I get up and I check my e-mail. I am shocked to see an e-mail from Lance written at *10:13 p.m.*

His letter is almost three pages long. It is a response to the e-mail I had written him earlier. He writes:

> *I am VERY upset at this e-mail. You say "I don't think there is anything more to discuss. We have said it all." And then "please don't make a big deal out of the phone call tonight. Happy New Year is fine" Well here's how I see it. There is MUCH that needs to be said and all I want to say now is 'Happy New Year' and skip the call.*

His next statement surprises me:

> *Lynne, I have been FALLING IN LOVE with you and YOU keep saying we don't have a relationship. Call it then what you want, but don't suddenly act like we don't have something of great value that can be lost, and is NOW BEING LOST. If my feelings for you begin to fade, we will have a very weak friendship because I will not nearly communicate with you that often.*

Lance has not been communicating with me "that often" for two weeks! He is sending mixed signals, and I am confused. Also, he has not indicated to me in any way he is "falling in love" with me. He continues:

> *I am really upset at your being so petty about this January 20 date. What is the big deal that I missed mentioning or seeing in your e-mail that you wanted to come out January 20??????? Why are you so disheartened??????? Was it cause you thought I didn't give a shit about what you said??? Is it because you think I don't respect what you have to say??? It is one thing to feel bad that I forgot to mention it and it is totally another thing to then ACT on it and cancel the reservations. THAT is what really upsets me. It turns "an innocent mistake I made" into "an inconsiderate act that I committed".*
>
> *What is there to be disheartened about if it was only an innocent mistake on my part??? Get it???*

Lance's e-mail is filled with abrasive caps, and double and triple punctuation marks. He is furious. He picks apart sentence by sentence my e-mail from the previous evening when I asked him if everything was okay, because I had not heard from him. He writes:

> *You have not had 'ONE REAL MESSAGE FROM ME' since you got back online. Excuse me, do we speak the same language here? What is a REAL MESSAGE, please define? To me, THAT is a sarcastic tone (yours AND now mine too).*
>
> *The sarcasm continues with your next sentence... "I think I heard more from you when I didn't have a computer".. what is THAT supposed to mean? OH I get it now, e-mails, e-mails, e-mails, you want me to send you e-mails. Well if that is what you want Lynne, then 'just say that'. Say, I miss your e-mails and please don't expect me to read between the lines ALL the time, especially with vague sarcastic language preceding that.*

I am in shock. I cannot believe this. He continues:

> *OK, now the next item is "Insecure"...3 times I committed the heinous crime of mentioning a word that I believe FITS you whether you like hearing it or not. IN trying to believe the BEST about you, I chose to say 'insecure' rather than 'sarcastic with an attitude'.*

He ends his letter with:

> *There is still plenty to talk about and I am not sure if I should call or just wish you a Happy New Year from here at the keyboard. Anyway, I am. If you would like me to call, express your feelings in another e-mail and depending how we both feel after I have read your response, I will decide if I should call.*
>
> *If God has US in mind for the future he will work this out for His good and glory and we must NOT sin.*
>
> *With much affection that I feel now that I have exhausted myself sharing my heart and soul with you. Lance.*

I am sobbing. This man is abusive. His e-mail is belittling, hurtful, and upsetting. Never in my wildest dreams did I imagine this would happen. I know my heart and my intentions. I am confused and bewildered, and I don't understand what I could have said or done to make him so angry.

I go back to bed. I lay, huddled up, a sorry sight, crying and hugging my cat. I am heartbroken.

CHAPTER 10

Trying to Patch Things Up

Monday, January 1, 2001-New Year's Day

I am up at 5:00 a.m. I have not slept all night. I am physically, mentally and emotionally exhausted.

How can I stay with a man who would send me an e-mail like this? But I don't want to lose him! What's wrong with me? Why am I like this? Again, I am giving pieces of myself away. Is it my fear of being rejected by a man I had adored, which began the day my father died?

I have to get myself together. My son, Jeff, and his wife, Marla, are coming at noon to assemble the computer desk and swivel chair they had given me for Christmas.

I call Tony around 8:00 a.m. I am crying so hard, he is having trouble understanding what I am saying. He tells me to calm down and talk slowly.

"I spent the whole night crying and laying in the fetal position, Tony," I sob. "I am so upset." I read Lance's letter to him.

Tony is aghast. "Lynne, first of all, we don't do fetal!" he says. "This guy is not for you. You don't need this in your life. You are upset all the time. He is not worth it, Lynne. Let him go."

Tony is right. He has known me for three years. He also knows my history with men. He is a dear friend and always supportive. He is also used to me not listening to him. Today is no exception.

I am relieved I have not told anyone in my family about Lance. In my subconscious mind lies the fear of another relationship not working out.

My family has watched me go through three marriages plus a couple of disastrous relationships. I want to be sure Lance is the "right one" before telling my family about him.

Tony calms me down. He will call later to see how I am doing. I hang up and go back on line. There is another e-mail from Lance titled "Us." Thus far, I have not responded to his New Year's Eve e-mail.

Although Lance is apologetic about his mean-spirited letter, he also justifies its content. He intimates all that has transpired to be my fault. He feels he has done nothing wrong.

I can tell he is concerned he has not heard from me. He wants me to respond to his e-mails. Now the tables are turned. *He* is waiting to receive an e-mail from *me*, rather than the other way around.

At this point, I have the control back. The person who cares the least in a relationship is the one who is in control. Had I been thinking clearly, this would have been the time to let him go. But I remain vulnerable. Vulnerability causes a person to make wrong choices.

I am also devastated. I don't want what "we have" to end. I don't even know what we have! I am in a state of anxiety, pain and turmoil. I love him!

I respond to Lance's "Us" e-mail with a short note telling him my son is on his way over. I will e-mail him later. He writes back immediately. I can tell he is relieved to hear back from me. Lance knows his New Year's e-mail was not nice.

I make it clear to him I am responding to the "Us" e-mail, not the nasty e-mail from the night before. I write:

> *This is in response to your "us" letter. I will not respond to the anger expressed in your letter New Year's Eve.*

He writes back that he may have been a little "sarcastic," but not angry.

I had the ball. I had gained control of the relationship before I e-mailed him back. I should not have responded to any of his e-mails. That would have given him time to think and realize he was out of line.

I am afraid to be honest with a man I care about. I have no trouble being assertive with other people in my life. However, when it comes to a romantic relationship, I am afraid to make waves. This has never worked for me before, so what makes me think it will now?

I pick up pizza and wings for Jeff and Marla. They arrive shortly thereafter, and I am able to conceal my anxiety. I am glad they do not know about my relationship with Lance.

Jeff assembles my new computer desk and swivel chair. I have a wonderful afternoon with them and am thankful for a loving family.

Tuesday, January 2, 2001

Lance continues e-mailing me. He will call me Wednesday night, January 3 at 9:00 p.m. to "discuss everything." He sends me a two-page letter listing eight things we need to "discuss." He is back to sending me lengthy e-mails at night.

Everything on his list is about what *I* said or did. There is nothing that makes him responsible for our "miscommunication." He starts with the January 20 date.

> *Why did you cancel the January 20 reservations so quickly? What was your basis for such a HASTY decision? This really hurt me, Lynne. Do you really think I just rush through your e-mails and don't read them carefully? Were you hurt? Would you say you were hissy or pissy about this?*

The answer to "do you think I am rushing through your e-mails?" is yes! Lance *is* rushing through my e-mails. If he were reading them, he would not have missed the paragraph that suggested the meeting in New York City on January 20. It was five lines long. This issue contributed to his blow up on New Year's Eve, so instead of standing my ground and addressing it, I withdraw. I do not want to "upset him" again.

There are seven other questions dealing with *my* insecurity, *my* misunderstanding him "not reading my e-mails" and *my* "not thinking we had a commitment." He also questions *my* honesty.

He asks:

> *Does it bother you or scare you, or mean nothing to you that I have been close to falling in love with you?*

I am totally confused. Lance's e-mails are not consistent with his behavior. He has not been acting like he's falling in love with me. His e-mails have been impersonal and sometimes distant.

He gives me the option of responding by e-mail before we talk on the phone. I don't e-mail him. There is nothing for me to say. I do not feel I should be on the defense.

Wednesday, January 3, 2001

It is almost 9:00 p.m. Lance will be calling me any minute. I am nervous. I am not up to going over his "list." Why should I have to explain, justify, or defend myself? I am dreading his phone call this night.

The phone rings at 9:00 p.m. sharp. Lance is right on time.

When I tell him his letter on New Year's Eve was abusive, he denies it. He states he was being "a little sarcastic," but the letter was not abusive in any way. I begin to think I must have misunderstood.

We are having a terrible time communicating. We are on the phone for over two hours.

I tell Lance, "I am not answering your questions or going over your list. You are picking apart everything I said and did."

Lance finally says, "I can't take this, let's just keep our relationship a casual friendship."

I panic! I want more than that! I have put so much time and emotional energy into this relationship, and now he is only offering me a casual friendship?

I tell him it is my fault. I say, "You are right, it is me, I am insecure, I just could not admit it before." Lance is thrilled I saw the light. We are back on track. Everything is fine now, and he will e-mail me tomorrow.

I hang up. Everything is not fine. I do not have a good feeling about our conversation. I feel sad, confused, unsure of myself, and stupid. None of this makes sense. Lance is back in control of the relationship.

I know in my heart I agreed with him to make peace. Also, I did not want to lose him. I gave the control back to him. Why can't I be stronger?

He thinks he was not at fault. I know he was. His behavior was out of line. I appeased him. This is my pattern, to take the blame if something goes wrong in a relationship. I want things to flow and be "okay." However, is the anxiety, frustration, and sadness I feel a fair trade-off?

Lance is happy and going about his business. I am miserable and hanging on, as usual. I am disgusted with myself. I have no peace. But I love him and want him. How sad is this?

Thursday, January 4, 2001

Lance e-mails me. He is glad that we "straightened things out". He is ending his e-mails with the smileys. They are meaningless to me at this time. In fact they are annoying.

We continue to correspond by e-mail. Lance is acting aloof, again. Nothing has been accomplished as far as I am concerned.

I record in my journal: "Sent Lance a long e-mail this evening. He was online and sent me a short note back saying he was tired and would call or write to me tomorrow. I don't trust Lance. I can't put my finger on why. His New Year's Eve e-mail did a lot of damage. I don't want to be like this any more."

Friday, January 5, 2001

Lance's e-mails are patronizing. He writes on this date:

> *And when I say to YOU, that I want to "HELP" YOU, I am not saying I want to be your hero, savior, counselor, therapist or anything of the like. I just want to be someone who UNDERSTANDS you, and can ACCEPT you, and see your heart, and be able to give you the wisdom and compassion, that God has been so gracious to give me.* [smiley added]. *Whether you end up with me or not as your lifetime partner, you will indeed benefit to be able to have healthy communication and develop a much better self image and have much better self esteem.*
>
> *I want to put together a list of the key things we have learned or discovered through these last several days, so we can build on them and not make the same mistake again. The past should ONLY be brought up to enforce the positive direction of the present and the future and bring peace and healing and deliverance. The truth, remember sets us FREE!* [smiley] *Thank you Jesus!*

Saturday, January 6, 2001

Lance e-mails me:

> *January 20th is a DATE! It should be a big day for us. We will have some real extended relaxing time together I think will be very good. Let me know what ideas you have and we (or I) will work out the particulars. Thanks!*

The Internet smiley caps this off, as usual. The magic and anticipation of meeting him on January 20 is not the same.

Had I followed my instincts, I would have canceled this meeting. There has been so much negative karma surrounding these plans. It is inevitable this day will be disastrous.

In this same e-mail he informs me:

> *I will be out sometime today and or busy with some other things. I tried to call you about 10:55 a.m. but there was no answer. I really need to get on with my day, but I hope maybe we can talk Sunday evening.*

This e-mail is written Saturday morning, and I will not be hearing from him until Sunday evening. I know that he is meeting other women. I can sense it. He states in another paragraph:

> *Anyway if you don't get any e-mails from me for a while, I should at least call you or e-mail you by Sunday evening, or sooner, if it works out that way.*

I am anxious, worried, and jealous. I always wonder where Lance is and what he is doing. I also realize we are not a committed couple. What right do I have to feel this way or say anything? I remain quiet and pretend not to notice or be concerned.

He has not mentioned the "list" that he wants to go over of the "key things we have learned."

Sunday, January 14, 2001

I record in my journal: "I am down. No self-confidence. Lance is clueless."

I can sense from Lance's e-mails that he is distracted. I am careful when I write to him. I reread my e-mails, making sure there is nothing offensive in them. I don't want to make him angry again.

As the January 20 date draws near, I notice Lance has not mentioned it. This is quite a contrast to his behavior a month ago when he was counting the days and "couldn't wait to see me face-to-face." I remain silent.

CHAPTER 11

Lance's Wife

Lance talks a lot about his wife, Karen. It has been two months since he moved out of their apartment. He lives walking distance from her in the same complex. His roommate, Roy, is fond of Karen and thinks Lance should be trying to preserve the marital relationship.

Karen is upset and hurt over the breakup. She and Lance have been married seventeen years.

It is cruel and emotionally hard for Karen to have Lance living near her. At this time, I don't see this. I am too busy focusing on Lance and me.

Lance says he truly "loves" Karen, but has never been "in love" with "anyone." He states he is fond of her, but she "drives him crazy." She is a Christian and judgmental of his behavior.

While they were living together, she disapproved of his being on the computer, corresponding with other women. This had lead to a huge argument one night, and Lance moved out shortly afterwards.

Even though Lance does not want to live with Karen, he appears to want her in his life. He can't understand why she won't forgive him for his past mistakes.

He wants to give her a year to get on her feet financially before doing anything legal regarding a divorce. He also wants her as a friend. He is taking care of her financially and checks on her often to make sure she is all right.

Karen lives with her seventeen-year-old son from a previous marriage. Her mother also lives with her. The boy is Lance's stepson. Karen cares for her mother, who is ninety-one years old, with Alzheimer's disease, and in a wheelchair. Lance tells me his mother-in-law lived with them for several years. Karen loves taking care of her mother. I picture her as compassionate, but also needy.

Lance feels terrible he left Karen with the responsibility of taking care of her mother by herself. It tears him apart. He feels much guilt. He also tells me it is not good for him to be around his wife for very long.

Lance has seen Karen recently. He stopped by to get his mail. He tells her she needs to find a job. He will support her for a while, but is expecting her to try to find some other means of support. He wants to give her as much time as possible so he doesn't become the "bad guy."

He is annoyed she "doesn't know what mail she is supposed to keep." I wonder why he doesn't change his address.

Karen tells Lance "I don't want to see you; I don't want you around here." Lance tells me her attitude is self-righteous. He is happy to be "out of there."

He says to me: "When I am away from her for a while, I start feeling so much love for her and care and compassion and want to see her doing okay."

I tell Lance she sounds like a nice person.

He says: "She makes me feel worse about myself. She will bring to light all of my failures. It frustrates me when anyone seems to feel I should go back with my wife."

Karen had said to Lance: "Who would want to go with a man who has broken his commitment to his wife?"

Lance has said to me "As a separated man, a lot of women do not want to go out with me. There are women who have replied to my ad that say 'you seem like a great guy, but I do not go out with a man who is separated.'"

I am in a constant state of confusion. It does not make me feel good when Lance talks about replying to other women's ads. Also, I do not need to hear all this talk about his wife.

Karen has not worked for years. I get the impression that even if she wasn't taking care of her mother, she would not be working. Her only means of support is her mother and Lance.

Lance is glad I understand his being married and wanting to stay connected to his wife.

I wonder why I am being so stupid.

CHAPTER 12

The Emotional Rollercoaster Continues

Saturday, January 13, 2001

I get Lance's usual Saturday-morning phone call. We talk for two hours. The January 20 trip to New York City is one week away.

Lance has not mentioned it.

Still no "list" of things we have learned. No intimate conversation. Where are all the sparks from December? Did I dream this?

This conversation is a farce. Lance tells me about an eighteen-year-old girl he corresponds with on the Internet. Her screen name is "Slave Girl," and he thinks he can be her "spiritual daddy." He contacted her, thinking anyone with a name like that must be hurting and need help.

I feel like puking.

He then brings up the events from New Year's Eve. "That little difference we had New Year's Eve concerned me. It made me realize everything is in this order in time and space for a reason. We shouldn't try and do things out of God's timing."

I think to myself that "little difference" *we* had? I know in my heart I was not responsible for the New Year's Eve blow-up.

He then says, "I have probably met maybe seven different women. They are one-timers, nice, but I can tell they are not for me. You are different. I see a lot of potential. But if for some reason, I meet somebody here in New Jersey and you were no longer in the picture the same way, I know that would hurt you."

What is Lance's point in telling me this? I don't respond.

Lance continues, "God has brought you into my life, and we have a good relationship. If it doesn't work out, there would be a lot of ways we would grow and learn. It may make us better able to handle other relationships God puts in our path. I have to find a woman I know I have the romance with, plus all the other things."

I cannot stand hearing Lance talk about "other women." What about me?

He picks up his call-waiting. It is Roy, his roommate, calling from Florida. Lance hangs up, ending the conversation with "very nice talking to you."

I am furious, hurt, and upset. I am mad at myself for being so passive. Why am I even bothering with this man? Why does he have to tell me about his other "women" and patronize "our" relationship? Lance is acting like I'm so lucky to have him.

Tony calls me a few minutes later. I relate the conversation to him and I ask him "what would you do if you were me?"

Tony says, "Ask him three questions: 'Do you love me?' 'Are you looking for another woman?' 'Are we a couple?'"

I tell Tony I don't want to address the situation. I am afraid to make waves.

Tony tells me to say, "'Lance, our relationship needs clarification; otherwise I am afraid it would be to our advantage to abort our association.'"

"He is a womanizer, Lynne," Tony says, sounding frustrated. "You are in constant turmoil. You are going to get hurt!"

Why am I hanging on? I lap up Lance's words of encouragement like a hungry dog lapping up crumbs. I ignore his words about other women.

As usual, I don't listen to Tony.

Monday, January 15, 2001

Lance is e-mailing me jokes! Pages of jokes. How intimate. The jokes comprise the majority of our communication during the next couple of days. The January 20 date draws near.

Tuesday, January 16, 2001

Lance e-mails me:

What would you like to do this weekend?

Lynne C. Epstein

I suggest the Wax Museum just off Broadway. Also, Lance's birthday is in February, and I would like to treat him to lunch at a place of his choice. He accepts my offer and chooses a steakhouse he went to as a boy. It will be nostalgic for him.

My feelings this time are very different from just five weeks ago when we met in New York City for the first time. I am hoping when we see each other, we can recapture the magic we had before. This meeting is very important to me, and will bring clarity to our relationship. I have a list of things to take with me. I want to be sure to take a camera.

CHAPTER 13

January 20 in New York City

Friday, January 19, 2001

I wake up excited! Only one more day, and I will see Lance!

I start getting ready for work. It is 6:00 a.m.

The phone rings. I am surprised to hear Lance's voice.

"I heard a weather report," he says. "I am having second thoughts about tomorrow. It is supposed to snow. They are expecting three to six inches tomorrow. If we are in New York, we will be dealing with that".

He wants to know if we can reschedule. I tell him I understand, and we can come up with another Saturday. Lance says he is disappointed, but somewhat relieved. He will call me tomorrow. He ends the call with "have a great day."

I hang up the phone. He feels better, but I don't. I am extremely disappointed and a little annoyed. What was I supposed to say when it was obvious he did not want to make the trip?

I go to work. Tony is shocked when I tell him that Lance is not coming. He thinks Lance's excuse is lame.

I call my sister, Lea. She has not known about Lance for very long. I tell her he does not want to take a train to the city because of a weather report. She says "Lynne, if a man wants to see a woman bad enough, he will ride a bicycle twenty miles to make it happen."

Throughout the day, I process Lance's phone call. I start to get angry.

I am willing to travel three and a half hours by bus to see Lance. He does not want to travel one hour and twenty minutes to see me.

I have my bus ticket, and it is paid for. I call my cousin Patti, who lives in New York City and make a plan to see her tomorrow. I decide to make the bus trip even though I will not be seeing Lance.

That evening I e-mail Lance, informing him I was unable to cancel my bus reservation. Since my ticket is paid for, I will be meeting my cousin Patti in New York instead. I hope he realizes he can still change his mind and make the trip. Maybe he will reconsider when he finds out I am still going.

Saturday, January 20, 2001

I am up at 6:00 a.m. I log on to AOL. Lance has not answered my e-mail from last night. I know he got it. I sent it before 10:00 p.m. He is always up until 11:00 p.m. Now I am really angry. Disheartened, I take a shower and get ready to drive to the bus station.

It is bitter cold. As I drive to Binghamton to catch my bus, I notice the sky is gray.

The bus ride is long and tedious. I arrive in New York City at 10:30 a.m. My cousin Patti is meeting me at 1:00 p.m. The bus drops us off in front of McDonald's between Forty-sixth and Forty-seventh streets. I go into McDonald's to get out of the cold.

I order a chicken sandwich and a hot cup of coffee. Sitting upstairs by a window overlooking Sixth Avenue, I notice how different everything looks from just five weeks ago. Even though it is morning, the sky is gray and dark. The tall buildings and the concrete pavement give the city a gloomy appearance. This matches my frame of mind. I am sad. I miss Lance terribly.

Why couldn't he have come? Even though the weather is cold and damp, there is not a drop of rain or a flake of snow in sight. I am here, and he is not.

Lance and I had planned to meet in front of Radio City Music Hall, just four blocks away, at 12:00 noon. After eating, I walk down the street. I cannot get over how cold it is. There is no activity in the city this day. The holidays are over, and people are either home or inside the stores. I duck into Rockefeller Plaza to get warm.

At 12:00 noon, I stand in front of Radio City Music Hall by myself. This is the moment I would have seen Lance. Where is he right now? Is he thinking about me and wishing he had made the trip after all? I cannot stand the cold. It is painful. I feel chilled to the bone. I am feeling cold on the outside; heartbroken and lonely on the inside.

I torture myself for a few more minutes by standing there, wishing Lance was with me. I am so cold that I go back into Rockefeller Plaza and browse the shops for an hour. At 1:00 p.m., I meet Patti. I am glad to see her.

We are hungry. We walk around trying to find a place to eat. I am freezing and cannot stand being on the street.

We take a cab to the Carlyle Hotel near Central Park. It is beautiful inside, and we enjoy a wonderful brunch. The food, drink, and atmosphere provide me with much-needed warmth, but the anxiety I am feeling inside is constantly present. I share my concerns about Lance with Patti. She is understanding and sorry for my disappointment. She gives me her sweater to put under my jacket. This makes me a little warmer.

I am too cold to shop. Besides, my heart is not in it. I am bordering on being depressed. The cold intensifies my somber mode. I don't feel like doing anything. Sightseeing would not be enjoyable in this weather.

We decide to go to Rolf's Bar and Restaurant on Third Avenue on the East Side. Rolf's is notorious for its fine dining and beautiful holiday decorations. It is Patti's favorite hangout, and she is friends with several of the regular patrons.

I am glad to get into the warm cab. The atmosphere at Rolf's is warm, friendly, and comforting to my wounded spirit. Patti's friends are there, and we have a great time talking and joking around. I use her cell phone and call Tony. I tell him there is not a drop of rain or a flake of snow in sight. He laughs and is not surprised. Three drinks and two and a half hours later, I take a cab back to catch my bus at 7:00 pm.

During the long ride home, I look out the window at the dark. I feel lonely. I process my relationship with Lance and the events that have lead up to this day. I realize the January 20 trip was doomed from the day Lance ignored it in my e-mail to him. Why was I so insistent to see him on this date? This is another pattern of mine; trying to make something happen.

Why don't I get it? This man does not care for me at all.

The bus pulls into Binghamton at 10:00 p.m. I get into my cold vehicle and drive home. My warm, cozy apartment feels wonderful. I am tired and cranky.

The first thing I do is check my e-mail. Lance has written to me.

CHAPTER 14

Ending the Relationship

Lance's e-mail is titled "Lynnie in New York City." I am irritated as I read:

> Oh Lynnie! I can't believe it! The weather turned out totally different than from what I heard on Friday morning's weather report, and YOU ended up going to New York anyway, and I stayed home disappointed that I didn't go. What a bummer – for me anyway!

I notice he capitalized "you" making me the perpetrator of the situation.

Lance continues:

> Considering you couldn't cancel your trip, you did the same thing I would have done, were I in your place. Well I hope you had a nice time anyway even though I couldn't be there with you. The weather wasn't great, but at least there was no snow storm. That was great you had friends to be with.
>
> How frustrating for me though. When I got your e-mail last night, I thought to myself, gees, if I knew you COULDN'T cancel I might have gone anyway.

Subtle Deception

I am furious! What a crock! Lance could have called me last night after receiving my e-mail and told me he changed his mind. He had plenty of time. As I continue reading Lance's patronizing words, I become more infuriated.

> *The reason why I told you Friday morning was because I thought you would still have time to cancel, but since you couldn't I might have waited a little longer to decide what I wanted to do. As it turned out, it worked out for you because you had time to make other arrangements. I am sorry I didn't get to spend the day with you. I really hope though you had a great time and that you will try and reschedule something for a Saturday in February.*

As usual, Lance is not taking the blame for anything that has transpired. He is justifying all of his actions.

I have no desire to reschedule or see him at this point. My patience reaches the breaking point when I finish his e-mail.

> *So tell me about your day. I just stayed home and slept a good part of my day. Maybe I just needed the sleep. I have been so tired at work.*
>
> *Well, I'll talk to you Sunday. I am going to the nursing home in the morning and then will be home during the day. I may catch you before I go. Later Lynne, sleep tight! Lance* [with three Internet smileys added]

I am too tired to cope. I go to bed exhausted after a cold, depressing, emotionally exhausting day.

Sunday, January 21, 2001

I am up early. The first thing I think of when I awaken is Lance's ridiculous e-mail. I reread it, thinking I may feel differently about it after a good nights sleep.

Not so; I am furious, sad, and very disheartened, again. The tone of his e-mail is not one of regret. Lance is handing me another crumb. I feel like a puppy being patted on the head by his owner.

Lance "ministers" at the local nursing home the third Sunday of each month. He loves doing this. He also sings to the elderly. I admire his respect and compassion for the elderly, but I am not impressed with anything Lance says or does this day.

I sit with my coffee and ponder the last few weeks.

I recall my phone conversation with Lance a week before. He had said:

"If, for some reason, I met somebody here [New Jersey], and things suddenly became different, and you were not in the picture, I know that would hurt you, and it has nothing to do with anything."

I had not replied to his words during this conversation. He had continued by saying:

"God has shown me how easy I could get into this thing of having multiple women. What I have to remember is when I find the right woman [obviously not me] I can totally make that commitment to God in my thought life."

At that point I had said "You are a lot like Solomon."

Lance had ignored my comment and said, "I have to find the woman that I know I have the romance with, plus all the other things. If I am going to commit to one woman, I will have to have the sense this woman can really complete me."

I wonder who "this woman" is. I have been thinking constantly about a man who is thinking and talking about other women.

I respond to Lance's e-mail with a short synopsis of my day with Patti in New York City. I don't reveal to him my depression, disappointment, and remorse. In spite of all that has happened I don't want to rock the boat. How crazy is this?

Lance sends me another e-mail. He does not comment on my e-mail telling him about my day in New York. Obviously, he is not interested, even though he had asked how my day went. Instead he talks about himself, as usual. He says:

> Well I have been busy clearing the snow and ice from my car that was supposed to be yesterday, only it arrived 12-24 hours late...

I wonder what he means by the snow was late. He ends his letter with:

> Now I have to run off to the nursing home. MY message for today will be RESTING in the Lord, perfect message for a REST home, huh and for me too! [smiley added].
> Will catch you later, have a great day. [smiley]
> Lance [smiley]

I cannot believe how oblivious this man is to my feelings. Of course he capitalized the word "my." Lance is very much into himself.

The phone rings. It is Tony. I am in tears. I tell him about my day in New York City and the patronizing, clueless e-mail from Lance.

"I can't take this, Tony, I can't stand feeling this way," I sob.

Tony is forthright, as usual. "Move him out, Lynne. It is time for you to get on with your life. This man upsets you all the time. He is not for you."

I have heard this before from Tony – many times.

"I think I should break it off, Tony, but I am scared to death. What if I make a mistake?"

Tony asks, "Do you want him in your life?"

"Not if I have to feel like this all the time," I answer. I am still crying.

"Send him an e-mail and move on!" Tony says.

With Tony's help, I jot down a short e-mail. I title the e-mail, "Our Friendship."

I write:

Dear Lance,

I have done much pondering the last two days, and you can interpret and analyze me any way you choose, but after yesterday and the weekend's fiasco, it is obvious to me you don't feel the same way about me that I feel about you, otherwise you would have certainly met with me yesterday.

As of this writing, I would appreciate no further contact with you, and I wish you luck with your mission in life. Lynne

"Do the e-mail and move him out!" Tony says.

I start to whimper. I am scared to death.

"Get that e-mail going and send it!" Tony is yelling at me and showing me no mercy. "You can call me later."

I hang up the phone and write the e-mail. I read it over. I reread it. I am shaking. I am terrified. Should I send it? Will it give me peace? Do I really want to end this? Can I cope with never seeing or talking to Lance again?

The e-mail stares back at me from the computer screen, intimidating me. I am frightened. I ponder my feelings over the past few weeks. I have a rock in my stomach.

I know I am not happy. I am constantly in turmoil. I am in love. I miss him. I want him to love me. I want to see him. I want him to feel the same toward me as I do him. He doesn't. It is a no-brainer. Yes, I am better off without him.

But what if he does care? What will I be throwing away? Will this e-mail hurt him? Maybe I am being unreasonable. Naturally his feelings matter more than mine.

I am a wreck. I have to do this. I have to let go.

Shaking, I hit the "send" button. It is too late. Lance has my e-mail.

CHAPTER 15

Blame-shift

I take a deep breath. I did it. I broke up with Lance.

It's over. I can't believe it.

Immediately I turn on my VCR and start doing step aerobics. I need to release my stress hormones.

The phone rings.

I look at my caller ID. It's Lance. It has been only two minutes since I e-mailed him, and he has read my e-mail already.

The bastard; he has been online all day and has not e-mailed me. Naturally he is talking to his other female correspondents. He could care less about talking to me.

I continue my workout. I hear his voice on the answering machine, but the loud music drowns out what he is saying. I feel cold and heartless. I ignore his message.

After finishing my aerobics, I stare at the telephone, feeling intimidated by the red, blinking light. Hesitating, I press the "play" button.

"I can't believe you are doing this. I don't understand. I would appreciate it if you would call me back so that we can discuss this. Goodbye." Lance's voice sounds bewildered and a little hurt.

I am unmoved by Lance's message. I am not going to call him back. This man doesn't get it!

I need to leave my apartment and change the negative energy I am feeling. I visit a couple of friends and return home a few hours later.

Nervously, I log on to AOL. Lance has written me. His e-mail is two pages long. He writes:

> Lynne, I believe you should have called me but since you like e-mails, here is my e-mail response. I do not understand this bizarre behavior, because it makes no sense to me at all.

As usual, Lance is not admitting any wrongdoing. He is emphasizing my behavior and calling it bizarre.

> I was a little depressed yesterday thinking I could have been with you in New York, but wasn't. I was also kind of disappointed that when you couldn't cancel your reservations, that you didn't call me back to give me an opportunity to wait out the storm before you made other plans.

What is he talking about? I had e-mailed him Friday night telling him I couldn't cancel my reservations and that I was going. Lance had plenty of time to call me and change his mind. He continues:

> If I had known you couldn't cancel your reservations, I wouldn't have made the decision not to go that soon. But I guess it's easier for you to take my canceling as personal rather than try and understand my being concerned about snow storm's lest you find out I almost died in one, and have had a few other NJ Transit horror stories due to freezing rain and snow.

To me, this is a crock. If he was truly "afraid" of a train ride, why didn't he say that when he canceled? He is making me the one at fault. The blame-shifting worsens with his next sentence:

> Why does this one cancellation have to have so much deeper meaning to you? In my mind this is UTTERLY RIDICULOUS!
> But you know, IF you communicated to me, that it WAS important to YOU that I try and go, we could have talked it out, but YOU acted like everything was okay. Well, I guess I don't know you at all, and you don't know me either, although you make decisions like you do.

I cannot believe Lance did not know how important this weekend was to me after all the conflicts we had had over the January 20 date. He continues to pile on the guilt.

> *If I don't feel for you as much as you feel for me it is because of THIS kind of bizarre behavior that you do. If I am going to analyze you, then let me say, you do self-fulfilling prophesies of rejection to yourself, and as a result you DO get rejected. This is the second time you have done this to me, and both times it has been in YOUR mind, and has had NOTHING to do with me or what I feel for you. This makes NO sense to me at all.*
>
> *This is totally ridiculous to me. I am very hurt, disappointed and even a little broken hearted about this, but I won't beg you back.*

I feel empty. Have I really hurt Lance? He seems so bewildered. What if I made a mistake?

> *I do hope that you will reconsider and be reasonable about this, but then, who knows if you will do this again! Any time anything indicates in your mind that your feelings exceed mine for you, you back away COMPLETELY. And you don't let my feelings evolve naturally, but squelch the ones I do have for you with this petty nonsense.*

I have already forgotten how sad I was the day before in New York City. I am totally focused on Lance and his feelings. This is now about him, not me. His feelings matter, mine don't. He is minimizing my feelings, and I am going along with it. Lance has convinced me that I am the one at fault.

> *I am not convinced that I cannot fall deeply in love with you, but I become less and less convinced that I can, every time you back off like this. I guess you do not think it is either worth the time, because you sure put a lot of meaning into THIS past Saturday.*

Oh, no. Lance could have fallen in love with me if I had just been a little more patient; I am in tears as I finish reading…

> *I will truly miss you and all the fun we have had and the deep feelings we shared. I thought they meant more to you. They certainly meant a whole lot to me, and it really saddens me that everything is ending like this. This is a very sad day for me, and I almost can't believe you have decided this fate for us. I care for you deeply, and think this is the silliest most ludicrous thing to end our friendship now, but what can I say? I will really and truly miss you and I have no idea why I am losing you, and why it has to be this way at all.*
>
> *I guess I wish you success and happiness in YOUR mission in life too. Lance*

My heart and soul are flooded with guilt. What have I done? Was it a mistake to break up with Lance? I am a little girl again. I feel the same way as I did when my dad was mad at me and then I never saw him again. I start to panic. Will I ever see or talk to Lance again?

CHAPTER 16

Asking for Forgiveness

Monday, January 22, 2001

I wake up, lonely and heartbroken. The first thing that hits me when I wake up is Lance's e-mail. I have not answered it. I am upset and guilt-ridden. My emotions are in turmoil. I don't know how to fix this.

I call Tony. He is adamant that I did not make a mistake, but I am listening to my emotions and ignoring Tony's advice.

At work I am a basket case. I am unable to focus on my job. Tony works in another unit not far from me. I call him on the phone, crying. "I don't know what to do, Tony. What do you think I should do?"

Tony's patience is wearing thin. "What do you want to do, Lynne?"

"I want to give it another chance. I am going to send him an e-mail apologizing."

"Go ahead," Tony says with a sigh. He is fed up from trying to make me see the reality of the situation. "I'm here for you."

I quickly type an e-mail to Lance and send it to him at his workplace. I write:

> *I am so sorry Lance, for what I have done to you. I truly care for you, and I truly did not think you wanted to see me. I thought your excuse was lame (about the weather). I was on the bus for a total of seven hours, and all I could think of was that we could have met.*
>
> *I am terrified of a relationship. The way I feel about you terrifies me. Yes, you can call me insecure. I am not good at handling relationships at all.*

> *I wanted to see you. I miss you. I care about you. All I wanted was a few hours with you.*
>
> *I thought you were backing away from me the last few weeks and were trying to disengage yourself from me. I sent you that e-mail to let you off the hook. Yes, call me whatever you want. I am just an insecure, loving, and caring person that wouldn't hurt a fly and especially would never intentionally hurt you. I have never had anyone tell me that my behavior was bizarre.*

My next sentence is a beauty:

> *I totally agree with all you said. You are fine. I messed up. Please forgive me Lance and give me another chance.*
>
> *If you don't forgive me, I will go on, in peace. I am so sorry. I truly did not think you cared. You said on the phone a week ago you were afraid you would hurt me if you met someone who lived near you.*
>
> *I am at peace with whatever you decide. I would like us to continue the way we were. If you say no, I don't blame you. Again I am so sorry and I am asking your forgiveness. Lynne*

I can't wait to hit the send button. My e-mail has been sent, and I am praying that Lance understands and gives me another chance.

I go on a break with Tony and show him my e-mail to Lance. He is disgusted and says to me, "This e-mail is pathetic, Lynne. You are groveling."

I pay no attention to Tony's comments, although deep down, I know he is right. When I return from my break, I immediately check my e-mail. Lance has responded. He writes:

> *Just a quick response to let you now I got your message and we are fine. I will write you in length also, but just sending this quick note to give you some peace of mind. We are fine, all things can go back to the way they were. Lance [with three smileys]*

Lance is giving me another chance. What a wonderful man! He even cared enough about my feelings to e-mail me right away, because he knew how upset I was.

I breathe a sigh of relief.

CHAPTER 17

Communicating and Understanding Each Other

I arrive home after a long day at work, emotionally exhausted. I cannot believe I actually broke up with Lance. I am relieved and happy he is being so wonderful about it. He is giving me another chance!

Immediately I check my e-mail. Lance has sent me a four-page letter titled "Understanding Me." It begins:

Lynnie, Lynnie, Lynnie, what am I going to do with you? (lol)

"Lol" is a computer acronym used on the Internet meaning "laughing out loud." Lance uses it a lot. I find this acronym annoying and impersonal.

He then says:

Lynne, I am NOT in love with you! I have never been truly "in love" before.

Infatuated, yes. I was very infatuated with you when I first saw your picture. The more we communicated, the more infatuated I got. Then we met, and a little reality set in. Nothing terrible, mind you, but just reality. Then things started heating up again in my mind, until we had that bad e-mail communication.

Lance is recalling the New Year's Eve blow-up, which I believe was not my doing. He then admits:

> *I did cool off slightly and did begin to desire to meet other women a little more.*

Lance admits he cooled off. It was not my imagination. He continues:

> *I have spent a couple of hours each with many women I have met since my split up, and I could tell there would be no future with any of them. YOU are the only person I have had any desire to want to get to know more in person after a first meeting.*

Lance's next sentence will turn out to be prophetic in the months to come, and I will remember it. It is the reason I stayed with him for so long.

> *IF I get to the point I know for sure you and I do NOT have a future as a couple, I will say exactly 'that' to you and that I would enjoy remaining friends with you.*

Remaining friends with a man I have been romantically involved with is not an option for me. I know this about myself, but at this time, it is not relevant.

Lance informs me he was sad he could not be with me in New York City last Saturday and informs me I put too much emphasis on these "little things."

> *You put too much emphasis on these little things. The only time you should put emphasis on little things is when they really are a small expression of a BIG thing. You have to learn to communicate and confront before reacting or DON'T react at all!*

Lance will not admit he did not want to meet me. He refers to my breaking up with him as a "reaction."

Lance is minimizing my feelings and emotions and justifying his behavior.

It is not a little thing when someone tells you they care about you and suddenly cools off.

It is not a little thing when someone cancels a romantic meeting for a lame reason.

It is not a little thing when a person you care about is sending you mixed signals and has you in constant turmoil.

At this time, I am not rational. I want so badly for everything to be okay, even at the expense of my believing he is right and I am wrong. I actually think to myself that Lance may be correct in assuming I "overreacted."

He continues:

> *Your mission in life is NOT to make someone else's life easier by giving them a way out if they want to end their relationship with you, but to put it in God's hands and let HIM either give you the words to say, or just to trust Him to work in the other person and/or circumstances.*
>
> *Even if I was looking for a way out, I wouldn't have been happy letting the relationship end this way. It devalues everything we had.*

I wonder what "we had."

Lance ends his letter by telling me:

> *You have been a great comfort to me these last three and a half months. I have enjoyed your silly sense of humor. I know you have a big heart. This increases my respect for you.*

Lance is getting personal again and noticing my qualities and my sincerity. He ends his letter with:

> *Let's make a reservation for the next Saturday you have free in February and try and do what we planned to do January 20th. After we have spent a whole afternoon together, hopefully we will both have a little better idea where we are going.*
>
> *All is forgiven! Let's just learn so we don't make the same mistakes again* [smiley added].

I answer Lance's e-mail. I tell him his backing off and cooling down had me confused.

He writes back saying he has a history of not maintaining "hot" in a relationship. Is that supposed to make his cooling down okay?

I respond:

> *I will put one hundred percent into the RIGHT relationship. I love to give of myself to that one special person. I am the kindest, most sincere woman you will ever know. In spite of my insecurities, I also have the confidence in what God can and will do in and through me.*

I should not have said I am insecure. Lance grabs the opportunity. He writes back:

> *Just remind me it is your insecurities you are asking or inquiring about and I will try even harder to be honest and reassuring. Once I am aware you are insecure about something, I will be more conscious about keeping you reassured about it.*
>
> *You need to face your insecurities head on because if you don't it will undermine any good we have in our relationship.*

Lance likes thinking I am insecure. It gives him power. Lance likes weak women. Right now I fit the profile. Why didn't I stay strong when I broke up with him yesterday?

I am vulnerable, and my feelings for Lance override my common sense.

Again, Lance is sending me long, e-mails two or three times a day. The communication continues for the next month. We set a date to meet in New York City on February 24, 2001.

The strong feelings I had for Lance after our first meeting return. I cannot wait to see him again.

CHAPTER 18

Two Wonderful Invitations

Tuesday, January 23, 2001

Lance and I are back on track! Today he writes:

> *We must be honest with ourselves, honest with God and then honest with each other, otherwise honesty will NOT prevail in our relationship.*

Lance compares me with his wife, Karen. He will do this a lot in the months to follow:

> *I have made many of the same mistakes with Karen, which you have made in our e-mail communication. I trust and hope you won't do what I did and keep making the same mistakes over again. It ruined whatever a good marriage I could have had, and it has the potential to ruin whatever relationship we CAN have.*

Lance is saying the mistakes in our "relationship" have been made by me, not him. I believe him at this time and am cautious in my interaction with him. I don't want to "screw up" again.

Wednesday, January 24, 2001

Lance e-mails me:

> *You know, YOU have a lot of wisdom. I am pleasantly surprised. I guess it should be no surprise because YOU have recognized the wisdom in me...and that is wise! LOL*

Lance's arrogance and self-absorption are not apparent to me at this time. He continues:

> *I am glad we are on the same page now. I don't think there is anything we have not completely resolved.*

I record in my journal: "Lance finally saw my heart in my e-mail to him. I think we have resolved everything up to this point."

I am surprised to get a telephone call from Lance this evening. He informs me he has been invited to a wedding on March 31, 2001.

A former neighbor of his, Jacob, who he babysat for years ago, is getting married. It is a black-tie affair at the Roslyn Claremont Hotel in Roslyn, New York. Lance invites me to be his date to this formal affair! I would love to go.

This is wonderful. I will be meeting Lance in New York City in February, and I will also be seeing him in March.

Lance and Jacob are Jewish. Lance has not seen him since his bar mitzvah years ago. I tell Lance I have never been to a bar mitzvah and would love to attend one someday.

Friday, January 26, 2001

Lance and I are getting closer. Breaking up with him was the right decision. I can tell he has feelings for me again. He needed that wake-up call.

Today, Lance e-mails me at work and tells me to call him. He has a surprise for me and wants to hear my reaction on the telephone. I call him immediately, my heart pounding with anticipation.

He tells me his sister is having a bar mitzvah for her twin boys, Donald and Edward, on April 25. He wants me to be his date. It will be in Long Island. He remembers I had expressed my desire to go to a bar mitzvah, and he thinks it is something I would enjoy. Of course I would love to go.

I will be seeing Lance three times in the near future! What a change from a week before, when I thought it was the end of our relationship.

I have to find a special dress to wear to the wedding in March. I want to look beautiful for Lance.

Friday, February 2, 2001

Today is Lance's birthday. I surprise him with a phone call wishing him a happy birthday. I also send him a card in the "regular" mail, stating that I would like to treat him to lunch at a restaurant of his choice when we meet in the city. He gladly accepts.

The trip to New York City is just four weeks away!

CHAPTER 19

Deep Conversations

Lance has been calling me Saturday mornings, and we have been e-mailing each other every day.

I look forward to his calls. I love hearing his voice. Our conversations have been casual and about *him*, *his* wisdom, *his* job, and how God is using *him* to help others.

I want to talk about "us." I am patient and glad his e-mails have been somewhat personal.

Saturday, February 10, 2001

I receive Lance's Saturday-morning phone call. Today's conversation is different. Lance is talking about "our" relationship. He says, "I just know I have a lot of good feelings about you. I can't wait to see you."

My heart skips a beat. Our meeting in New York City is two weeks away, and Lance can't wait to see me.

He continues, "I like you so much. I just think about you, holding you, and being close to you…"

I close my eyes, imagining being in his arms. I freeze when he adds, "…lying naked with you, and being inside you."

I am taken aback by Lance's sexual innuendo. I am offended and flattered at the same time.

I respond by saying, "I wasn't thinking about that. I guess I will take that as a compliment."

"I had to tell you," he says. "A part of me felt the last few days I could almost lose control. If you resisted, though, I would lose my desire immediately."

"That speaks volumes to me," I stammer. My heart is pounding. This is the first time Lance has talked to me about sexual intimacy. I like it.

"Here's how I rationalize this," he says. "Since I have been a Christian, I have not had intercourse. I really don't want to because I don't believe it is right. But if I felt we were going to end up together, I could justify it in my mind. You can be monogamous and not be married, but to me it is not right, according to God's Word."

"I am glad you brought this up," I reply. "We are definitely on the same page. I agree with you. It would not be right to have sexual intercourse if we were not married."

It is a thrill to hear Lance talk to me like this. I am extremely attracted to him physically, and hearing him speak these words makes me feel close to him.

Lance continues, "Psychologically, I was afraid you might lose control. Your innocence just makes me love you. It is an honest innocence, not stupidity"

I am glad to hear him state that I am not stupid. On this day, I am in denial of his condescending flattery.

I am relieved when he says, "It strengthens the relationship to not have sex. I like what I have with you. I think the next time we are together will be very confirming. You are a sweetheart. I love you."

Wow, Lance said, "I love you!" I am smart enough to know he is not saying he is "in love" with me, but the words "I love you" are music to my ears.

This has to be more than a friendship. A male and a female who are just friends do not use the term "relationship," nor do they discuss the possibility of having sex. Lance continuously refers to us as being in a relationship.

Before hanging up, I say, "It has been wonderful talking to you today."

Lance says, "Yes, it was an 'us' talk."

An "us" talk! Yes, it was! Our relationship has gone up a notch. We are closer. I am on a cloud. I am glad we have the same sexual views. I think about Lance the rest of the day and dream of being in his arms.

That afternoon, I mail a valentine to him in the regular mail ("snail mail," as Lance calls it). I pick out a special card; caring, but not too forward.

The evening before Valentine's Day, Lance e-mails me and asks me if I am the "secret admirer" who sent him a "warm, fuzzy, furry, online valentine." He thinks it is me who sent it to him. It isn't! I tell him I did not send it.

Wednesday, February 14, 2001 - Valentines Day

Lance surprises me with a "Happy Valentine's Day" phone call before I go to work. He tells me to check my e-mail for a surprise. I receive an online musical valentine with a song titled "The Test of Time."

"Let your heart know what's on your mind
Let your love grow and it will shine
If the love you find is by design it will surely stand the test of time"

I know Lance's and my love will surely stand the test of time!

I look at my online valentine again. It is fuzzy and furry-looking.

I say to Lance, "I noticed the valentine you sent me was fuzzy and furry-looking. Didn't you say your 'secret admirer' sent you a furry-looking valentine?"

Since Lance is "honest," he answers, "Yes, it is the same one. I liked it and thought I would send it on to you. I also sent something back to the secret admirer and asked 'who are you?'"

Lance did not take the time to find a special online card for me. Instead, he recycled a valentine sent to him! I ignore this flag.

I also wonder about the valentine sent to me in the regular mail from Lance. The year is whited out. It must be a recycled card meant for someone else a different year.

Saturday, February 17, 2001

Lance and I have another long telephone conversation this morning. We are communicating and getting closer every day. I love it.

"I like you a whole lot," he says. "I want to hug you, be close to you. When I say I want to be inside you, I mean I want to be close to you. It is a wonderful feeling I have when I think of you."

I long to be in Lance's arms. My entire body tingles when Lance talks to me about sexual intimacy. I have never felt such strong chemistry with any man like I do with Lance.

Before I can respond, Lance suddenly shifts the conversation to his wife, Karen. I had almost forgotten he was married.

"I was over at my wife's apartment a couple weeks ago. She asked me if I had started things with the divorce."

"Does she want the divorce?" I ask.

"I want to make sure she is financially stable," he says. "She is always judgmental about my character. She doesn't want to stay married to me. She gave everything to the marriage, and it wasn't reciprocated. She thinks I am cunning and crafty."

Lance's wife is right. I don't see this yet. I have blinders on.

Lance says, "I think I want it all now with us. But at the same time, I am not ready. I am still married. I know in a marriage things can fade, but you can grow if you have love. You have to cherish the love and do whatever it takes to be sure you don't lose it."

I will be patient. I am always patient, always waiting. Waiting for what? I want to conform myself into the perfect partner for him and wait until he is ready to devote himself to me. Lance presents himself as a man who knows it all and who has great wisdom.

Lance is married! This is a no-brainer. But I am not paying attention to my brain.

CHAPTER 20

Lance's Ministry at the Nursing Home

Lance was previously a worship leader at a church near his home. He led the congregation in singing, praising, and worship. This ministry was taken away from him when the board of deacons and the pastor found out he had been corresponding with women on the Internet while living with his wife. The church was very supportive of his wife, Karen. Because of this, Lance had stopped attending church. Karen and her mother are still attending.

Lance also has a ministry at a nursing home about twenty minutes from where he lives. He sings and preaches to the residents once a month. He is still continuing this ministry, even though he has stopped attending his regular church. Karen used to join him at the nursing home, but has not gone there since their separation. On February 19, he writes:

> *I love them at the nursing home and they love me. I do think I am a real bright spot for them. They love my singing and my messages. I work hard at trying to keep them awake and touching them and asking them questions requiring one-word answers. What I do for them is a drop in the bucket but I know they appreciate it so much and look forward to it.*

It is easy for Lance to talk about himself in his e-mails. Also, I have gotten used to not hearing back from him until the next day even though he is online all day. He tells me my e-mails are "always welcome," as long as I "don't mind not hearing back until the next morning." He adds:

> *Your e-mails make me smile and laugh and warm my heart… that's good any time.*

I wonder why it takes him twelve hours to hit the reply button. I ignore the possibility that he may be chatting with other women online.

The church is right in taking Lance's ministries away from him. If Lance is married, dating another woman (me), and corresponding with other women on the Internet, it is hypocritical for him to be in any kind of ministry.

I am glad Lance feels close enough to me to share his personal problems regarding his ministry.

He ends his e-mail by saying:

> *Well, on a more pleasant note 'US'……yes, you and me…the bright exciting part of my life right now. You are just a wonderful person and so in tune with me. I think of you and my heart melts. How nice it would be for you to spend some relaxing time in my arms. My lovely Lynniekins* [smileys added].

I can't wait to see Lance! The New York City trip is just five days away.

CHAPTER 21

Second Meeting in New York City

Saturday, February 24, 2001

I am up at 5:30 a.m. Today I will be seeing Lance!

During the bus ride to New York City, I pray and ask God's blessing on this day. I know in my heart everything is going to run smoothly and will confirm Lance and I are meant to be together. It has been over two months since our first meeting.

Lance had e-mailed me the day before:

> *I am truly grateful to God that I can be a special blessing in your life. I can't think of a person I would rather pour my love and energy into than you, because it is always so well appreciated. I really hope (with the help of God) we have what it takes to make the feelings grow and last a lifetime* [three smileys added]. *I shouldn't have any trouble being at Radio City at Noon.*

The bus arrives at 10:30 a.m. and drops us off in front of McDonald's on Sixth Avenue, between Forty-sixth and Forty-seventh streets. I go inside and enjoy a hot cup of coffee upstairs where I had sat, four weeks ago, peering out the window and feeling lost and alone. It is different today. The sun is shining, and the street is alive with tourists. Some are shopping; others are at the vendor on the corner enjoying a hot dog. The city is alive today with excitement and magic.

I walk outside and feel the brisk, cold air on my face. It is less than an hour before I will be meeting Lance. The Hilton Hotel is four blocks away. I have time to go there to primp and make sure my hair and makeup are perfect.

At 11:50 a.m., I stand in front of Radio City Music Hall. Suddenly, Lance appears! His dark brown wavy hair is blowing in the breeze. He looks so handsome and appealing. We smile and hug each other. There is an instant chemistry.

I take his arm as we walk toward Broadway. Lance has chosen Tad's Steakhouse for lunch. It is a restaurant he frequently went to as a boy and he wants to go back there to reminisce.

We arrive at Tad's, and we order a steak dinner. I buy him lunch as a belated birthday gift. After we eat, I hand Lance a small, wrapped package. It is a daily devotional titled "God Calling." Lance is pleased. He says he has seen this booklet before and has always wanted one.

We enjoy talking and exchanging photos of our families. We have been at our table over an hour. The time flies. Everything is flowing smoothly. The energy and interaction is wonderful.

Upon leaving the restaurant, we head for Madame Tussaud's Wax Museum, which is located in the heart of Times Square. I touch Lance affectionately on the back while he is buying the tickets. We both feel an immense chemistry.

We are there for over two hours. The wax figures look so realistic! Lance poses with Barbara Streisand, President Bush, and Celine Dion while I take his picture. He then takes a photo of me sitting with Marilyn Monroe and Jennifer Lopez. We are having a ball being childlike and enjoying the wax figures on the several floors of the large museum. I dance with Madonna, and Lance clowns around with Johnny Carson.

It is dark by the time we leave the museum. Lance would like us to go somewhere for a drink. I suggest the Hilton Hotel. It has a cozy lounge with cushioned chairs and little tables. It is only a few blocks from where I will be catching my bus in an hour.

The lounge is warm and manifests a nice ambience. Lance and I sit across from each other at a small table. He orders a glass of white zinfandel for each of us.

The loveseats are all occupied. Lance keeps hoping we will be able to get one so we can snuggle. Finally, a couple gets up and leaves. We dash over to the empty couch. Lance puts his arm around me. We are like two lovebirds, gazing into each other's eyes and kissing occasionally.

Lance's arms feel wonderful around me. I want to sit there with him forever. Lance asks a patron to take a picture of us together. We sit there, laughing, talking, and kissing until it is time for me to go back to my bus.

Lance walks me the few short blocks to McDonald's. He waits with me until I board the bus back to Binghamton. He kisses me, and he promises to have an e-mail waiting for me when I get home.

As the bus leaves New York, again, I look across the river at Manhattan. The lighted city against the black sky, with colorful reflections in the water, takes my breath away. I have the same feeling as I did after our first meeting.

I know, without a doubt, that I am meant to spend my life with Lance.

CHAPTER 22

The Relationship Blossoms

Monday, February 26, 2006

It is two days since my romantic meeting with Lance in New York City. The magic we shared still lingers. I record in my journal: "Had a wonderful e-mail from Lance. We are getting closer, and we are reading 'God Calling' together every day."

Lance's e-mails confirm our time together in New York was meaningful. He writes:

> *I think about you a lot and how close I felt with you walking through the streets of New York and in the Wax Museum and in the Hilton - and without one sexual thought! I just felt myself getting turned on writing this…AMAZING huh? It is like; how deep can we really go in our love? What potential of love can we have here if we both set ourselves out to cherish and nourish? And it must be this way, or it could fade or disappear like it has with so many other couples.*

He then adds:

> *The whole day with you was wonderful. When I touch other women, most often it is either just kindness, affection, or MOSTLY sex, but with YOU, it does come from a heart of pure love, and ALL my senses do get involved with each component of my being: mental,*

> *emotional, physical and spiritual. Being with you, for me to experience this is also very different and something I am not used to.*

He is looking forward to seeing the photos I took while we were together. They are already in the mail.

My daughter Jane's birthday is coming up on March 16. She lives in New Jersey, about fifteen minutes from Lance. Lance and I consider this to be a "divine coincidence." I haven't seen Jane and my grandchild, Brian, since November. I would love to visit her on her birthday and then see Lance the next day for a couple of hours while in New Jersey.

I telephone Jane. I tell her I would like to take a bus to Port Authority in New York City and then take a train to the Hamilton Station, which is five minutes away from her home. Jane is glad I am coming, and says she will pick me up at the train station on Friday, March 16.

I tell Jane about Lance. I ask if it would be all right for me to spend Friday evening with her family, all day Saturday with her and Brian, and then have Lance pick me up on Saturday night. I would like her to meet him.

Jane is fine with this suggestion. I am anxious for her to meet Lance. I know she will like him.

Lance is pleased that I will be coming to New Jersey in two weeks. I would rather take the bus and train than drive. My car is a used Toyota and has several miles on it.

Saturday, March 3, 2001

I meet my friend, Naomi. I have been talking to her about Lance for weeks. She is happy for me and offers to help me find a dress for the wedding in Roselyn, which is just four weeks away.

I try on a beautiful champagne-colored gown with golden flecks all over it. The spaghetti straps are jeweled, and there are slits going up each side of the gown. The dress is gorgeous, and the jeweled straps and slits make it appear sexy. This is the dress!

I find a pair of gold pumps that match the dress perfectly. Naomi and I pick out a beautiful gold shawl and a sparkling gold handbag. I am all set for the black-tie wedding.

The relationship with Lance is growing in our e-mail communication. He writes:

> *You bring out the best in me and inspire me to do everything I can to make you happy. I don't ever want to be a disappointment to you, but an inspiration, and a source of strength, wisdom, knowledge, help, comfort and encouragement.*

Our interaction has escalated since the meeting in New York City. I think about Lance constantly. He continues in the same e-mail:

> *We haven't spent enough time to honestly say we are "in love" with each other, but I do see clearly that the potential is there. I want it all Lynnie, and I know you want to make it happen as much as I do! We must NEVER allow things to cool down to the point where we are not going forward. Even stagnancy is not good. We must go forward at a pace that is comfortable for the two of us. Thank God, that He made the pace possible with us.*
>
> *I look forward to receiving your e-mails, for they minister LIFE to me! I feel the love coming from them.*

Sunday, March 4, 2001

Lance and I are excited about seeing each other in New Jersey. We enjoy sharing ideas for what we should do on Saturday night, March 17.

Lance lives near Princeton in an apartment he shares with Roy, a man from his church. He can't wait for me to see his room, meet his cat, and have some quality time together.

He is considerate of my time with my daughter, and he is willing to see me later in the evening if I want to have dinner with Jane, her husband, and Brian. I check with Jane and she suggests I have dinner with Lance. He can pick me up at her house, and she will meet him.

Lance e-mails me this afternoon. He writes:

> *Oh Lynnie I think about you a lot* [two smileys]

In the same e-mail he tells me about his sister, Susan. I will be meeting her at the wedding on March 31, and of course, I will see her at the bar mitzvah in April, since it is for her twin boys, Donald and Edward.

Susan is divorced and has a boyfriend, Patrick. He will also be at the wedding.

I also tell Lance about my sister, Lea. Lea is supportive of our relationship, and she is looking forward to meeting him at some point.

Lea is astounded when I share a cute story with her regarding Lance. I tell her Lance once had a cat and would say to it, "I love you to pieces, Pussy Kot." Lea and I have used the phrase "love you to pieces" many times when talking about a person we care about. I tell Lance that my sister could not get over another person using that phrase, since she and I have never heard anyone else use it.

Lance responds:

I loved hearing about the fact that your sister thought she and you were the ONLY ones that would say 'love to pieces' and that she loved the fact that I said it too! Now maybe she will feel good about me becoming a part of your family, if of course we get married. That may just be another divine sign.

He then adds:

Maybe in May, I will make my first trip up there to visit. If I do, I would love to meet her and all of your family if possible.

Oh Lynnie, I just love you!! You are such a wonderful, loving, sweet, caring, funny, humble beautiful person and really I could go on and on and on. You are such a blessing to me, and I always want to be a blessing to you. Cherish, Nourish, and then flourish.

I will catch you later my Sweetheart! Lancecat

The "love you to pieces, pussy kot" becomes the closing in our e-mails. We abbreviate it to LYTPPK.

I think to myself, this cannot get any better. Lance is falling in love with me. He wants our relationship to grow, he wants to see me in New Jersey, and now he is talking about traveling to my home and meeting my family. He has even mentioned marriage.

Spring is coming. Romance is in the air; I am walking on sunshine!

CHAPTER 23

Seeing Lance in New Jersey

Monday, March 12, 2001

Lance continues to send me loving e-mails. He is also calling me more often.

Today, he writes:

> *Spring has never been romantic to me because I have not had real romance in my life. I have found a beautiful woman who touches my heart and soul every day; one who always puts a smile on my face and melts my being.*
>
> *These feelings are not superficial sappy stuff. They are based on a true connection we have. I am getting turned on just writing this. You are awesomely adorable!* [three smileys] *I love you, Lynnie* [three smileys]

I am ecstatic at how well our relationship is going. My trip to New Jersey is just four days away.

I pick up my gown at the dressmakers, which I had altered for the March 31 wedding in Roslyn, New York. I can't wait to wear it. I want to look beautiful for Lance.

Friday, March 16, 2001

Today is my daughter Jane's birthday. I board the 10:30 a.m. Greyhound Bus from Binghamton, New York to Port Authority Bus Terminal in New York City. Penn Station is just a few blocks away from Port Authority, and I can walk to it after arriving in New York City. Then I will take the next available train to Hamilton Station in New Jersey.

I give Lance a quick call on my cell phone. He is glad to hear from me. He offers to pick me up at the Hamilton Station. I inform him Jane will be picking me up and thank him for the offer.

I look forward to seeing Jane and celebrating her birthday with her. I have a small gift for her, a glass elephant. Her husband, Paul, is an avid Republican and works at the campaign headquarters during elections. The figurine will be a nice addition to their elephant collection. I also look forward to seeing Paul and my grandson, Brian.

I successfully board the train at Penn Station around 2:30 p.m. Jane and Brian greet me at the Hamilton Station about an hour later.

I have a wonderful evening at my daughter's home. Paul's sister, brother-in-law, and son come over. We have pizza and ice cream and celebrate Jane's birthday. Later Jane, Brian, and I take a walk around the neighborhood. It is warmer in New Jersey than in New York. I can smell the spring air, and I think of Lance.

When we get back, I get a short call from Lance. Jane talks to him and gives him directions to her house. I can't wait for her to meet him tomorrow night. After all my disastrous relationships with men, she will see I have finally met the right one.

Saturday, March 17, 2001

Jane, Brian, and I go to a nearby mall this morning. We have a great time browsing the shops. I buy Brian a couple of outfits. He is starting to know who I am. He calls me Gin Gin, and I love it. He is a doll.

We return home around 3:00 p.m. Brian has to take his nap. Lance will be picking me up in just four hours.

I start getting ready for my date with Lance around 5:00 p.m. I take a hot bubble bath, wash my hair, and spend an hour primping and putting on my makeup. I want to look perfect. Jane asks me with a smile. "Are you wearing *those* pants?"

"Yes," I say, "What's wrong?"

"Mom, you look like an old lady! Here, wear these." She finds me a pair of black dress pants. They fit perfectly and complement the lime-green sweater I am wearing. I get Jane's smile of approval.

It is 6:55 p.m. My heart is pounding. Lance will be here any minute!

Jane says, "Mom, let me answer the door when he gets here, okay?" I can tell she is amused at my nervousness.

The doorbell rings. Jane lets Lance in, and they introduce themselves to each other. He is wearing a bright, red jacket. I love his dark, brown, wavy hair. He looks gorgeous. Jane is surprised he looks so young. She later tells me she was expecting a tall, gray-haired, older-looking man with glasses. Lance is short, young-looking, and handsome.

Lance gives me a big hug. The chemistry is brewing already.

I ask him to join my daughter and me in the den. Lance and I hold hands and sit together on the couch. I introduce him to the family cat, Lucy, and to Brian, who is happily playing. We spend about fifteen minutes talking to Jane. I am so proud of Lance. I am sure Jane is impressed.

Lance and I say good night to Jane. I inform her I will be back at a reasonable time. Lance and I chuckle at the mother telling the daughter when she will be home from a date.

Lance has the evening planned. After we get into his car, he calls the local Chinese place from his cell phone and orders us dinner to take out. We will dine at his apartment. I will also meet his roommate, Roy.

We park at the Chinese restaurant. Lance tells me to stay in the car. The owner of the restaurant knows Karen and him. Lance does not want to be seen with "another woman." The evening is flowing too smoothly for me to notice this flag.

I ignore another flag when he asks me to "duck down" in the car when we drive by Karen's apartment complex, two buildings away from his. He doesn't want to hurt Karen and is adamant about her *not* finding out that he is "seeing someone." I feel foolish ducking when we drive by.

We pull up to Lance's complex. It is dark out. He lives in a cluster of brick apartments that all look alike. Before separating, Lance and Karen had lived just two buildings away. I wonder why he chose to live so close to her after they separated.

Lance's apartment is plain-looking. There is a brown, shabby couch to the right as we enter the living room through the front door. The dining room is to the left of the living room, which completes an "L" shape. Lance and Roy have used the dining area to store boxes and other miscellaneous items. I notice a guitar case on the floor.

The small kitchen is off to the left of the dining area. The door on the opposite side of the kitchen leads to a hallway. Lance's roommate, Roy, has a room on the right of the hallway. Lance knocks on his door. Roy is sitting at a computer desk in his small cluttered room. Lance has told me Roy is a Christian and does not approve of our relationship because Lance is a married man.

Lance introduces me to Roy. I smile and say hello. Lance then tells Roy that he and I will be in his room. I can tell Lance is indicating to Roy he wants privacy with me. I am all for that!

Lance opens the door to his room. I am astounded at how different it looks from the rest of the apartment. It is so large that Lance could almost live in this space by himself. I surmise the reason he has the large room and Roy the small one is he is paying the monthly rent himself. Roy is obviously struggling financially.

Lance's room is painted light blue. His computer is on the left as I enter. I am pleased he has several pictures of me on the wall and on his desk. Straight ahead is a bulletin board. Lance has tacked pictures of his parents, grandparents, and siblings on it. There is also a picture of Karen and her mom. Karen is an attractive redhead.

To the right of the room is his couch. It is covered with a light-blue velour throw. There is a picture of Jesus on the back wall behind the couch. I meet Lance's adorable shorthaired white cat, Puffy. I pet her and pick her up, and she purrs happily.

Lance has set up a small table with candles, a tablecloth, and dinnerware, in the center of the room. He has also downloaded songs onto his computer. The lights are low, and romantic music is playing. It is a perfect setting for a romantic dinner.

Lance opens a bottle of wine and pours me a glass. We toast to our future and enjoy a wonderful candlelit dinner. I am heartened that he has made such an effort to make sure everything is perfect for our time together. Lance and I cannot stop touching each other and looking at each other. The chemistry is very strong. I want him to kiss me.

After dinner I take pictures of Lance at his computer and he takes a picture of me sitting on the couch with Puffy.

Lance takes the dishes out to the kitchen. I follow him like a puppy dog, playfully putting my hands on the back of his shoulders. He turns around, grabs me, and kisses me. I love being in his arms. We have fun eating ice cream out of the container.

Back in the room we sit on the couch, holding hands. He starts talking to me about Karen. He is almost in tears as he tells me he drove by her apartment earlier that day and saw his mother-in-law's wheelchair sitting outside by the door. It tears him apart that he has left Karen with the full responsibility of caring for her mom. I admire Lance for being so concerned and caring for his wife and his mother-in-law.

Lance has rented a video, *Meet the Parents*. He likes comedy. He is also an avid Jerry Seinfeld fan and enjoys *Seinfeld* reruns. We will watch the movie, and if there is time, also watch a couple of *Seinfeld* reruns that he has videotaped.

Lance moves the couch up near the TV, which sits on a dresser to the left of his computer. He puts his arm around me, and we enjoy the movie while sipping another glass of wine. We laugh a lot and kiss in between the laughter.

After watching the movie we are back on the couch again. I feel very sensual as Lance kisses me and touches me. I would love to spend the night but we have decided ahead of time not to because my visit to New Jersey was initially to see my daughter. I lay there in his arms, and he holds me tight. We almost fall asleep.

Suddenly we realize it is after 2:00 a.m. Lance and I chuckle as he drives me home. I feel like a teenager who has not kept her curfew.

Lance drives slowly into Jane's driveway at 2:30 a.m. We hope no one hears us. He kisses me goodnight and says he will call me tomorrow. I slither in through the garage, feeling like a burglar. I successfully make it to the guest room without being caught. Around 3:00 a.m., I snuggle under the covers and fall sound asleep, dreaming of being in Lance's arms.

CHAPTER 24

"In Love"

Monday, March 19, 2001

I am on a cloud. What a wonderful time I had with Lance two nights ago! We are getting closer and more intimate on the telephone. Lance is talking about "our" relationship more than he ever has before.

Lance feels the same as I do about our time together. He tells me in a telephone conversation this morning:

"That night was the first time we were really 'alone' with each other. I felt so connected to you in every way; physically, emotionally, and spiritually."

I am breathless listening to his words, and I tell him I felt the same way. He continues:

"Just spending time with you after watching the movie, listening to the music and not even saying anything, lying in each others arms; it was magic. When you left, I was able to receive something from God, and I felt at peace with myself."

Lance calls me again this evening. I can't believe how often I have been hearing from him. Also, my concern about his talking to other women is starting to wane. He says:

"I don't need to be online chatting with anybody at all. I see the difference now, why I was so drawn to so many women. I was hungering. But with you and me, if we have the love, everything else falls into place. My feelings for you are very deep. They really incorporate everything into my entire being. When I put my hand on your soft skin, I feel your softness through and through. You take such good care of yourself."

Lance is talking about an exclusive relationship with me. I know in my heart we were met to be together. My patience has paid off. He is starting to see it now. He continues:

"I guard our relationship with my life. I don't even want to go around with another girl. I am a man, and I can look, but now when I look, I can say, 'so what!' What I have with you is worth so much."

"When did you start to feel this way?" I ask.

"When you said goodbye," he says. "I felt like I had lost a part of me. When you sent me that e-mail saying that you did not want to see me again, I told Roy, 'I got dumped. Lynne doesn't want to go out with me any more.' I felt terrible. That was the turning point."

I smile to myself as I recall that horrible lonely day in New York City and how Lance had canceled meeting me at the last minute. Yes, I definitely did the right thing by breaking up with him the next day. Lance needed to know he was not God's gift to women. It got his attention.

It is too bad that I don't remember, in the months to come, that Lance's narcissism needs to be recalled and kept in check. My heart is ruling at this point, and I am not paying attention to my head.

I almost forget Lance is married when we have these intimate conversations. My mind jolts back to reality when he starts talking about his wife.

"I started writing a letter to Karen. I want to try and communicate everything to her. If I said to my wife that I was willing to live with her and not go on the Internet, but that I am not in love with her and there is someone out there I know I could love, I am sure she would not want me back under the circumstances."

I smile when he adds, "I think you will make the most wonderful wife in the world."

I can tell that he truly cares for Karen, but I do not see her as a threat to our relationship. Lance is being so *honest* with me about everything.

Tuesday, March 20, 2001

The wedding in Roslyn is just eleven days away. I have my dress and accessories, and I cannot wait to go to this black-tie affair with Lance. I picture how beautiful I will look in my gown and how handsome he will look in his tuxedo.

Lance and I have a wonderful conversation on the telephone this night. He says: "We have a combination of a friendship and an intimate, special commitment, day-to-day, in how we are to each other. There is now a new entity. It has to be nourished."

I have emotionally emerged in Lance. I am happily surprised when he adds: "I am ready to pluck all my ads off of the Internet. It is not appropriate for me to be going out with lots of women. When I was married, that was all I could think about."

Wednesday, March 21, 2001

When I arrive at work, I receive an e-mail from Lance written at 6:52 a.m. He writes:

> *Good morning my love. I loved so much talking with you last night. We had some deep conversation and apparently you were not aware of how serious I am about you. I know you feel the same about me. I love you.* [three smileys]
>
> *Have I told you I love you? Have I told you I love that you love my arms, my touch and my voice and that I make you happy and that I make you smile?* [three smileys]

I am filled to the brim with emotion, and my eyes are watering when I read:

> *I once said in an e-mail to you that I am not "in love" with you; in fact I have probably said it to you more than once. Well that is NOT true any more...*
>
> *I know now that I AM "in love" with you!* [five smileys added]
>
> *God calling today: ALL IS WELL. God is planning your journey and OUR journey. Courage, courage, courage! Look forward to hearing from you later, my love* [Three smileys]
>
> *LYTPPK, Lancecat (Love you to pieces Pussy Kot)*

Lance is in *love* with me. I knew it! I don't think our love can possibly go any deeper.

I am in love with him, too. This is definitely the man I was meant to spend my life with.

CHAPTER 25

Wife and Church Issues

Sunday, March 25, 2001

Lance and I are in love! My heart is singing, and I think about him constantly. I cannot believe how fast the time has gone and how much our relationship has progressed in just a few weeks.

In five days, I will again be traveling to New Jersey to attend the formal wedding that Lance had invited me to in January. The ceremony and reception is in Nassau County, just outside of New York City at the Roslyn Claremont Hotel in Roslyn, New York. It is an exclusive seventy-five-room, European-style hotel nestled in the historic village of Roslyn.

Lance and I have discussed our plans for this weekend. I will be traveling to New Jersey on Friday, March 30, and I will spend the night at my daughter, Jane's house. Lance will pick me up late afternoon on Saturday, March 31. Since Roslyn is over two hours away, we have decided to spend our first night together at the Roslyn Claremont Hotel. Lance has made reservations for us as "Mr. and Mrs." How nice that sounds!

We are looking forward to sleeping together and have set boundaries for our intimacy. We can be close and not have sex. I have a set of pink-cotton shortie pajamas which will cover me appropriately and look appealing at the same time. I want to look attractive, but not too sensual.

I cannot wait for Lance to see me in my exquisite, sparkling, gold-champagne-colored gown. I want to look beautiful, and I want him to be enamored when he sees me.

On this day, I get a call from Lance at 2:00 p.m. I am surprised to hear from him since he never calls me on a Sunday afternoon. We had already talked this morning.

Lance is upset. He just hung up from a phone call from Karen. She told him her mom is declining fast. Lance loves his mother-in-law, Celia, and is very concerned. Apparently, there was a lot of tension in his conversation with Karen, and communicating with her was very difficult.

I notice this time that he is calling her "Karen" rather than referring to her as "my wife."

"Karen knows I am not in love with her. I think on some level she knows I still do love her, but she will come to realize that it is not as a husband. I told her I tried to set up an appointment for counseling, and I was only doing it for her."

Lance's voice is frustrated and defensive. I quietly listen.

"I have been to my pastor for counseling. I understand my problems. I really tried to explain to him I couldn't stay married to Karen. He's clueless. He thinks I have a problem. Sometimes these pastors jump on a particular sin, and if that is the sin you are in, then that is the one they crucify you for."

I am shocked when Lance says, "Pastor thinks I need help. He knew I had that cyber thing on the Internet. I didn't have sex with my wife for ten years. That is not normal."

This is the first time Lance has said anything to me about *"cyber sex"* with other women on the Internet when he was married. I knew he was e-mailing and instant-messaging other women, which ultimately lead to the breakup of his marriage.

Before I can respond, Lance says, "I didn't feel romantic when I was married to Karen. I could have had sex just to have sex, if one day I wanted to. I had biological needs. Karen was content to not have sex and have us get along fine as long as I treated her nicely. That is all she asked for."

Flag! As long as he treated her nicely? Is Lance not nice?

I almost choke when he says: "I didn't get into telling the pastor I would masturbate. 'You need sex,' was the thing that he [the pastor] was focusing on."

Lance continues: "You are the first person I can say this to who understands me completely."

Still in shock, I ask, "You had sex with women on the Internet?"

"That is not actually sin," he says. "You don't know who the person is. It is better than if I actually went out and did it."

Lance is being defensive. Since he is such a "Godly" man with "special gifts of wisdom," he should know better.

I should know better, too! Why am I even in the picture? I am in too deep to be rational.

I am appalled at this conversation. If a partner in a marriage has been betrayed, I do not believe counseling can help. I do not understand why Lance is being so defensive. It was wrong for him to be cybering on the Internet with other women, especially as a married man.

Lance continues talking, almost as if I am not on the phone: "I couldn't put together a worship team. The Holy Spirit doesn't have to do much to quicken scripture in my head. I spend a lot of time in the Word. I live by His principles every day. It is with me everywhere I go."

Lance is upset because Karen is his conscience. When he talks to her, he is reminded of the mistakes he has made. He wants to live the way he is living and still be involved in the church. The church is not going to tolerate his behavior.

Lance pauses. I sit there. Neither of us are talking for about five seconds. I hear a clacking sound on Lance's end of the phone.

"Are you on the computer?" I ask.

"I thought our conversation was basically over," Lance says. "Then I see someone was instant messaging me. I will turn my monitor off."

I am furious! Lance has called me to complain and vent his feelings. I am giving him my heartfelt attention and he is talking to someone else (a woman, I am sure) on the Internet at the same time!

While I am fuming over his rude behavior, Lance starts talking again.

"I feel good in the Lord that I am handling the situation respectfully. Pastor did not come back at me with anything of substance. I explained to him what ministry does for me. I have tried to get a minister to meet with Karen and me."

Lance lost me somewhere in this conversation!

He is in love with me.

He is frustrated with his wife.

He is upset with the pastor of his church because he is not allowed to "utilize his spiritual gifts" since he was on the Internet, cyber-sexing with other women while being married.

And he wants Karen and him to go for counseling! To what end? To what purpose?

I ask him, "Is Karen is still attending the church?"

"She stopped going," Lance says. "It is hard for her to get her mom there. She tried different churches. She was not getting what she needed. I explained to the pastor what ministry does for me. Every time I got up and ministered to the people, I was transparent before God."

I reply, "I don't think this church is doing you that much good."

"All this pastor does is basically tell you what you should do," Lance says. "He is not allowing me to use my spiritual gifts."

I think to myself, how can Lance think he can minister in a church, utilize his spiritual gifts, and jack off at the computer on his own time?

Lance loves me. I truly believe that. The cyber sex is a past issue. I know it.

I try to ignore the flag from a few minutes ago when he was talking to someone else on the Internet during his call to me. I am thinking one thing and feeling the opposite. If Lance is in love with me, why do I suddenly feel like I am in turmoil?

I have noticed Lance always feels guilty after he talks to Karen. I can understand why Karen feels betrayed and hurt. Lance wants to be her friend and doesn't realize if a marriage or a romantic relationship ends, it is almost impossible to back it up to a friendship.

"At least I have a sense of where *we* are going," Lance continues. He is now talking about him and me. I am glad he knows where "our" relationship is going. Right now, I don't.

"I need to start looking for another church," Lance says, interrupting my thoughts. "My spiritual gifts are being stifled here. How wonderful I felt last weekend when I saw you. I felt at peace with myself."

Before I can respond, he suddenly switches the conversation back to Karen. "I told her I would like to take her out to lunch and talk. She is not being honest with herself. Any thing is possible with God."

I do not understand what he needs to talk to Karen about, or what he thinks is possible with God. I am in a total state of confusion.

"What if she wants to go back with you?" I ask.

"Karen knows I am not in love with her. I think, on some level, she knows I still do love her, but will come to realize that it is not as a husband. She thinks I have abandoned her emotionally."

I reply, "Transitions are hard, Lance. She is probably processing everything and needs time."

Wow, what a wise wizard I am! I have all the answers and am here for Lance whenever he needs to talk. My focus is on my love for Lance and his love for me. All of this other brouhaha makes no sense.

Lance is married! Why don't I get it? I am the loving, caring, understanding "girlfriend." I am sure my patronizing words are a comfort to Lance.

Lance replies, "I am glad I had a chance to talk with you. I am finally talking to somebody who agrees with me. There is nothing we can't talk about. I just love you."

Lance needs to have agreement and approval. I don't see it at this time.

He adds, "I understand where I made my mistakes, too. God is giving me the okay. We have all done things wrong. I learned a big lesson."

I think to myself that Lance realizes his past behavior was wrong, and he will not make the same mistake again.

I reply, "The good news is you learned."

"Thanks for being there for me, as you always are," Lance replies. "I can always trust you."

Lance can always trust me, but can I trust him?

Lance is married! He is seeing another woman, and the other woman is me!

But this day I am focusing on "Lance and me," "us," and "our love." In five days, I will be with him again.

Karen is right. Lance has abandoned her emotionally. He does this every time he has a relationship with a woman. I will find this out soon enough.

CHAPTER 26

Preparing for the Wedding in Roslyn

Monday, March 26, 2001

I record in my journal after talking with Lance last night: "I feel crappy over Lance's phone call. He was on the computer. It was rude. I can't take loving him and feeling threatened and jealous at the same time."

I know Lance is not in love with his wife. He has told me several times he loves her like a family member. Actually, it pleases me Lance is good to Karen and is truly caring and concerned about her and her mom. It tells me he is a good man.

However, Karen is a distraction from my relationship with Lance. I don't see at this time how twisted this thinking is. Who am I to think I have a right to a man who is married? I am the intruder. Lance is Karen's husband.

"I thank God you understand me," Lance says to me during today's telephone call. "So many other women would only be focused on their relationship with me. They wouldn't want to hear all this about my wife. That attracts me to you; the fact you understand my situation with Karen and how I feel."

Wow, my keeping silent and listening these last two days has paid off. It has caused Lance to be more attracted to me. I'm glad I did not confront him and kept quiet.

Lance also tells me he does not want to be with young girls any more. He says, "I wanted to have someone whose kids were grown up. I am very grateful for the way you are. You are a Godsend to me. You are just the best. I guard what we have. I love you."

We hang up on a wonderful note. I record in my journal: "Lance called me this evening. I love him, I really do." I go to bed, dreaming about being in Lance's arms. In just four days, I will be on the bus to New Jersey to attend the lavish, black-tie wedding.

Thursday, March 29, 2001

I can't wait to see Lance this weekend. I will be leaving tomorrow. I have put hours of preparation into this special event.

Again, I will be traveling by bus to New York City and then taking a train to Hamilton, New Jersey.

I have to transport my gown in a large shopping bag. By the time I have traveled by bus and train to New Jersey and paid for my dress and accessories, I will have paid over three hundred dollars for this date. This does not concern me. What I have with Lance is priceless.

I have a hair appointment today to touch up my blonde highlights. I am taking tomorrow off from work to be sure I am rested and ready for my trip. I plan to leave early afternoon and arrive in New Jersey around 5:00 p.m. Jane will be picking me up at the Hamilton Train Station.

I will have plenty of time on Saturday to primp and get ready for my formal date. Lance is picking me up at Jane's, late afternoon. I can't wait to see the look on his face when I answer the door in my beautiful, sparkling gown. The trip to Roslyn is a couple of hours from New Jersey; not too far to travel in our formal wear.

Lance surprises me with a telephone call at work this afternoon. He tells me there has been a change in plans for our date on Saturday.

A couple hours ago, Lance found out that his friend, John, who lives in Long Island, has had a death in the family. His father passed away. John is Jewish, as is Lance.

It is a Jewish custom to call on people who have had a death in the family. It is called *"shiva." Shiva* is a period of mourning in Jewish tradition where people come and pay condolence calls at your house throughout the day.

Lance informs me John will be sitting *shiva* at his residence in Long Island for the next few days. Lance wants to pay John a condolence call on the way to the wedding in Roslyn. Lance also tells me John's wife is good friends with Karen.

I can see Lance has already made a decision to do this and is simply informing me of the change in plans. I tell Lance that would be fine, however, wouldn't it be awkward for us to walk into their home, with me wearing an evening gown and he a tuxedo? Lance has this covered. He tells me we can wear appropriate clothing for the visit and then change into our evening wear *at their house!*

I can't believe what I am hearing! I don't even know John and his wife. Also, how is Lance going to explain my being with him to these people who are close friends of Karen's?

I need to find something to wear to this condolence call along with lugging my gown and accessories on a bus and a train. I was looking forward to being all dressed up in my gown and preparing for the wedding at my daughters, where I have all my makeup and can fuss with my hair. Now I will be wearing two different outfits on this overnight date.

Of course I don't say any of this to Lance. He would never understand. He is calling the shots. He never asks me how I feel or if it is convenient. He simply calls to let me know there has been a change of plans.

The compassionate side of me understands that Lance means well in wanting to visit his friend. However, the timing is awkward and inconvenient. Since I am not Jewish, perhaps I don't have a clear understanding of Jewish tradition and how much this call would mean to John.

I am glad I did not make waves about it with Lance. That is not my place. I will happily comply with this change of plans. I am sure we will still have a wonderful time at the wedding. This blows holes in my dream, though, of greeting Lance at the door in my beautiful evening gown.

Later this evening, I go through my closet. I find a brown, sleeveless dress with an accompanying brown jacket. This outfit is appropriate for the condolence call. I neatly place it on a hanger, along with my gown, in the large shopping bag that I will be transporting on the bus and train ride to New Jersey.

Friday, March 30, 2001

I am up at 6:00 a.m. I am so excited and cannot wait to see Lance. I will be boarding the 8:30 a.m. bus from Binghamton, New York to Port Authority. I quickly check my e-mail.

Lance has sent me a surprise. It is an online "Happy Anniversary" card. I had forgotten we had met online on September 30, 2000. Today is March 30. It is our six-month anniversary.

The musical card is beautiful, but it is Lance's message that touches me the most. He says: "Happy Anniversary, my sweet Lynniekins. My anniversary gift to you is I am going to remove all of my personal ads off the Internet. I love you, Lance."

My heart is singing. Lance wants us to be exclusive. No more personal ads for him to check. He is removing them all. He loves me!

I look up his site on Yahoo where he was using "Lanceangel" as a screen name. No ads! They are gone! He really did remove them all.

During the bus ride to Port Authority, I dream about the wonderful time Lance and I will have at the wedding in Roslyn. As I board the train at Penn Station after exiting the bus and walking the eight blocks from Port Authority, I make sure my large shopping bag with the evening gown, my dress for the condolence call, and my accessories are with me, along with my suitcase.

My daughter, Jane, picks me up at the Hamilton Train Station at 5:00 p.m.

I enjoy the evening with my grandson, Brian. We all have pizza and ice cream. Lance calls me twice this night. I am sound asleep by 10:00 p.m. I have a wonderful weekend ahead of me.

CHAPTER 27

The Condolence Call in Long Island

Saturday, March 31, 2001

I am awake at 7:00 a.m. My heart is beating with anticipation. Today is the big day! I have looked forward to this formal wedding for weeks.

Lance is picking me up at 2:30 p.m. We will call on his friend John to express our condolences, change our clothes for the formal wedding, and be on our way.

10:00 a.m.

My grandson, Brian and I are happily playing in the living room when the phone rings. It is Lance. Jane looks annoyed as she hands me the phone.

Lance tells me he received a call from his wife, Karen, last night. Her mother, Celia, is failing fast. Lance had gone to Karen's apartment to visit with Celia and offer support. Karen is heartbroken to see her mom in this condition.

"Celia was out of it," Lance says. "She stopped breathing at one point, and it appeared she was seeing something for about a minute. I thought maybe she was looking into Heaven."

"I am glad you went over there," I respond. "I know you have a special relationship with your mother-in-law."

Not noticing my response, he continues, "I told Karen I was going to a wedding this weekend. I was hoping she wouldn't ask me if I was going with anybody, and she didn't. I told her I would call her when I get back tomorrow. Her brother and grandchildren are there."

Lance is very concerned about his mother-in-law. I admire him for his loyalty to his wife in this situation. Lance is a caring person.

He continues, "There are three families that live close by. Karen's son is there also.

"I am glad her family is with her," I respond. "I….."

Lance interrupts me. "I have been really sleeping well. I know I am getting good rest if I have those periods where I get sleepy. It has a lot to do with boredom, sitting and relaxing. If I brought you here to New Jersey, there would be different things to do."

I can't believe how quickly Lance has changed the subject. My antennae go up when he mentions bringing me there. Is he thinking of me moving to New Jersey in the future?

Before hanging up, Lance confirms he will pick me up at 2:30 p.m. "When we leave, we will be going to my friend's house. You will be comfortable there. You can change into your dress for the wedding and touch up before we leave."

"I can't wait to see you," I respond.

"Oh, by the way, our room at the hotel is a hundred and eighty dollars," Lance says.

"Oh, okay", I answer. We hang up. I sit there with the phone in my hand. Does Lance want me to pay for half the room? What is the protocol for a couple going on a date and sharing a hotel room for the night? I don't have an etiquette book handy.

12:00 Noon

I start getting ready for my date. I want to take my time with my hair and makeup. Jane is folding laundry. I can tell she is annoyed. "Jane, are you all right?" I ask.

"You are acting like a teenager, mom," she says. "You are a grandmother and not acting like one."

"Jane, you know how much I love Brian," I answer. "Just because I am going on a date doesn't mean I don't love my grandchild."

"I think Lance is arrogant," Jane says. "Last night when he called here, he said, 'Hi, Jane,' as if he had known me for years! I hardly know him. We do not have that kind of familiarity between us for him to talk to me like that."

Jane is right. Lance is quick to get to know someone. I recall how he wanted to meet me right after I answered his ad. Jane's statement does not concern me at this time. I am too wrapped up in my magical fairy-tale date.

I change the subject. "Jane, Lance told me the hotel room will cost a hundred and eighty dollars. Do you think he meant that I should pay for half the room?"

"Did he ask you to?" Jane says.

"No, but why would he tell me the cost of the room if he doesn't expect me to pay part of it?"

"Mom, just offer him the money and see if he takes it."

That is a good idea. I forget about the hotel room and continue to primp.

2:30 p.m.

I am dressed and ready. Lance will be here any second. I check myself out in the mirror. I look very attractive in my trendy, brown, sleeveless dress covered by a matching brown jacket. My gown is on a hanger, covered with dark plastic. Lance will not see the gown until I am wearing it. I have my gold handbag, gold shawl, gold shoes and other accessories in a large shopping bag. My toiletries and shortie pajamas are packed in a small, overnight bag. My heart is thumping with excitement. I can't wait to see Lance!

The doorbell rings. He is here! When I open the door, he is smiling at me. Lance is wearing a navy-blue sports jacket and dark pants. He looks so handsome.

I say goodbye to Jane and Brian. As I get into Lance's car, I see his tux hanging on a hook in the back of the vehicle. He carefully lays my gown on the back seat. Lance starts up the car. We are on our way!

During the drive, I ask Lance if he told John I will be accompanying him on the condolence visit. He tells me John knows "someone" will be coming with him. Lance has also told John we are on our way to a formal affair and will be changing our clothes at his house.

Lance is worried about Karen's mom. I can tell it is weighing heavily on his mind. He has assured Karen that he will get in touch with her the minute he returns from the wedding tomorrow.

We arrive at John's house around 4:30 p.m. The wedding is at 7:00 p.m. Roslyn is over an hour away.

Lance rings the doorbell and John answers. It is a very nice home in a residential neighborhood.

Lance introduces me to John. I shake his hand and tell him how sorry I am to hear his father has passed away. The three of us walk through the living room into the dining room. John's wife is sitting at the dining room table with two other women.

Lance says hello to John's wife and introduces me. I sense a terrible tension in the room. I can tell these women have taken an immediate dislike to me. I recall John's wife is close friends with Karen. She looks at me as if to say, "Who are you, and what are you doing with Lance?"

There is food on the table. No one offers us anything to eat. That is fine with me. My stomach is already churning.

The situation is awkward. John says to Lance and me, "Let's go back into the living room." I am relieved to get away from these women.

I sit there silently while Lance and John reminisce about their childhood and recall fond memories of John's father. I feel extremely uncomfortable. This visit is like being in a torture chamber. I cannot get over how unwelcome I feel.

John says to Lance, "So where did you two meet?"

"We met on 'Love at AOL!'" Lance replies with a big smile. He is holding my hand. For some reason, "met on Love at AOL" sounds shallow to me. I can tell John is thinking the same thing.

"Oh, that's nice," John responds. What else can he say?

I cannot wait to get out of this house. The three women in the next room are buzzing and whispering, and I know it is about me. I cannot stand the karma here. How could Lance have put me in this uncomfortable situation? Isn't the *shiva* custom a few days? The drive was not that far. Why couldn't Lance have seen John on another day? Why combine a depressing visit with a formal wedding date?

It seems like hours before Lance finally says, "Well, I guess we will change now and be on our way."

John politely says, "Lynne, you can use our master bedroom. There is a bathroom there, also. Lance, you can change in the study across the hall from the bedroom."

I can't wait to change my clothes and end this torturous visit. Lance and I go out to the car and get our formal wear. I lug my dress and my shopping bag full of accessories up the stairs of this stranger's home. What will these women think of me when I come down the stairs in a sparkling evening gown? My dreams of answering the door and Lance seeing me in my beautiful dress are shot to hell!

I go into the master bedroom and shut the door. I start getting undressed. My friend, Naomi, has given me some glitter to sprinkle above my chest on my bare skin and shoulders, which will be surrounded by the beautiful jeweled spaghetti straps. While changing my clothes, my feelings of excitement return. This is it! This is the moment I have been waiting for!

I take off my "condolence clothes" and put on my gown.

I look in the full-length mirror in the bedroom. I look stunning. There are two slits, one on each side, that go halfway up my dress.

My taupe pantyhose give my legs a smooth, dark, shapely, and sexy appearance. The gold pumps with small heels add to this. My hair looks beautiful. I put on a pair of gold, dangling earrings and touch-up my makeup. I add the glitter to my bare skin above my breast and sprinkle some in my hair. I put on my lipstick and spray on my Rain cologne.

I look beautiful! I forget I am in a stranger's home. I carefully fold up my brown outfit and put it in the paper shopping bag. I have my gold handbag and my gold shawl.

Shaking with anticipation, I open the door and go out into the hallway. The door to the study is opened, and I see Lance trying to adjust his tie. He looks so handsome in his black tuxedo. The white shirt against the black jacket and cummerbund looks striking. He turns around and smiles at me.

"You look great, Lance!" I say. He smiles and says thank you. I stand there, waiting for him to comment on my gown. He glances at me and mumbles, "Nice," then goes back to fidgeting with his tie.

John comes upstairs and helps Lance with his tie. Lance is concerned it is not straight. At this moment, the crooked tie is a crisis.

I grab a long trench coat Jane had loaned me. I put it on to cover my gown. Suddenly I am embarrassed to be in this situation. I want to hide my dress. I wait for Lance before going downstairs. Thank heavens the door is at the bottom of the steps. I cannot wait to get out of this house!

The trench coat I am wearing is open in the front, exposing my evening wear. John's wife is standing at the bottom of the stairs by the front door. Surprisingly, she tells me she likes the gown. I am grateful for the compliment.

I think to myself that maybe Lance is not one to give a woman a compliment. I start worrying about my dress. Maybe it is too formal?

We say goodbye to John. I am relieved and happy to get into Lance's car and be out of there. I think to myself, "Thank God that is over!"

Lance gets out a map and directions to Roslyn and asks me to navigate. I sense Lance's impatience when I have trouble understanding the map that has been drawn for the guests. In addition, it is dark out, and I am having trouble reading. I am worried sick that maybe my dress is too formal. I feel like an idiot! Lance notices none of this.

Suddenly Lance gasps, "I forgot my cell phone! It is in my sports jacket and I left it at John's house!"

"Do we have time to go back and get it?" I respond.

"No!" he says in a panicking voice. "We are already running late! I can't call my sister for directions! We don't have time to go back there now. We will have to stop there tomorrow on the way home to pick up the phone."

I think to myself, "Wonderful."

"I didn't bring my cell with me because I knew you had yours," I say to him.

Lance snaps, "I wish you had brought it. We need it!"

I glance out the car window. It is dark, cold, rainy, and dismal. We are lost. The wedding is in forty-five minutes. I feel sick inside.

CHAPTER 28

The Wedding in Roslyn, New York

Saturday, March 31, 2001, 6:45 p.m.

Lance leaves the Long Island Expressway and pulls into a gas station and studies the map.

"Look for Exit 37," he says.

He gets back onto the Expressway, heading east. I spot the exit. "There it is!" I say. "We need to take a left at the second light onto Roslyn Road and bear left onto Old Northern Boulevard. The hotel is about a quarter of a mile on the right."

I am relieved we are no longer lost. I look at my watch. It is 6:50 p.m. The wedding starts in ten minutes!

Five minutes later, we pull into the parking lot at the Roslyn Claremont Hotel. It is brightly lit; a beautiful, large, traditional-looking structure that stands out in the darkness.

Lance parks the car. "We can get our luggage and check in later," he says. "We have to find out where the wedding is."

He takes a small, plastic bag from the glove compartment and quickly places a wedding band on his left hand. "We will register as Mr. and Mrs.," he says.

I had forgotten about that. I am glad that Lance and I will be checking in as a married couple. I think to myself, though, it is because of his appearance and not mine that he is doing this.

We dash across the parking lot, into the hotel, and through the elegant lobby. There is a sign pointing to the elevator that says "Wedding Upstairs," with the last names of the bride and groom on it.

We take the elevator to the fourth floor. The door opens. Straight ahead is a private room. We are just in time. The chairs are covered in white satin. There is a canopy up front where the wedding ceremony will take place. There are flowers at the end of each aisle and pink-and-white bouquets up front, under the canopy.

A woman waves to us. "Over here, Lance," she says. "We saved two seats for you."

We walk over to her. She is an attractive woman with shoulder-length auburn hair. I immediately recognize her as Lance's sister, Susan. She is with her boyfriend, Patrick. Lance introduces us.

"Karen just called me on my cell phone," Susan says to Lance. "Her mom passed away about an hour ago."

The music begins. The bride starts walking down the aisle.

"I will call her as soon as the ceremony is over," Lance whispers. "Oh, that's right; I don't have my cell phone!"

"You can use mine," Susan whispers back.

I am still wearing Jane's long, beige trench coat and holding my gold shawl and gold handbag. I feel scattered and awkward.

Susan is wearing an elegant, black, sleeveless evening gown, covered with tiny, feathery-shaped flocks, each one surrounded by tiny black glitter. She looks beautiful. I look around at the other guests. Many of the women are wearing black. I am relieved to see a few of the women in glittery pastels. My dress is fine and not out of place!

Rose, the bride, passes us as she makes her way down the aisle to the front of the room. Cameras are flashing. She looks beautiful in her strapless, white-satin gown. The bridesmaids are wearing black. Jacob, the groom, joins her under the canopy. They are both beaming with joy.

The ceremony is less than half an hour. Lance smiles at me and squeezes my hand when Jacob and Rose recite their vows to one another. I smile back. For a moment, all is well in my heart and soul.

After the exchanging of vows, the rabbi recites seven blessings over the second cup of wine. This theme links the bride and groom to their faith in God as creator of the world, bestower of joy and love, and the ultimate redeemer of their people.

The ceremony ends with the traditional "Breaking the Glass." A glass is placed on the floor, and the groom shatters it with his foot. This act serves as an expression of sadness at the destruction of the temple in Jerusalem, and identifies the couple with the spiritual and national destiny of the Jewish people.

After the breaking of the glass, with shouts of "*Mazel tov*," the bride, *kallah*, and groom, *chatan*, are given an enthusiastic reception from the guests as they leave the canopy area and head toward a private room to be left alone for the first time as man and wife.

The wedding guests are told to proceed across the hall for appetizers and drinks. The reception will begin in half an hour.

"I have to call Karen," Lance says to me. Susan hands him her cell phone.

"I'll let you have your privacy," I say to Lance.

"Lynne, stay with Susan and Patrick. I will be right back," Lance says to me and dashes out of the room.

I follow the guests across the hall. There is a large, round table in the center of the room, with a fountain in the center. The fountain is surrounded by a montage display of assorted fruits, vegetables, meats, and cheeses. Hors d'oeuvres are being butlered. To the left of the room is a buffet of hot appetizers, meatballs, kabobs, mushroom caps, and wings. I spot an open bar to the right of the buffet.

I head straight for the bar. I need a drink! I order a glass of white zinfandel.

Drink in hand; I slither over to Patrick and Susan, who are filling their plates with appetizers. They are cordial, friendly, and easy to talk to. I finish my drink and feel more at ease. Patrick offers to get me another glass of wine. I gladly accept his offer.

Lance appears out of nowhere. He puts his arm around me and says "Karen is doing okay. She is with her family. She has many friends, and they are with her. I told her I would come over and see her the minute I get back tomorrow."

He hands Susan her cell phone and says to me, "Can I get you a drink?"

"No, thank you, Patrick is getting me one," I say.

Patrick returns with my drink and I thank him.

"Let me introduce you to some people," Lance says.

He puts his arm around me, and we are back in our own world, as if Karen never existed.

We walk over to an attractive young lady. She is wearing a brown evening gown, covered with gold glitter. Lance says to me "This is Lydia, the groom's sister."

Lydia smiles and says to us, "Lance and Karen, how nice to see you!"

"Uh, this is not Karen," Lance says, embarrassed. "Karen and I separated a few months ago. This is my girlfriend, Lynne."

Lydia turns red and apologizes. "I am so sorry, Lynne. I have only seen Karen a couple of times!"

I smile at her. "Not a problem, Lydia. So you are the groom's sister?"

"Yes, Lance and Susan used to babysit for Jacob and me when we were kids. We lived on the same street."

"Oh yes, I remember Lance telling me about that," I respond.

Lance and Lydia hug and reminisce for a few minutes. I look around. Lydia then says to me, "Lynne, again I am so sorry I called you by the wrong name, I feel terrible."

"Lydia, don't worry about it. I understand." Lydia is genuine and friendly. I like her.

Lance and I make our way to the reception, which is being held in the ballroom. Victorian-style windows adorn the white walls. The round tables are covered with white, brocade/linen tablecloths. A dozen white roses in a glass vase serve as centerpieces, surrounded by white burning candles. The room is dimly lit and has a romantic ambience.

Lance and I sit down. I finally take off my trench coat and put my gold shawl around me. We are up front by the band. I am glad Susan and Patrick are at our table. Lance and I do not know the other guests, and we introduce ourselves.

The seven-course meal begins. The band starts to play. I have my camera. I take a picture of Patrick and Susan. I ask them to take a picture of Lance and me together. I want to capture this moment. Another guest takes pictures of the four of us together.

The rest of the night is magical. Lance asks me to dance to "Unchained Melody." He holds me tightly on the dance floor, strokes my hair, and kisses me gently on the lips while we dance. It is just him and me.

After the seven-course meal, the crowd gathers in a circle as the traditional circle dance, *Hora*, is played. The bride and groom are lifted in two chairs while we all sing and clap to "Hava Nagila."

The food and drink are wonderful. The band plays the entire evening.

Lance and I eat, drink, dance, sit together, talk, touch, and dance again. Even amid the conversing with the other guests, it is just him and me.

I feel relaxed and happy. I forget all about Karen, the condolence call, and the brouhaha that lead to this moment. Lance has his arm around me and is attentive every minute.

The festivities end at 1:00 a.m. Lance and I say goodnight to Patrick and Susan and wish Jacob and Rose a wonderful life. They will be going to the bar mitzvah in April. I look forward to seeing them again.

The cold weather goes unnoticed as Lance and I retrieve our luggage from the car and register and Mr. and Mrs. I am in love and ecstatic!

Our room is warm and quiet with Victorian style furniture. I have had enough food and drink to warm my heart and spirits. I can't wait to be in Lance's arms.

I go into the bathroom and change into my pink, shortie pajamas. Lance changes into a tank top and shorts. When I come out of the bathroom, he raises his eyebrows and says, "Umm, cute!" Lance likes what he sees.

We turn out the lights and fall into each others arms. We are under the covers, kissing and touching each other. I can't get enough of Lance. I love his kiss and his touch. We fall sound asleep in each other's arms.

Sunday, April 1, 2001 -9:00 a.m.

I awake next to Lance's warm body. He stirs a little and then gets out of bed and goes into the bathroom. I lay there, smiling, remembering last night.

Lance comes out of the bathroom and walks over to my side of the bed and sits on the edge to see if I am awake. I smile at him. He strokes my hair and says good morning.

We sit in bed together in each others arms talking and laughing. We fall back asleep. Suddenly it is 10:30 a.m.!

"We have to check out," Lance says. We don't want to miss the continental breakfast."

Suddenly I remember the cost of the room. I take ninety dollars cash out of my purse and put it on the desk. "This is for my half of the room," I say to Lance.

"Thank you," Lance replies and puts the money in his wallet.

I am ready in fifteen minutes. We quickly pack our bags, proceed downstairs to check out, and then head to the lounge for the continental breakfast.

The Library Lounge is quaint and cozy, with cherry, wood-paneled walls, a bookcase, and a fireplace. At the end of the room, by the fireplace, is a long table covered with a white-linen cloth. It is decked with an aray of fruits, muffins, bagels, and croissants, along with a pitcher of orange juice and milk.

To the left is another small, round table, also covered with a round, white-linen tablecloth. The second table has a coffee pot, silverware, and white cups and saucers on it.

I am pleased that Lance and I are the only two people in the room. We sit next to each other on a comfortable loveseat and enjoy a leisurely breakfast.

"How about coming to my apartment for awhile after we get back to New Jersey?" Lance says.

"I would love to," I respond. I am pleased we can hug and kiss and be together some more. I am not concerned about having to take a train and a bus back to New York State later on. I savor every second that I am with Lance.

After breakfast, we leave the hotel and begin the trip back to New Jersey. It is bitter cold out and very windy. I am glad I have Jane's trench coat, but it is not lined, and it provides little warmth.

I had forgotten about Lance leaving his cell phone at John's house in Long Island. We have to pick it up, along with his sports jacket.

Lance parks the car in front of John's house and jumps out. "I'll be right back," he says.

Relieved at not having to go inside, I sit in the car and wait. Ten minutes passes. What is he doing? Why is he taking so long? After another five minutes, I start fuming. How can he be so rude and leave me sitting out here in the car? I start to get cold.

Suddenly, the car door opens and Lance gets in. "I was telling them all about Karen's mom passing away," he says as he starts up the car. "They knew her real well."

Lance continues talking non-stop for another five minutes about his conversation with John and his wife. He does not mention leaving me alone in the car for fifteen minutes, nor does he notice how angry I am.

As usual, I keep quiet.

Lance has many religious tapes in his car and puts one into the tape deck. He pulls me over next to him, puts his arm around me, and starts singing with the music.

We pull into a gas station. "Let's get a hot drink," he says to me. Lance holds me tight to keep me warm as we walk into the convenience store, the wind blowing against our faces. I am chilled to the bone. After we get back into the car, Lance leans over and kisses me. "I love you," he says.

I forget everything else. Lance loves me.

As we enter New Jersey, Lance says, "You know, I think I better get over to Karen's house. I don't think there will be time for you to come over to my apartment today. I will be sure to have you come over when you come back here to go to the bar mitzvah."

"That's fine," I say, feeling disappointed, but understanding.

We pull into Jane's driveway. Lance helps me with my overnight bag and dress and walks me inside. Jane motions for us to be quiet, as Brian is napping.

"We had a great time," Lance says to Jane.

Jane doesn't answer him. I walk Lance to his car. We embrace for several seconds. He strokes my hair and kisses me passionately on the lips.

"I am going straight to Karen's apartment," he says. "I will call you."

"Thank you for a wonderful time," I say. I stand in the driveway and watch his car disappear into the distance. I miss him terribly already.

CHAPTER 29

Back to Reality

Sunday, April 1, 2001 - 4:00 p.m.

After Brian's nap, Jane takes me to the train station.

I decide to leave my gown at her house in order to make my traveling easier. The brown dress and jacket I wore to the condolence call along with the gold accessories from the wedding are with me in a large paper shopping bag.

8:00 p.m.

The bus pulls into the Greyhound Station in Binghamton. I get into my car and drive home. It is colder than in New Jersey. My apartment feels wonderful and warm. I am glad to see my cats, Happy and Stubby.

I immediately check my e-mail. Lance has not written. It has been six hours since he dropped me off at Jane's house. Is he still with Karen, I wonder? I feel a twinge of jealousy. I miss him already. He must be with her; otherwise I surely would have had an e-mail. There is no telephone message, either.

While unpacking, I realize I don't have the shopping bag. Where could it be? I am sure I had it on the bus. Or did I leave it on the train? I call the bus station, and they have not seen it. I had my brown dress, my jacket, my gold handbag, shawl, and accessories in that bag. I cannot afford to lose it!

I take a hot bubble bath to relax and then drive over to my friend Marge's house. Marge is eighty-eight years old and a close friend of the family. She is like a mom to me, and has known me since I was a baby. I visit her every day.

Marge knows all about Lance. She enjoys hearing about my weekend. I have a glass of wine with her and return home around 10:00 p.m. Again, I check my e-mail. Nothing from Lance.

Monday, April 2, 2001

I check my e-mail the minute I awaken. Lance still has not written to me. I can't believe it!

My mind starts racing. How could he do this? I am sure he has been home. Did he spend the night at Karen's? How long does it take to write a short e-mail? Does he care whether or not I made it home safely? Doesn't he miss me and want to talk to me?

And my bag; I am livid that I cannot find the bag with my dress in it. Where could it be? How can I be so scattered? Where is Lance? Why hasn't he called me? How long does it take to make a phone call? Is he *that* clueless? I know he cares. Or does he?

I will not e-mail him. If he doesn't care enough to contact me, I will not get in touch with him, either.

I arrive at work and mechanically perform my clerical tasks. I can hardly concentrate. I run upstairs and have coffee with Tony. He can tell I am worried and upset.

At 9:45 a.m. Lance calls me.

"I am surprised I haven't heard from you," he says.

I sit frozen. I can't believe what I am hearing. "I was giving you your space," I reply.

"I appreciate that so much," Lance says. "I was with Karen until midnight last night. I asked her what I can do for her. She wants me to write out her bills and do her laundry. I am going to do that today."

Did I hear right? Lance appreciates me giving him space? Didn't we just spend our first night together and enjoy a wonderful romantic weekend?

Lance continues; "I just wanted to touch base with you. I am home now. I am on my way back to Karen's."

Lance stops talking. I don't answer him. "Are you all right?" he asks.

"Yes," I stammer. "I just wondered why I hadn't heard from you…"

"Oh!" Lance groans and sighs. "Of course, oh my God, I understand. I can see why you would be upset. I am so sorry I didn't get in touch with you sooner. I lost all track of time. Look, I have to get over there, but I will call you this evening, okay?"

"Okay," I say. I hang up the phone and burst into tears. I am an emotional wreck, and I don't know why. What is my problem? Is it selfish of me to have hoped I would have heard from Lance before now? Couldn't he have sent me a quick e-mail at midnight? Am I overreacting? Am I jealous of Karen?

Lance and I spent a wonderful romantic weekend together. He says he loves me. Karen has his time and attention, though.

A part of me admires him for his caring and devotion to his wife, especially during her bereavement. Lance loved his mother-in-law and is also grieving. I have to pull myself together.

But can't he say *something* to me about *us*, our weekend together? Am I losing my mind? I wonder what the protocol is for a married man to say to another woman the Monday after spending a romantic weekend with her.

I remember my bag of clothes. I am furious that I lost that bag! I didn't have a chance to tell Lance about it. Would he even care?

I mechanically get back to work. During my lunch hour, I drop off my disposable camera at the one-hour photo. Even though I am distraught and scattered, I am anxious to see the pictures from the wedding.

After work, I pick up the photos on the way home. While driving, I open the envelope and start looking at them. They came out beautifully. Both of us look great.

My eyes are not on the road. Suddenly I hit the brakes, but it is too late. Crash! I have rammed into the back of a jeep!

A fender bender is the last thing I need! I just spent over four hundred dollars for the weekend. I am on a strict budget.

Fortunately, the jeep I hit doesn't show a scratch. The female driver is lovely and drives away. I am not so lucky. The front of my red Toyota is dented. I am furious. I turn around and drive to my mechanic. He assures me he can take the dents out tomorrow for only seventy-five dollars. "Only" seventy-five dollars? I am broke enough as it is.

Upon arriving home, I take a hot bath and try to calm down. I visit Marge. She enjoys the photos taken at the wedding. All of them came out wonderfully. I have photos of Lance and me with Susan and Patrick, Lance and me alone, and a couple of Rose and Jacob, the bride and groom. There are a few others showing the lavish dining area and the other guests.

I return home around 9:00 p.m. Lance has left a message, asking me to call him back. I dial his number, and he answers.

"How are you?" I ask.

"I really had a good day," he says. "I could tell the appreciation [from Karen] was flowing the whole time. My wife said to me, 'This makes up for the last six months. I can't believe you stayed here with me.'"

I wonder how Karen would feel if she knew Lance had spent the weekend with me. She thinks Lance attended the wedding by himself. Of course, if she had asked Lance if he went alone, he would have no choice but to tell her he took a date with him, because Lance is always so "honest".

Lance continues, "She will be doing some things after the funeral. She is going to Pittsburgh for ten days to be with friends. I told her to let me know when she returns. I offered to spend evenings with her so that she would not be alone."

"That is very nice of you..." I start to say.

Lance keeps talking as if he did not hear me, "She has planned a few trips in the summer; I think she is going to California."

I sit quietly and listen. I can tell the last thing Lance has on his mind is the weekend we spent together. It is like it never happened.

Again, I am torn emotionally. Lance is being good to his wife and supporting her during her time of grief. But Karen does not know he is seeing another woman, me. Karen still loves Lance. Is he giving her false hope?

My thoughts are interrupted as Lance keeps talking. "I did seven loads of laundry for her and folded it."

He must be reading my mind. He says, "We didn't get into anything about the marriage."

I think to myself, "Why am I dating a married man?" It is too late. I have fallen in love with a married man!

"They didn't put my name in the obituary!" Lance says, sounding hurt. "I always called Karen's mother 'Mom'. I never called her by her first name, Celia."

"Why did she leave out your name?" I ask quickly while he pauses for a second.

"Karen doesn't like to pretend," Lance responds.

I am glad Lance's name was left out. I feel a slight twinge of guilt for being happy about it. He doesn't deserve it. He is dating me and deceiving his wife. Karen and I are on the same page. I don't like to pretend, either!

"A lot of people know how close I was to Celia and that I always called her 'Mom,'" Lance continues, sounding very distraught.

"I can understand how you must feel."

"But you know, the next couple of days will be very healing," Lance continues. "More than missing me, she will miss taking care of her mother. That was one of the most meaningful things in her life, taking care of her mother. She is very humble about that."

I sit still, listening and doodling on a piece of paper.

"There are two viewings tomorrow. One is in the afternoon and the other is in the evening. Her body will be sent to Pittsburgh. The family is renting a fifteen-passenger van to Pittsburgh. They will have a special service there. Karen will stay in Pittsburgh for ten days. She has a tremendous support group."

Lance continues talking about Karen for another fifteen minutes. "She was enough like my mother to almost become my mother. It is hard for her to say she is sorry. She used to say to me, 'What's the matter with you, what's wrong with you, why can't you do this right?'"

I think to myself, "I am nothing like Karen. I would never talk to Lance like that." I rationalize to myself how lucky Lance is to have someone like me.

"I really see your worth," Lance says to me. "I see your worth very much. I see your attitude; how you want to do the right thing. You are a very entreatable person. You sit there and listen and admit that maybe you are wrong."

"I am glad you feel that way about me," I respond.

"My sister told my uncle that I brought a very nice girl to the wedding. I had such a wonderful time with you. Everything is great. I just think when you are with me, you relax. You rest in the relationship and don't think as much about doing and being. I can't get over how much fun I had at the wedding."

"I had a wonderful time, too, Lance," I say.

"I am going to give you a 'Lance hug' and go now. I will talk to you tomorrow."

"Okay, goodnight," I say.

I hang up the phone. I wonder what we talked about. Lance did all the talking, and all the talking was about him.

He never asked me how I was doing. I did not have a chance to tell him about losing my bag, the fender Bender, or that I had picked up the photos.

We were on the phone for almost an hour. Lance talked about us for less than five minutes.

CHAPTER 30

Getting the Relationship Back on Track

Tuesday, April 3, 2001-6:00 a.m.

I am up and getting ready for work. I think about my conversation with Lance last night.

I can't believe how he minimized our time together this past weekend. My heart is so full, and he is acting like the weekend never happened. How could he forget so quickly?

I can understand the position Lance is in. Karen needs his help. He was close to Celia, Karen's mom. This whole situation has me scattered and confused emotionally.

During my morning break, I show Tony the photos from the wedding. I can tell he does not like Lance.

"Lynne, I don't trust this guy," Tony says to me.

"Why?" I ask.

"Look at you!" Tony replies. "You are a mess. You are in constant turmoil. He is a womanizer, Lynne. He doesn't care about you."

I try to defend Lance by explaining to him about Karen's mom.

"It's a no-brainer, Lynne. He is married!" Tony shows me no mercy.

I don't listen to him. I don't want to think about Lance being married.

Lance calls me at work at 10:45 a.m. He is on his way to the funeral home. The viewing for Karen's mom is today.

He tells me a neighbor whom he and Karen knows, has suddenly passed away. They will be going to *that* funeral tomorrow! It is in Clinton, New Jersey, which is about an hour from where Lance lives.

I don't think I can take anymore. Why am I even in the picture? I have no business dating a married man. Lance belongs with his wife. I should bow out of this relationship. I am in too deep emotionally to have the strength to do it.

After work I drive to Binghamton to cash my check at the local credit union. The Greyhound Bus station is not far away. I had called them two days ago and asked about my bag. The person I talked to had not seen it. Maybe by some miracle it has shown up.

I drive to the bus station. I tell the clerk who I am and ask about the bag. She says "I am so glad you stopped by. After you called here Sunday night the driver brought this to us. It was left on the bus."

She hands me my bag. I am ecstatic. I needed those personal belongings. I am not able to share my joy with the man I love. He doesn't even now I lost the bag. Do couples in love share these little things?

When I get home I call my sister and Tony and tell them I found the bag. I am thankful for friends and relatives who care about my well being and *know* about these little things.

I spend the evening teaching an aerobics class. After class I visit Marge. I arrive home around 9:30 p.m. Lance has not called nor e-mailed me. There is no way I am going to e-mail him. If he was thinking about me I would have heard from him.

I stay up until 11:00 p.m. hoping Lance will call. He doesn't.

Wednesday, April 4, 2001

I arrive at work distraught. It has been almost 24 hours since Lance has contacted me. It feels like a century since the wedding in Roslyn even though it has been just three days.

The phone on my desk rings at 8:55 a.m. It is Lance.

He tells me the funeral service for Karen's mother is today. Afterward, he and Karen will be attending the wake in Clinton, New Jersey, for the neighbor who passed away two days ago. The call is brief, and he will get back to me later.

Tony and I go out for lunch. Again, I share with him my feelings about Lance. He continues to remind me that Lance is a married man.

"Wake up and smell the coffee, Lynne. You are being a total ass!" Tony says.

"Thank you for your support, Tony," I say sarcastically.

After work, I check my e-mail. Lance has written me a short note:

> *I am picking Karen up in a few minutes. We will be driving together to the wake in Clinton, NJ. I will call you later. LYTPPK, Lance* [Internet smiley added]

The LYTPPK (Love you to pieces, pussykot) means nothing to me in this e-mail. In fact, it is inappropriate as is the smiley. The word "together," referring to him and Karen, cuts me like a knife.

My mind is spinning between Lance being married and my feelings for him. Like it or not, I am the intruder in his marriage. Emotionally, though, I feel like Karen is the intruder into *my* relationship with Lance.

When will it ever end? Karen's mom's funeral is over. Now there is another wake for Lance and Karen to attend. He and Karen are going out of town *together!*

At this point, it would have been right, fitting, and proper for me to end my relationship with Lance by telling him I am sorry, but I made a mistake getting involved with him while he is married. His loyalty belongs with his wife. If, at some point and time, he is legally divorced, he could contact me.

But of course I don't do this. I am thinking with my heart and not my head.

I cannot wait for Karen to go to Pittsburgh. She will be gone for ten days. I recall that Lance told her he would sit with her evenings when she returns, so she does not have to be alone. This is another reason I do not belong in his life.

I call my friend, Naomi.

"Hi, Lynne," Naomi says. "How was the wedding?"

Naomi had helped me pick out my gown and accessories and had loaned me jewelry for the wedding in Roslyn. She knew how excited I was and how much this date meant to me.

I start crying. "The wedding was great, Naomi, but things are not good right now."

"Why, what's wrong, Lynne?"

I tell her about the weekend, the funeral, and the events up to this moment.

"Lynne, this will all die down," Naomi says. "Just be silent and give it a little more time."

Naomi wants me to be happy. She does not like the fact I am dating a married man, but is supportive of my feelings this day.

I drive to my dance class. It is good for me to be with my peers. The dancing releases some of my anxiety, and I feel better. I needed to get my mind off Lance. It occurs to me that Lance does not know I take dance classes.

Afterward, I visit Marge and return home around 8:30 p.m. The phone rings at 9:00 p.m. It is Lance.

"I feel terrible for my wife," Lance begins. "I want to see her happy, but there are things she cannot do for herself."

I sit and quietly listen, thinking to myself how hard it must be for Karen to have to relate to Lance as a "friend" after being married to him for seventeen years. My heart goes out to her. She has no idea Lance is seeing another woman. If she knew, she would be devastated.

"God has used these last three days, Lynne. Karen really sees me as a friend, not as a husband. She has resigned herself to the fact that this is the way it is, and I think she is ready to move on. All of her friends acknowledged how much I did for her mom, and she knew it, too."

I don't believe for one minute that Karen views Lance as a friend at this time. He is still her husband. As usual Lance is talking about how much *he* did for her mom and how all her friends acknowledge *him*.

"She lived with my roaming heart and mind. Today it is so obvious to me I could not love this woman as a wife, only as a friend. I never stopped loving her as a friend. I wanted to give us both the sense that we don't have the same relationship as before; set boundaries; but I *will* give her more freedom to call upon me when in need."

I gasp silently. Lance is going to give Karen more "freedom" to "call him when needed?" Am I hearing right? He is setting boundaries for his wife? How patronizing!

I sit, silently fuming. Why am I so stupid? Why do I love this man?

Lance senses my silence and feels uneasy. "Umm, well, back to work for me tomorrow..." he says.

"Um hum," I reply.

"I am so glad I have my Lynnie," he says. "I love my Lynnie." He is trying to break the ice now.

Sensing I now have his attention, I respond, "I am glad you love Lynnie, too." I pause and then say, "I have missed you."

"After spending twenty-four hours with you last weekend, we have hardly spoken at all!" Lance says.

Finally Lance remembers our weekend together!

He continues, "I have wanted to talk to you, really. I just value the intimacy with one woman that I can be *honest* and devoted to and enjoy. I have this wonderful beautiful, soft, slender woman with a twenty-year-old body; and you want so bad to please your man."

That's putting it mildly, I think to myself.

Lance continues, "It makes me love you more. It makes me want to try and make you happier."

"You do make me happy, Lance," I reply. "But, to be honest with you, it has been very rough for me these last three days."

"A part of me knew you had to be thinking about Karen and me being together," Lance says in an understanding tone. "I was anxious to get home tonight and call you. I knew a part of you had to be worried or concerned because I had this long ride with Karen to the wake."

"I thought maybe you and Karen would be getting back together," I say. I can tell Lance hears the emotion in my voice.

"Oh, Lynnie," Lance says, "I wish you were here, right now so that I could give you a big hug! I love you. I am so blessed to have you."

Tears are welling up in my eyes. I am so in love with this man.

"What you did these last three days, Lynnie, made up for the last six months. God used it to redeem a lot of things. You are so understanding and accepting."

"Oh, Lance, I feel so much better. Thank you for communicating this to me," I respond happily.

"Everything is multiplied when you have God," Lance says. "Two people, you and me who are in total agreement working together, loving each other. I would be crazy to let something like that go."

"Yes," I say.

"If I was married to you," Lance says, "I just think I would enjoy having you here and nature would take its course. I am so turned on talking with you right now. I loved being with you in bed; just hugging you and feeling your softness against me, touching you and holding your hand."

"I loved being with you, too, Lance," I say. I am filled to the brim emotionally.

The last three days have been awful for me, and this moment is making it all worth it. Lance loves me! My worrying was needless.

"I feel so bad," Lance says. "I haven't even asked about you. I was almost rude. It was a very rare situation. I couldn't leave my wife."

"Oh, Lance," I say. "Do you have any idea how much it meant to me seeing your character and concern for Karen's welfare during this horrible time for her? I so understand. Yes, it did hurt me, but at the same time, I knew that, because of who you are, you were doing the right thing. I think so much of you for your kindness to her."

"We understand each other, because we know each other's intentions," Lance replies.

"Being in bed with you, when I think of sleeping with you in Roslyn, that is the image I have; experiencing your warmth, your skin, your heart, and your soul. You bore some of my pain. I knew you felt my frustration, and you wanted to help."

I am glad I was silent and passive. God has blessed me for it. Naomi was right. The situation died down. Lance and I are back on track. Remaining silent was the right thing to do.

"That is a very special quality," Lance continues. "Most people would have 'reacted' to this situation."

I did react, but Lance never knew. I am thankful I was able to vent to Marge, Tony, and Naomi.

"You had more of a calming effect," Lance says. "There was a real tenderness and gentle concern and understanding on your part. That is one of the things I love about you."

"I just sat and did nothing," I said.

"Doing nothing is the best thing," Lance says approvingly. "You know, we didn't have a minute to reflect on the beautiful weekend we spent together."

"That is okay, Lance. We are doing it now."

"To be able to connect with you on so many levels so quickly tells me how faithful God is," Lance says. "I just value the intimacy I can have with you. I can be honest and devoted to you. It is so easy for me to love you, and I know when we talk we see things the same way. That is so important."

I can't stand it anymore. I feel like I am ready to explode.

"I love you, Lance," I blurt out.

There is silence at the other end of the phone.

"Oh," Lance says. "I am so filled up hearing you say those words to me."

Lance and I talk a few more minutes and hang up on a wonderful note. It has been an enriching and enlightening conversation. He will e-mail me in the morning.

I happily breathe a sigh of relief after saying goodnight to Lance.

I did it. I finally told Lance I loved him! Why shouldn't I? After all, he has told me several times on the phone and in his e-mails that he loves me.

So why doesn't it feel right?

CHAPTER 31

Taking the Relationship to the Highest Level

Thursday, April 5, 2001

I wake up feeling exhilarated! Spring is in the air! I am in love!

I reflect on my conversation with Lance the night before. How wonderful it was being intimate and close again. We truly communicated. Lance loves me and I love him. It is a beautiful day.

I drop my car off at my mechanic's on the way to work. I cannot wait to get rid of the dent on the front of my car. Tony meets me, and he drives me to work.

"You seem happy today," Tony says.

"Yep," I answer, grinning like a Cheshire cat.

"Did Lance call you last night?" Tony asks.

"Yes, and we communicated," I answer. "We are fine now."

"Good…for you!" Tony answers sarcastically.

I told Lance I loved him! It was time. He has told me he loves me several times on the phone and in his e-mails. I have his e-mail dated March 21, where he says "I am *in love* with you."

Yes, it was time for me to say it back to him.

At work I check my e-mail. Lance has sent me a "Good Thursday Morning" message. He writes:

Hello my love! When you said the words "I love you" last night, I want you to know I melted. I was pacing the floor like I normally do but I fell face down and my head was just hanging over the side of the bed with my mouth touching the edge and I was looking down at the floor space between the wall and the bed. That's why I started speaking so softly and sort of muffled. See what you do to me?

He says he will catch me later and ends the e-mail with the familiar LYTPPK and adds three Internet smileys.

I notice he did not say "I love you" back. What's wrong with me? I am being a woman and reacting emotionally. Of course he loves me. He is the one who told me in March our love has to be cherished, nourished, and flourished. Part of nourishing our love is to say it to each other, right?

I do not hear from Lance the rest of the day. I pick my car up after work. I am pleased to see my car looking nice again, minus the dent in the fender.

I mail Lance the photos from the wedding. I begin to feel normal again.

The bar mitzvah for Susan's twin boys, Donald and Edward, is on April 28. I will be seeing Lance in about three weeks. I cannot wait. It will be nice seeing Susan and her boyfriend, Patrick, again.

Saturday, April 7, 2001

I receive Lance's Saturday-morning phone call. He tells me he received the photos from the wedding. He likes them, but is not happy about his tie being crooked. He will scan them on the computer and send them to Susan and me.

He tells me Susan noticed how happy he and I were at the wedding in Roslyn.

"I just want to be with you right now," I say.

"I am smiling," Lance replies. "It is nice to hear you say those things, I would like you here, too."

He continues, "I see you as an almost definite part of my future. I already know I want to be with you. I love you."

Lance and I talk for four hours this day. He talks about Karen, his ministry, and God, but most of the conversation is about "us." We are getting closer, intimate, and more loving with each other.

He expresses his sadness about Karen. He says, "There's lots of things going on inside of me; sadness about the wife. I am so focused on my sadness for her."

I can see Lance is a kind, compassionate person, and that he truly cares that his wife is hurting.

"I love the fact we know each other now for over six months and have handled everything in a godly manner," Lance says. "I don't anticipate any more tension like we had on New Year's Eve."

I had forgotten about the New Year's Eve blow-up. It was months ago. Lance and I are on a different level now. He is right. There will be no more misunderstandings like there were on New Year's Eve. We have seen each other three times since then. We are in love.

"We have it all," Lance says. "We will not blow it. We will seek God together and do it right and keep it right. I appreciate your heart so much. We both now have a chance to have everything we have always wanted."

"Yes!" I say...

"You are like an egg without the shell; just as soft. It would be so easy to crack that soft shell; I don't want to do that, ever. I will handle you gently always, like my heart wants to. I have been cruel and mean but I am now a new creation that God is creating. Maybe one day 'we' will be another creation; marriage."

Before hanging up, I invite Lance to join my family and me for Easter dinner. Marge is taking us out to dinner and would like Lance to join us. The time has come for my family to meet the man of my dreams.

Lance will let me know before the weekend is over if he can make it. We hang up on a wonderful note.

That evening, Lance e-mails me:

> *Hello my love. Just a brief message to tell you I love you and appreciate you for who you are and for all you do and say! You inspire me to Godliness and righteousness and I thank God for you! I do wish I could be with you more, but our relationship is in God's hands, so all is well! LYTPPK* [smileys added] *Lancekins* [smileys added].

I attend a cabaret that evening at a church where Tony is performing. Tony has been singing for years and has been in several local productions. His passion is singing, and he hopes to perform on Broadway someday. I e-mail Lance and tell him about Tony's great performance. Lance writes back:

So what was Tony performing? Did I miss something about him?

I am glad Lance is reading and commenting on my e-mails. I write him back, telling him about Tony's talent and career.

Sunday, April 8, 2001

Lance declines my invitation to join my family and me for Easter dinner. He writes:

> *I remembered this morning that I have the nursing home ministry on Easter Sunday. Since it IS Easter Sunday I think my place for next weekend should be here in New Jersey with my cousins and at the nursing home. I know you understand. I was looking forward to meeting Marge and your family next weekend but it seems God's timing won't make that happen for another month.*
>
> *Please thank Marge for extending her invitation to me for dinner. We can think about the weekend of May 12 for a visit from me if that sounds okay to you. Have a great day and know that I love you to pieces (PK). Lancekins*

I write back that I understand and will relay the message to Marge.

That evening, Lance e-mails me again. I cannot believe how much he is calling and e-mailing me. Lance truly loves me! He writes:

> *Hello my love. How great it is to hear God is enabling you to become the person He created you to be and what an honor it is for me to be a part of helping the true Lynnie to emerge. I love that Lynnie very much.*
>
> *That is so cool about Tony. He is a professional writer and a professional singer too!*
>
> *You are a constant blessing to me! I hope your day was great! I love you to pieces Pussy Kot! Lancekins* [smileys added].

Monday, April 9, 2001

Lance sends me his usual "Good Morning" e-mail. He starts with "Dearest Lynniekins, love." He tells me to have a great day.

He later calls me at work. He would like us to go away for a weekend. How romantic that would be! He is looking forward to taking me to the bar mitzvah in three weeks.

Things could not be better between us. It is spring, and I am in love!

Tuesday, April 10, 2001

Daylight savings was this past weekend. I had to move my clock forward an hour. I hate it. I keep oversleeping. I have an awful time adjusting to the time change.

Lance offers to call me when he gets up at 6:00 a.m. to make sure I am awake. I love this idea. What a wonderful way to start the day!

This morning, he calls me at 5:45 a.m. What a thrill to hear his voice first thing in the morning. He tells me he has scanned our photos from the wedding in Roslyn and sent then to his sister, Susan. She loves them.

Later at work, I hear the song, "You Light up my Life," by Debby Boone, on a coworker's radio. I think about Lance. He truly lights up my life. I e-mail him the song. I write:

"You…………light up my life……………………you give me hope…… to carry on…………………."

Lance writes back:

"And you light up my days……………….and fill my nights… with…song………!
It can't be wrong, when it feels (in our spirits) so right……………!
And you……….light…up…my……life!!!!!!!"

Tears of happiness are streaming down my face. This is a magical moment. It is Lance and me and our love. We have reached the highest peak.

I do not know this is one of the last times I will feel this from him again.

CHAPTER 32

Overnight Change

April 11, 2001 - Wednesday

I love getting Lance's early-morning telephone calls! He is calling me several times a day, in addition to sending me loving, caring e-mails.

When I arrive at work this day I receive an e-mail from Lance quoting the *God Calling* book I gave him for his birthday. He writes:

> *God Calling:* "Pray for love. Pray for God's spirit of love to be showered on all you meet! He will fill you with His love."
> And I love you very very much! [smileys added] *Lance*
> PS: Loved talking to you this morning.

April 12, 2001 - Thursday

Tony's friends, Joe and Pat, are performing tonight at Don't Tell Mama, a piano bar on Forty-sixth Street in New York City. Tony has asked me to accompany him to their performance. We will be taking the late-morning bus from Binghamton to New York City and staying overnight at the Comfort Inn, which is located right off Broadway.

I tell Lance about the trip and send him an e-mail with my itinerary and the phone number of the hotel where Tony and I will be staying. I sign the e-mail with the the usual LYTPPK.

Easter is three days away. I have picked out a beautiful card for Lance. I drop it in the mail on the way to the bus station. I want to be sure he gets it on Saturday, the day before Easter. The front of the card has a basket of colorful flowers on it. The message inside reads:

> *Our lives have been so blended together that I can hardly remember yesterday without thinking about you. And I can hardly imagine tomorrow without feeling that you will be the brightest part of it.*
> *Happy Easter.*

I write "Dear Lance," at the beginning of the message on the card. I then add a personal note at the end which says, "You are such a blessing, Lance, and I truly love you and thank God for you. A very, very Happy Easter to you from my heart. Lynne."

My heart is so full when I drop the card in the mailbox! Lance will be touched when he gets it! He will probably be in tears! I can't wait for him to receive it. I am sure he has sent me one, also.

I also mail a card and a package to my grandson, Brian, who lives fifteen minutes away from Lance. I want to be sure Lance and Brian receive their greetings the day before Easter.

Lance has affectionately started calling me "Schmoopy" He got the name from a *Seinfeld* episode where Jerry and his girlfriend called each other "Schmoopy."

Lance responds:

> *Hello Schmoopy,*
> *Hope your time away is peaceful and strengthening. Will be in touch. LYTPPK very very much too! Lancekins* [with several smileys added]

Tony and I arrive in New York City around 2:30 p.m. and check into the hotel. After grabbing a bite to eat, we take a walk.

"I have to find the Cyber Café on Broadway," I say.

"Why?" Tony asks.

"I want to see if Lance has e-mailed me," I respond.

"Oh, for God's sake, Lynne! You just talked to him a few hours ago," Tony says, sounding frustrated.

"I know," I say, "but I miss him and want to see if I have an e-mail from him."

Tony is livid. We find the café. Excited, I check my e-mail. Lance has sent me a message at 4:45 p.m. He writes:

I will call you in the hotel tonight if it works out conveniently. Let me know what time you think is a good time to call and give me the number of the hotel again if you can. I hope your day is fun and pleasant. I tried calling your cell a few times but couldn't get through. Time to leave work and head for the gym.

Missed our afternoon telephone calls, pussycat!
Enjoy yourself now!
I wish you were with me!
LYTPPK [several smileys]
Lancecat [smileys] *PS Hugs and kisses to you* [smileys]

I happily answer his e-mail. Tony is annoyed as my fingers go a mile a minute on the keyboard. I again give him the telephone number of the hotel. I wonder why he doesn't have it, since I already e-mailed it to him.

Back at the hotel, while getting ready to leave for the show, Lance calls me. Tony is livid and keeps interrupting. I duck into the closet with the phone and shut the door, so I can talk to Lance without any distractions. Tony is furious at my giggling and at the way I am carrying on.

The show at Don't Tell Mama is wonderful. Joe and Pat invite Tony and me to a gay bar after the performance. There are over two hundred gay men at this bar. I am the only woman. I enjoy a couple glasses of white zinfandel while Tony clowns around with his friends. He deserves to have fun after tolerating my asinine behavior with Lance all day.

Two hours later, we walk the eleven blocks back to the hotel. The weather is warm and spring-like. We are both a little high and laughing and having a great time. We arrive back at the hotel around 1:00 a.m.

The red light is blinking on the telephone in the hotel room. Lance has left me a wonderful message! He misses me and hopes I had a great time. He will call me in the morning.

April 13, 2001 - Friday

The hotel telephone rings at 8:05 a.m., waking me out of a sound sleep. It is Lance! I thought he knew we would be sleeping in. I sit on the floor by the bed, whispering into the phone so as not to disturb Tony. It is too late. Tony is awake and not happy.

Lance chats away, unaware of the time. He is used to talking to me early on Saturday and does not know he woke us up. Of course I don't tell him. I love hearing from him, any time. I hang up, feeling happy and giddy.

"Lynne, you are such a horse's ass," Tony says and turns over, trying to get back to sleep.

Later, we board the 2:30 p.m. bus. I notice Tony never talks or asks about Lance. I wonder why he isn't happy for me.

I arrive home around 6:30 p.m. I immediately check my e-mail. Lance has sent me a letter at 4:33 p.m. with the title, "Welcome Home from New York." He writes:

> *Well Lynnie you survived two days in NYC with Tony and the gays everywhere so you can probably survive anything now. I look forward to speaking with you tomorrow morning. Sleep tight Princess Pussy Kot.*
>
> *LYTPPK very very much. Lancecat*
>
> *PS Have I told you I love your laugh?* [smileys added]

I sit at my computer pondering this e-mail. Why is he telling me to sleep tight at 4:45 p.m.? He knows I will be home around 6:00 p.m. Doesn't he want to call me to make sure I arrived home safely?

Am I overreacting? Am I expecting too much?

I will send him a loving e-mail. Lance will call when he realizes I am home this early. That's it! He forgot I was getting home at 6:00 p.m. He thinks I am getting in later. Men never remember those things. I am positive he will at least send me another e-mail after he hears from me.

I write him a note at 6:20 p.m.

> *Dear Lance,*
>
> *Just want you to know I am home now. I had a wonderful time in New York, but one thing was missing - you! I can't begin to tell you how much I thought about you when I was walking up Broadway. It reminded me of our times together in this magical place. I am looking forward to a wonderful future with you and many trips for us in the city.*
>
> *I want you to know I treasure what we have, Lance. I love your voice, your touch, your personality, your kindness, your thoughtfulness - and your touch - did I say that?* [smileys added] *I just love you to pieces, Lancecat. I can't wait to hear your wonderful voice again.*
>
> *Love, Lynniecat*

I hit the send button. It is 6:30 p.m. I know Lance is home and on the computer. He is on it every evening. I also know his service provider sends him a pop-up message the minute he receives a new e-mail, so Lance will know immediately I have written to him.

I take a hot bubble bath, unpack, and leave for a while to visit Marge. She enjoys hearing about the show and my escapades with Tony.

I arrive home at 9:00 p.m. I eagerly check my e-mail. I can't wait to see Lance's response to my heartfelt words!

Lance has not written.

I check my telephone. No message and he is not on my caller ID. I start to feel a lump in the pit of my stomach. It is a familiar feeling; the same one I had a few months ago.

I watch TV for two hours. At 11:00 p.m., I check my e-mail one last time before going to bed.

I stare at the blank inbox on my computer; no e-mail from Lance. It has been almost five hours since I wrote to him. I know he is online. He always is. I know he got my e-mail.

The silence is so loud I can hardly stand it. I am alone again.

CHAPTER 33

Flip-flop of Emotions

Saturday, April 14, 2001

I wake up at 7:30 a.m., feeling lonely and distraught. These feelings are familiar. I had them months ago when Lance admittedly "cooled off" from the "relationship."

Mechanically, I check my e-mail. Maybe Lance has written to me since I signed off last night.

He hasn't; not a word.

My mind is going a mile a minute.

I think to myself, what could have happened? What's wrong with me? Am I imagining this? Am I insecure? Maybe I am overreacting. Am I expecting too much by wanting to hear from Lance last night?

No, I am not being unreasonable! Lance loves me! So why couldn't he have contacted me after finding out I was home from my trip? Didn't he want to talk to me? He has been calling and e-mailing me regularly for weeks.

What is bothering me the most is the e-mail I sent him when I got home. I shouldn't have sent it! Damn! That's what did it! I know it! He is afraid now. He thinks I am getting too serious!

Suddenly I remember the Easter card I mailed to him on Thursday! Oh no! He will get it in today's mail! If my e-mail scared him, the card will surely make him back off! I should know better than to be "too" serious! Maybe I shouldn't have added the personal note on the card! What's wrong with me?

No, wait! Lance has been telling me for weeks he loves me! He wants to meet my family. He has mentioned marriage more than once. He took his ads off the Internet. He wants our relationship to be exclusive.

Then why are my insides churning? Because I know my intuition is always right.

I put on a pot of coffee. I will be getting Lance's Saturday-morning phone call shortly. Perhaps the conversation with him this morning will eliminate my fears and cause me to realize I am, indeed, overreacting.

8:00 a.m.

The telephone rings. It is Lance.

My heart sinks as he begins the conversation with, "I am wondering how my wife is going to handle coming back into her apartment."

Karen is still in Pittsburgh, Pennsylvania. She will be there another week. Lance thinks she should move. I tell him moving is stressful, even under "normal" circumstances. He agrees.

This conversation is a farce. Nothing Lance says today makes me feel any better. In fact, it validates my concerns about the relationship.

He talks about Karen, doing his taxes, his CPA course, and his parents. He even mentions politics.

I listen impatiently, feeling distraught. Lance doesn't notice or feel my anxiety on the other end of the line. He is too busy talking about himself. I eagerly wait for him to say something meaningful about "us."

He does not mention my New York City trip, which was only twenty-four hours ago, my e-mail from last night, or anything pertaining to what I have been doing.

"Social skills are one of the things I learned from my wife," he says. "She taught me very well. It helped me become a very balanced individual."

What social skills? I wonder.

I think to myself, "Why do I have to hear about Karen all the time? What's that about? And why didn't you call me last night when you knew I was home from New York City? Why haven't you mentioned the loving e-mail I sent you?"

"I love your long, blonde hair," Lance says, suddenly switching the subject to me. He is jumping all over the place in this fruitless conversation. "It makes you look younger. There is something very attractive about straight hair, like you have."

Before I can respond, he says, "What a gorgeous day it is! It is going to be a perfect day. I can hear the birdies."

"Yes, it is nice out," I respond, feeling empty.

Lance is changing the subject every minute. My nerves are shot!

"Where I grew up was Rockaway Beach. One of these days, we will go there. I will show you the house. We can shop and visit whoever is there that I grew up with."

"I would love to hear all about it," I say, gulping up this crumb. It is the first time he has mentioned "us'" in this conversation.

"As a kid, I didn't have any faith in God," Lance says, reminiscing about his childhood. He talks about his childhood and his mother another ten minutes while I doodle on a piece of paper.

"I know my mother never told me she loves me," he continues. "It is nice to hear it once in a while."

I think to myself, "Yes, it *would* be nice to hear 'I love you' once in a while!"

"I had issues with my mom. She blew it, big time. I am in control, and the Holy Spirit is in control. I had to realize my issues with her can't control me. I am as free as I can be. It has made me more sensitive to others."

I wonder what the hell he is talking about. He is certainly not sensitive to what is going on with me right now.

"My mother was a very caring person," he continues. "A lot of her *good* qualities *I* have picked up. I have great attentiveness to details."

I almost choke on this statement! Lance never picks up on my karma, my anxiety or my feelings. He is too wrapped up in himself. He knows nothing about being attentive to details!

"I am not bad in any way because of my mother. She did not respect me as a child nor teach me what was right. It is great that *you* appreciate me!"

Lance is now comparing me to his mother instead of his wife, Karen. *He* is like his mother in my opinion. Lance does not respect our relationship or my feelings in any way. I still have not come to realize this.

"I just sit back and know everything is okay," I respond.

What a crock this statement is! I am lying! I know everything is *not* okay. I can feel it.

"That has made me see the *real* you," Lance says. "Even when you are not perfect, you are perfect. That is why it is easy to accept what might annoy me."

I have no idea what he is talking about. I am finding out as time goes by, Lance gets annoyed quite frequently.

"We have to go with the flow," Lance says knowingly. "I think the flow *God* is setting up between us is good; keeping it that we see each other every four weeks."

Lance uses "God" to explain all of his own actions. Lance has set up the time frame of our seeing each other. I would gladly see him more often.

"All of the girls at the gym I talk with know about Lynne," he says. "I tell them I have a girlfriend. It is great. I am really happy. We are really an item."

Lance is so subtle. He is being *honest* now, and letting me know in a casual way he has several female friends at the gym. I am glad he considers us an "item."

He continues, "I am letting you know there are women out there I am talking to, and they understand what the situation is. If we were married and living together, there would not be a need to continue talking to them."

I feel like I have been hit by a truck! Even though Lance has taken his personal ads off the Internet, he is continuing his communication with several women. His statement defines his character. He has a "need" to communicate with them at the present time. In addition, he is referring to our relationship as a "situation!"

I am furious. Lance is being *honest* by letting me know there are still other women in his life. This is his mask. As long as he tells me what he is doing, he is justifying his inappropriate behavior.

He is clever. After this statement he immediately says "I forgot I had another ad out there on an ISP [Internet Service Provider] that stated I was 'single and looking.' I changed it to 'single and not looking.' I put our pictures from New York City and the wedding in Roslyn up on the site for everyone to see. I refer to you as my girlfriend. I will send you the link."

Lance's mixed signals have me crazy. He is calling me his girlfriend on the Internet and talking to several other women at the same time!

I am to blame for allowing this relationship to continue. I should have confronted him this day. My desire is to be exclusive. I remain silent because I fear confrontation. Lance is good at twisting the truth and making me feel wrong.

Lance has all his bases covered. He has me as his "girlfriend" and is enjoying the perks of corresponding with other females on the Internet.

Since he is so *"honest"* by letting me know about this, he is content with his lifestyle.

This is not the case with me. My heart is full, and my relationship with him is exclusive. It will take me months to come to my senses. I am still trying to be the "perfect" person for him.

Lance interrupts my thoughts by saying, "I want to get showered and prepare my message for the nursing home tomorrow. Hopefully, God will give me fresh insight and a revelation. I pray for His anointing."

"Okay, nice talking to you," I say, feeling disheartened.

"Okay, my love. I will probably talk to you tomorrow sometime."

Lance hangs up. I will be hearing from him "sometime tomorrow, probably."

What happened to all the calls and e-mails I was getting the last three weeks? What was today's conversation all about?

Lance will be receiving my Easter card this afternoon. Perhaps it will touch him, and he will call me to thank me and let me know he received it.

I am an emotional wreck. Who are these "other women?"

CHAPTER 34

Easter Sunday

Easter Sunday, April 15, 2001

I am awake at 6:30 a.m. I have not heard from Lance for almost twenty-four hours.

I know he received my heartfelt Easter card in the mail yesterday, because my daughter, Jane, who lives near him, had called me and thanked me for the package I sent to Brian.

Lance sent me the Yahoo link yesterday afternoon with his ad stating he is "Single, not looking" The only personal note from him was, "Click on my briefcase to get the photos."

Along with this ad, he posted pictures of us in New York City at the Hilton Hotel, along with three other photos of us at the wedding in Roslyn. Under "More about me," he states: "I have a great girlfriend! Check out my briefcase!"

My spirits are not lifted by his ad.

The phone rings at 7:00 a.m. It is Lance.

He informs me this is a "quick call," because he is working on his message for the nursing home. He has to be there by 10:00 a.m.

"Did you get my card in the mail?" I ask.

"Yes, thank you," Lance says. "It arrived yesterday. You are so sweet. I had a busy day yesterday. I was supposed to attend a birthday party for the little girl next door. I missed it! They never told me where it was!"

He then asks, "Did you check out my site on Yahoo with our pictures?"

"Yes," I say, "very nice, thank you."

"We really look good in both those pictures at the wedding," he says.

"Yes," I say, agreeing.

"I wish my tie wasn't crooked though," Lance says.

I think to myself, "that stupid tie!" He is *still* worried about it!

"I am going to my cousin's for Easter dinner," Lance says inattentively.

"That's nice," I respond, feeling empty and annoyed.

"My message today at the nursing home is 'Don't Give Up! The Best Is Yet to Come,'" Lance says enthusiastically.

I almost laugh out loud at the irony of this statement.

Lance continues vehemently, "Today is Resurrection Day! It may be tough now, but believe God, hang in there, and do what God has called you to do! There *will* be a resurrection!"

Lance waits for a response from his audience of one.

"Oh, excellent, very nice," I say.

"Don't give up! The end is happy!" Lance says.

"Atta boy!" I think to myself.

"Well, I just wanted to give you a quick hello," Lance says. "Happy Keester!"

"Happy Keester to you, too, Lance," I say.

We hang up. What's "Keester?" I wonder.

I check my e-mail. Lance has sent me an online Easter card. Half-heartedly, I open it.

It is a musical card. A rabbit pops up. The furry tail is moving back and forth to the music. The card says "Somebunny loves you."

"Adorable," I think to myself sarcastically.

Lance adds his own note. "Thank you for the snail mail yesterday. I love you, too, very much."

I sit for a few seconds, watching the tail of the bunny move back and forth while listening to the music. This is the type of card I would send to a child.

Later that afternoon, I celebrate Easter with my family at a nearby restaurant. My son, Jeff, and his wife, Marla, are there along with my sister, her husband, and two brother-in-laws. Her daughter, Dawn, and family are there and, of course, Marge. We all go to Marge's after dinner for a couple of drinks and some fun conversation. I embrace my wonderful family and am thankful for a nice day with them.

That evening Lance surprises me with a phone call. I am thrilled to hear from him!

"I had a very nice day," he begins.

"That's nice," I say, wondering if he will ask me how my day went. He doesn't.

He says, "When I went into the shower this morning, the power went out. I couldn't use my computer to print out my message at the nursing home. I just had that overwhelming sense that God was in control. Instead I dug up some photos of the people at the home I had taken years ago. I was able to share the pictures with them. They loved it."

"I am glad it went well," I say.

"I am expecting a call. It is from someone who is going to be helping me do my taxes," Lance says.

"I have to go to work, tomorrow," I respond. "If I had my druthers, I would be with you," I say boldly, hoping to get a response from Lance about "us."

"I thought about you today, too," Lance says. "I showed your picture to a couple cousins. They liked the picture. My one cousin, Tom, said you were pretty."

"That's nice," I say.

Lance goes back to talking about his taxes; "What I want to do is call this person back before I get too tired. I had wine and drove over two hours. I will call you tomorrow morning."

"It was a pleasant surprise hearing from you," I say.

"Okay, hon. Goodnight." Lance hangs up.

I notice the "tax" person he was referring to has no gender. Lance does this a lot. He makes a reference to "a person" and eliminates the gender. I know it is because it is a female. I would prefer he just be "honest" and say "she."

I reflect on my relationship with Lance the last few weeks. We were getting closer and more intimate. Lance told me he was "in love" with me. He mentioned marriage. I finally told him I loved him. Things have been going wonderfully until two days ago. What could have happened to cause the sudden change in Lance's interaction with me?

Suddenly he has cooled off, overnight! The conversations are *again* casual and meaningless. I can feel the difference.

A part of me detests Lance for his sudden change of heart and his complacency. How can he do this to me? This is not my imagination!

Perhaps this is simply one of Lance's "cooling off" periods, I think to myself. I still have hopes our relationship will heat up again.

I have a hard lesson ahead of me.

CHAPTER 35

The Bar Mitzvah

Friday, April 27, 2001

I board the train to Hamilton, New Jersey, from New York City. The bar mitzvah is tomorrow.

I think about my relationship with Lance the past two weeks. It is been up and down for me emotionally. I feel like a yo-yo.

My heart is not full this trip. I feel anxiety, not anticipation like I did four weeks ago before the wedding in Roslyn, New York.

Lance has sent me mixed signals the last two weeks. Our phone conversations have been short and casual. There has been little e-mail communication. Adding to my discomfort is the fact that Karen, his wife, has returned from her trip to Pittsburgh. Lance has been spending evenings with her. This reminds me he is married. Why am I dating a married man?

Jane picks me up at the train station at 5:00 p.m. I spend a pleasant evening with her and Brian. Her sister-in-law and family visits, and we have the usual Friday night pizza.

Lance calls briefly to tell me he will pick me up at 7:45 a.m. tomorrow. We have to be at the temple by 10:00 a.m.

Saturday, April 28, 2001 - 6:00 a.m.

Lance will be picking me up in less than two hours. Suddenly I feel excited and happy! Perhaps my anxiety the last two weeks is unfounded. Maybe I am overreacting.

I spend over an hour primping. I have a new black, sleeveless dress. It is street length and has an accompanying sheer, flowered coat, the same length as the dress. It looks beautiful with my accessories.

Hopefully, this weekend will provide the opportunity for us to regain our closeness. I long for us to be intimate again.

7:30 a.m.

Lance will be here any minute. I check myself out in the mirror. I look great! My black shoes and sparkling jewelry accent my outfit beautifully.

Jane dashes out the front door with Brian in the stroller.

"Where are you going, Jane?" I ask.

"I am taking Brian for a walk."

"This early?" I ask.

"I don't want to be here," she says curtly.

I feel sad, knowing Jane does not approve of my relationship with Lance. I had thought her living near him to be a positive factor. Jane has viewed it as a negative. At this time, I am unaware of Jane's perception of Lance's true character. My mind is clouded with infatuation and love.

The doorbell rings! It is Lance! My heart is thumping.

I open the door. Lance is wearing a black sports jacket and black pants. His burgundy-and-blue paisley tie accents his white shirt. He looks gorgeous. I am crazy about him, and I cherish our time together.

He grabs my overnight bag and dashes to the car. Obviously, he is in a hurry.

"You look nice," he says as I get into the car.

"Thank you," I respond happily, thrilled that he noticed my outfit.

Lance hurriedly backs out of the driveway. Suddenly we hear a "Crash!"

He has hit two aluminum garbage cans! Frustrated, he jumps out of the car and stands them back up before driving away. I notice several people on the street watching us. I wonder why everyone is up so early and standing outside. I later learn there is a garage sale going on involving the entire neighborhood.

"I am sorry about that," Lance says. "I didn't see the garbage cans."

"I will call Jane tomorrow and explain to her it was an accident," I reply.

Lance talks constantly during the two-hour drive. He is looking forward to my meeting his friends and relatives at today's celebration. His

Uncle Ralph and wife, Shirley, will be attending. I look forward to meeting the twins, Donald and Edward, who will be honored at the bar mitzvah. They are Lance's sister Susan's boys.

Lance and I will be spending the night at Susan's apartment in Farmingdale, Long Island. I wonder why he didn't reserve a hotel room. Perhaps he does not want to spend the money.

Rabbi Haviv will be officiating at the bar mitzvah. He is a member of the God Squad, a campus ministry that motivates college students to follow the call of Christ. He has been a guest on several television talk shows, as well as radio.

9:30 a.m.

We arrive at the temple in Farmingdale, Long Island. The ceremony will begin in thirty minutes.

I see Susan and Patrick in the foyer. I smile and say hello. Lance walks away and greets a gentleman. He motions me to come over.

"Lynne, this is Bill, Donald, and Edward's father," he says. I recall that this man is Susan's ex-husband.

"How do you do, Bill? So nice to meet you," I say, shaking his hand.

A woman walks over to us and stands by Bill. This must be Dolly, his girlfriend. We introduce ourselves to each other while Lance and Bill are talking.

An older couple approaches us. Lance walks over and hugs the gentleman.

"Lynne, this is my Uncle Ralph, my dad's brother, and his wife, Shirley," he says.

"How do you do?" I say to them, smiling and shaking their hands. "I have heard so many nice things about you."

Our group indulges in small talk for a few minutes until we are ushered into the sanctuary for the religious ceremony.

The men put on the traditional "yarmulkes," or "skull caps," worn by Orthodox Jewish males in the synagogue.

The initiatory ceremony begins promptly at 10:00 a.m. This occasion marks the time when a young person is recognized as an adult in the Jewish community.

The boys separately start by chanting the blessing in Hebrew. Susan, their mother, is up front with them and chants, reciting the Torah. Lance joins them. I am impressed with his fluent speech in Hebrew.

After the reciting of the Torah, Lance returns to his seat. He puts his arm around me and smiles.

Rabbi Haviv delivers a wonderful, heartfelt message of encouragement and guidance to the boys regarding their search and goals in life. I can tell Lance is proud of his nephews.

The energy between Lance and me is not the same at it was at the wedding in Roslyn. Even though Lance occasionally smiles at me, we are not connecting like we did just four weeks ago. I can feel the difference. I cling to the hope that, as the weekend progresses, Lance will be more loving and attentive. He has not said anything meaningful to me this day.

After the ceremony, the rabbi announces the celebration will be at a nearby restaurant. A yellow school bus pulls up out front. Susan has hired a bus to transport over seventy of Donald and Edward's school friends to this affair.

Upon arriving at the restaurant, we are directed to a small reception area to the right of the large dining room. There is a buffet, a bar, and several small, round tables for the guests to converse while waiting for the celebration that will begin shortly.

Lance and I sit with Uncle Ralph and Shirley. I am glad to be sitting with this older couple, as they are easy to talk to.

Lance asks me if I would like a drink. "Yes, please," I say.

"I will be right back," Lance says as he gets up and dashes away from the table.

I enjoy conversing with Ralph and Shirley. They tell me about their house in Florida.

"How long have you lived there, Shirley?" I ask.

"About five years," she says. "We love the weather there. I don't like the cold."

"Me, neither," I say. Ralph tells me about some of the trips they have taken since their retirement.

Rose and Jacob suddenly appear. They are the bride and groom from the Roslyn wedding. I invite them to sit with us. They are living in New York City. I tell Rose how often I travel to the city. We exchange e-mail addresses.

Fifteen minutes go by. Where is Lance, I wonder? I look around. He is nowhere in sight.

Uncle Ralph is perceptive. He looks at me and says knowingly. "He's taken off again, hasn't he?"

"Um, he went to get us a drink," I respond, feeling embarrassed. What does he know about Lance that I don't?

I start to feel annoyed. Where is Lance? Is he talking to some woman? I don't trust him.

Lance suddenly appears and sits down. He hands me my drink and starts chatting with Rose and Jacob. He does not mention where he was or why he was gone so long.

Naturally, I don't ask.

He grabs some wings off the hors d'oeuvres tray without asking me if I would like one. "May I have one please," I ask on purpose, trying to show him how rude he is.

"Oh, I'm sorry," Lance says, handing me the tray.

I am livid and not hungry. I take the wing and put it on my plate.

An announcer beckons the guests to the celebration. We all proceed to the large, adjoining dining area. A band is playing. Susan has hired two professional dancers, a black funky male and a blonde female to energize the seventy to eighty teenagers. Several of the teens are dancing in a line with them.

A huge video screen is in the center of the room, capturing the actions of the guests. Video cameras are everywhere. Lance and I see ourselves on the screen and wave.

The tables are adorned with white, linen cloths. In the center are huge pedestals with black, white, and silver balloons and a model of a sports car on top. Apparently the cars are a theme of this celebration. There is a flag on each car, identifying its model. Lance and I are at the "Corvette" table. I look around and see "Mustang," "Jaguar" and other models. There are also candles and flowers surrounding the centerpieces.

There are favors and CDs everywhere. I can't get over the preparation that went into this lavish affair.

The meal consists of beef, chicken, potatoes, vegetables, salad, rolls, and of course, plenty of wine. The band plays nonstop. We all enjoy dancing in a circle. Lance is attentive and has his arms around me constantly. I embrace every moment he is touching me.

I ask Rose to take some pictures of Lance and me. He smiles at the camera, hugging me from behind. I love being close to him.

After dinner there is a candle ceremony. The boys recite a heartfelt poem for individuals in their lives who are close to them and light an accompanying candle. After each reading, the person mentioned in the poem joins them in the lighting of the particular candle. Lance is one of these participants. I smile proudly and take several pictures of him with the boys.

The dancing resumes for two more hours. I notice Bill's girlfriend, Dolly, sitting alone at a round table, staring out at the dance floor while sipping her coffee. I look out and see him dancing with another woman. I recall seeing him dancing with several women earlier. I feel sorry for Dolly.

"Why buy the cow when you can get the milk for free?" Lance says to me, knowing what I am thinking.

I think to myself, "You will not get any free milk from me, buddy!" Bill and Dolly have been living together for a couple of years.

The festivities end around 5:00 p.m. As the guests trickle out, Lance and I assist Susan in cleaning up and gathering all the gifts and favors.

Susan lives about five minutes away. I stand outside, waiting for Lance and me to leave. Even though the sun is shining, I feel cold. The wind is blowing. Lance is talking with some of his friends about getting a new car.

He puts his sports jacket around me, noticing I am cold. I am grateful for the kind gesture.

Finally we get into his car. We arrive at Susan's in a matter of minutes. We enter her apartment and walk down a long hallway. The boys' bedrooms and one bathroom are located on the right, with a second bedroom to the left. At the end of the hallway is the living room and the kitchen. Straight ahead is another bedroom and a second bathroom. I wish Lance and I were staying at a hotel. I feel uncomfortable in this strange place. I hardly know Susan.

"You can change your clothes in the bathroom," Susan says to me.

I go into the second bathroom at the far end of the apartment. I change into my casual slacks and a tank top. There are no clean towels any where. Susan will probably provide us with fresh linens later.

Susan has ordered a couple dozen submarine sandwiches from Blimpies. Uncle Ralph and Shirley arrive. We all sit around, eating sandwiches and chatting. Lance brings me a Coke.

We spend the evening watching *Seinfeld* reruns. Lance's favorite is the "Soup Nazi" episode, which we all enjoy. The conversation is pleasant, but there is no time for Lance and me to be "together" alone. I look forward to that moment when we go to bed. We will be sleeping in the living room on the pull out sofa bed.

It seems like hours (it is) before Ralph and Shirley leave, the boys go to bed, and Susan and Patrick say goodnight. I go into the bathroom off the hall. No clean towels. There are two damp bath towels hanging over the shower and a damp, crumpled hand towel on the rack by the sink. I wet the corner of the hand towel and try to "wash up" as best as I can. I brush my teeth.

I go back into the living room, still dressed. I don't feel like I have any privacy. Lance has disappeared. I hear laughing and talking coming from Susan and Patrick's bedroom. Lance is in there, talking with them.

I sit in the living room alone and wait for Lance to come out. Fifteen minutes go by.

Finally, Patrick comes out and sees me sitting by myself. "You can join us, Lynne," he says to me. Patrick is more attentive to me than anyone in the apartment, including Lance. I can tell he likes me and thinks I am a nice person.

I go into Susan's bedroom. Susan is lying comfortably on the unmade bed, laughing with Lance. We all chat for a while. I am tired. I can't wait to go to bed. Finally, Lance says, "Well, we better get to bed, goodnight."

"Good night," Susan and Patrick say. I can't wait to get undressed and into bed and feel Lance's arms around me.

I proceed back into the hallway bathroom. I hate putting on my clean, short, lilac pajamas I had bought for this night, without having a shower or a bath. I wonder why Lance hasn't noticed the lack of towels. I don't feel comfortable asking for them. I go back into the living room. Lance makes no comment about my new cute pajamas.

He pulls out the sofa bed. The mattress is lumpy and saggy. Wires are sticking up. It is so low that it almost hits the floor! Lance doesn't seem to notice as we make it up with the sheets Susan has provided.

I get into bed and wait for Lance to come out of the bathroom. We are finally alone. Lance comes out in his shorts and tank top. He gets into bed and puts his arm around me. He kisses me. This is the moment I have been waiting for. I love his touch. We hug and kiss for about two minutes.

"I'm tired," Lance says, turning over. "Goodnight, see you tomorrow."

"Good night," I say, turning away from him. Lance is snoring loudly in less than five minutes. I lay awake most of the night, feeling lost and alone.

CHAPTER 36

Painful Departure

April 29, 2001 - Sunday

I am up early. Everyone else is asleep. I retrieve my used damp hand towel from the night before and try to freshen up as best as I can. Hastily, I apply some makeup. There is no place to sit and primp.

Lance says good morning to me when I return to the living room. He gets up. No alone time or intimate interaction.

Shortly afterward, Susan, Patrick, and the twins arise. Susan puts out the Blimpies from the night before and makes a pot of coffee.

Lance goes outside and plays ball with the boys while Susan and I engage in small talk. I have a long trip ahead of me and am looking forward to my "alone" time with Lance, which will be the drive back and the time at his apartment. I am hoping for some love and affection at the apartment, since we have been around people the entire weekend.

Lance comes back inside and chats with Patrick and Susan for what seems like hours. He finally says, "Well, we had better get going…"

I thank Susan and Patrick for their "hospitality," and we are on our way. The conversation in the car is fruitless. Lance puts on his religious tapes. I am close to tears and feeling empty on the inside. A woman knows and senses when the love of her life is backing away from her.

Why am I being so stupid? Because I keep telling myself things may change. After all, Lance cooled off before and then came back to me. Maybe this is a "cooling-off" period? I am in denial. This is another time I should have ended the relationship.

We pull into Lance's apartment complex.

"Duck," Lance yells, panicking and worried Karen will see him in the car with another woman.

I quickly duck, feeling like an intruder and an idiot.

How different his apartment looks from six weeks ago when it was nighttime, and he had his room dimly lit with a romantic ambience. It is now late afternoon. The sun is shining in his room, making it appear like an office. His computer desk takes up the entire left wall, and of course, he has his file cabinet. I noticed last time he had a file with my e-mails. How many files on other women does he have, I wonder?

Puffy the cat greets me. She is glad to see me. I pick her up, and she purrs happily.

I sit on the couch, hoping Lance will join me. He will be taking me to the train station in thirty minutes. I long to be in his arms and I want him to kiss me.

Lance sits at the computer desk and motions for me to sit on his lap. We spend the next twenty minutes looking at certain websites. I could care less.

Suddenly, I remember Lance hitting the garbage can at Jane's two days ago. I quickly type an e-mail to her, relaying Lance's apology. He tells me to inform her he will pay for a new garbage can.

"I better get you to the train station," he says.

Disheartened, I pick up my things, and we head for the station. Of course I have to "duck" again, so I am not seen in Lance's car.

We arrive at the train station in less than ten minutes. Lance stands behind me on the dock, with both of his arms around me. He feels so wonderful. I am so in love with him and hate the thought of leaving and being away from him.

I hear the whistle. I look down the long track at the approaching train. I will be leaving Lance in a minute or two. The loud, lingering screech as the train comes to a halt adds to my anxiety and sadness.

I pick up my suitcase and turn around, facing Lance. I look him in the eyes and smile, waiting for him to say something meaningful to me. Perhaps he will tell me what a wonderful weekend it was, and he will miss me and see me soon. I would love for him to tell me once again he loves me. I need an assuring word from him to carry with me on the long trip home.

Lance looks me in the eye.

I wait for him to speak.

"See ya," he says. He turns around and walks away.

I stare at the back of his head as he walks toward the parking lot. I will never forget it. He is wearing a red shirt. I can tell from his body language he has instantly forgotten about me. He cannot wait to return to his apartment.

I wait for him to turn around and wave. He doesn't.

I enter the door of the train numb and frozen. I have no idea when I will be seeing Lance again.

CHAPTER 37

Torturous Reflections

I sit, frozen on the train, as it departs from Princeton junction. I have a long trip ahead of me - almost five hours! I want off this train! I can't stand being imprisoned in this seat with only my thoughts and tumultuous emotions keeping me company! I need to talk to someone or just scream!

"See ya???? See ya????"

Is that all you had to say to me after spending the weekend with me? "See ya?" What's that about, Lance? You bastard! Who do you think you are talking to?

Tears are streaming down my face. I feel, empty, alone, heartbroken, and enraged!

How could he be so uncaring, complacent, and nonchalant after spending a weekend with me? Lance has no clue as to how I am feeling at this moment.

I picture him driving back to his apartment, thinking of *himself!* I bet the bastard cannot wait to get back to his damn computer! Damn him! How could I be so stupid to think he actually cares about me? But I want him to care! Didn't he tell me he was *"in love"* with me just a few weeks ago?

The train stops! What is wrong? Keep moving, get me out of here! The draw bridge goes up over the Hudson River between Manhattan and New Jersey. A cargo ship slowly makes its way under the bridge. What is taking so long? I cannot stand being trapped on this train, feeling like this! I cannot wait for the train to move again. I sit there another fifteen minutes.

It seems like hours before the train pulls into Penn Station. I am in a rage as I lug my suitcase and carry on bag down Forty-Second Street to the Port Authority Bus Terminal. I hardly notice the sunny weather or the hundreds of pedestrians hurrying along the street. There is no excitement for me in the city this day.

I purchase a paperback book. I need to read something to occupy my mind.

I board the bus and feel relieved to be on my way home. The problem is, I cannot escape from myself, my inner being, my torment, my pain, and my rage!

I try to read, but to no avail. I close the book, never to open it again. Instead, I start reflecting on the last few weeks of my "relationship" with Lance.

The fact he changed overnight remains vivid in my mind. Yes, it was on April 15, the day before Easter. Suddenly, *overnight,* Lance stops being loving and attentive on the telephone! The e-mails have been short, patronizing, and meaningless!

The phone calls are idle chit-chat. Never once did Lance tell me he could not wait to see me and take me to the bar mitzvah! Not once!

In addition, he was not affectionate with me over the weekend. Why did we have to stay at his sisters? Why not get a room in a hotel by ourselves? Because you are a cheap bastard and because you did not want to be alone with me, you prick! Damn you, how I hate you!

I want to explode! I can't! I am stuck on this frigging bus! Damn you, Lance!

"See ya?" "See Ya?" You bastard! You narcissistic ass! God, how I hate you for hurting me and making me feel like this! Walking away from me with no one on your mind but yourself! Yes, I know, Lance! You just can't wait to get back to your computer and start talking with all your other women, can you? You Solomon bastard - oh thou with great wisdom and insight - you prick!

I am an idiot! Why don't I drop him now? What is my problem?

My problem is I have fallen in love with a narcissistic, arrogant, self-centered bastard! That is a big problem!

"See ya? See ya?"

How can a person feel love and hate at the same time? When a person loves someone, gives their heart and soul away and puts one hundred percent into the relationship, only to feel rejected, betrayed, and empty, the love can easily turn into hatred!

This relationship is emotionally over. I know it.

Okay, Lance if you are so *honest,* then you can end this relationship! I am not going to make it easy for you, you prick! You told me if a time came that you thought we no longer had a relationship you would say so because you are so frigging *honest!*

Deep down, I know I am terrified to address the truth with Lance. I am in emotional denial, as well as turmoil. I know if I ask Lance why he was so complacent over the weekend, he will say to me:

"Lynne, are you sure you want the *honest* answer to that question?"

I would respond "Yes, Lance, I want the truth."

Then the door would be opened for him to tell me we can be just *friends!*

Oh, no, you bastard, prick! No, no, no! I will not make it easy for you to back our relationship up to a friendship and be one of your hundred female *friends!* Nope, nope, nope!

If you can play this game, so can I, Lance you bastard! You pompous narcissistic ass!

I have made my decision to ride out this relationship until Lance ends it. Two can play this game!

The bus pulls into the station in Binghamton. I run to my car, feeling like I have been released from a ten-year prison term.

Twenty minutes later, I unlock the door to my apartment. My cats, Happy and Stubby, greet me. I feel loved again. I am so glad to be home.

After unpacking, I log onto my computer. Lance has sent me an e-mail.

Lance will again draw me back into his web of deception.

CHAPTER 38

Emotional Denial

I am livid over Lance's insensitive parting words and exhausted from the long, painful, torturous train and bus ride home, I open Lance's e-mail. It is his "welcome home" greeting!

> *Hello Schmoopy!!*

I am furious. I feel like a dog being patted on the head. He continues:

> *I had such a nice time with my hot date this weekend. Hope u had a safe happy trip home............*

He must be kidding, right? Happy trip home? His "see ya" made my trip home a nightmare. How can he be so clueless? I am fuming as I continue to read:

> *Will call you Monday morning! Sleep tight pussycat........Puffy sends her love. "Meow" (the meow was from me...lol) LYTPPK* [Four smileys added] *Purrs 4 U Lancecat* [three smileys added]

I am not surprised at Lance's shallow, empty, and meaningless e-mail. He can take his LLTPPK and his smileys and shove it!
I long for his love. How pathetic is this?

Subtle Deception

I also notice he doesn't call to see if I made it home okay. Doesn't he want to hear my voice? Of course not. He is too into himself.

Chemistry gives a man power. I feel such powerful chemistry when I am with Lance. I long to be in his arms.

Suddenly it occurs to me, when will I see him again? We have no future plans. I momentarily panic. Then I remember, I am furious with him and hate him. No, I love him. What is wrong with me?

Lance has stopped the intimacy. There is no substance in our conversation, e-mails, or interaction. I need to wake up and smell the coffee. I will not respond to his e-mail.

He is happily going about his business. I am sitting here, alone, feeling miserable. Lance is oblivious to how I feel. Our relationship is hanging by a thread. He is not even aware of this.

I pick up the telephone and call Tony. I need to vent.

Poor Tony. I scream at him for five minutes straight.

"Do you know what Lance said to me at the train station just before I got on the train?"

"No, what?" Tony asks. I can tell he is amused. He knows Lance is a phony. He has told me this a dozen times.

"He said, 'See ya!'" I shout at Tony angrily. "See ya? See ya? What kind of words are those, Tony? Who does he think he is?"

Tony is laughing so hard he can hardly respond.

"Oh, Lynne, I can't stand it," Tony says, laughing hysterically. "What a bomb this guy is."

"It's not funny, Tony," I say, crying. "I am devastated!"

"Don't say I didn't warn you," Tony says, still laughing. "I'm here for ya, honey."

"Yeah, right," I respond. "I'll call you later. I am going to Marge's."

"Okay, hon," Tony says, still laughing so hard he can hardly talk.

I take a hot bath, unpack, and go to Marge's. Her friend, Nellie, is there. This keeps me from venting and screaming at Marge. After downing three drinks, I go home.

I log onto my computer, thinking perhaps Lance noticed I did not respond to his e-mail.

He has not written. I am not surprised.

Bastard! God, how I hate him! I go to bed feeling lost, alone, and heartsick. Lance will be calling me in the morning.

CHAPTER 39

The Mixed Signals Continue

Monday, April 30, 2001

The phone rings at 6:00 a.m., waking me after a restless night's sleep. I know it is Lance. I am still in a rage over his heartless departing words at the train station yesterday.

"I slept real sound last night…" he begins. I don't answer him.

"I still haven't unpacked my bag yet," he continues.

Lance has no idea how upset I am. Why can't I address this? Because I have been afraid of rejection all my life.

I should be rejecting him, the bastard!

Before I can say anything, Lance surprises me by saying, "Happy anniversary!"

Suddenly I remember today's date. It is April 30! We met seven months ago online, September 30, 2000!

"Oh, yes, Happy anniversary," I say, feeling bewildered.

"I love your character and your honesty," he says. "You mean a lot to me."

"Thank you," I mumble.

"Have a nice day, pussy cat. I just love you to pieces."

"You, too, bye" I respond.

I hang up the phone, thinking to myself, what the hell was all that about?

Am I overreacting? Is Lance so clueless he doesn't realize what he did? I cannot believe he remembered our anniversary, and I forgot. How different I feel today from a month ago on our six-month anniversary, when he took his ads off the Internet and told me he loved me.

Lance calls me at work during the day with a quick hello.

I had totally forgotten about Lance hitting Jane's garbage pail the day of the bar mitzvah. It seems like it happened months ago. Jane e-mails Lance this evening and he forwards her note to me.

Jane writes to Lance:

> Hi Lance,
> Thank you for mentioning the garbage pail incident and for offering to replace it. I will be going to Home Depot some time this week and will let you know the price.
> What really concerned not only me and my husband, but also the neighbors was that there are at least 50 kids in the neighborhood, many are shorter than the garbage cans, and Saturday morning they were all out and about because it was a block wide garage sale. If you didn't see the garbage cans - it could have been a child and that would have been such a tragedy. Please be aware of the children in the neighborhood and go very slow in our area.
> Thank you!

Lance responds to Jane's e-mail:

> Jane, I am so sorry for being careless! Please relate my apologies to your neighbors and your husband from me, and assure them it will never happen again, and that I will drive much more carefully through the neighborhood. Lance

I am impressed that Lance owned up to his mistake and apologized to Jane. It is incredible how quickly Lance draws me back in emotionally.

Even though Lance sends Jane an apology, he shares with me he is offended at her e-mail. He feels she was talking down to him, like he was a child. He says to me in an e-mail:

> *Feelings of unworthiness came over me about the possibility of being part of your family some day. I would not want to personally*

> *make a big deal about it because of you, and because of yours and my relationship.*

The statement about the possibility of becoming part of my family jumps out at me. Does Lance still love me? He is talking about being a part of my family. That would mean marriage, right?

I forget all about the "See ya!" Lance probably doesn't remember saying it. He even mentioned "our" relationship.

There are two people who see through Lance's phoniness; Tony, and now, Jane. I will find out months later that Jane cannot stand him.

May 1, 2001 - Tuesday

I receive Lance's Tuesday morning call. He cannot stop talking about Jane.

"She made me feel like shit! God will take this negative and turn it around."

"I understand, Lance," I say. "I am so sorry you feel that way."

"It is based on how she felt with the neighbors," Lance continues. "You know this situation has made me feel closer to you, and my admiration and respect for you have increased."

Wow, I think to myself. Lance is feeling close to me again.

He continues, "Everything Jane is going through is much more about Jane than about anyone else. She is lashing out, because she is unhappy."

What a jerk he is! This is about a garbage pail, and Lance is using his "wisdom" and "psychology" to justify his position. The truth is, Lance cannot handle being corrected about anything. He is too wrapped up in himself and considers himself flawless.

He adds, "Jane needs to turn her focus to God."

No, Lance, you do!

Like a spider to the fly, Lance continues to pull me back into his web of deception with his mixed signals. I am in emotional denial and want the relationship at all costs.

The next day, Jane calls me. She tells me Lance does not have to pay for the garbage pail. She adds, "Let's wait to see if he will travel up to see you." Jane has Lance figured out.

It's too bad I don't.

It occurs to me I have traveled to New Jersey three times to see Lance. He has not come to New York State to see me.

Lance has not been the same since April 15, when he suddenly changed overnight. What could have happened? I wish I had not sent him that loving e-mail the evening of April 14. Feelings of regret are constantly gnawing at my insides. I am in constant turmoil.

Is this how love is supposed to feel?

CHAPTER 40

Getting My Hopes Up Again

Wednesday, May 2, 2001

I record in my journal:

"I am totally disheartened over Lance's hot/cold behavior and his backing off. He is not nourishing the relationship. I get three 'nothing' phone calls a day from him. I am so angry at him for pulling back like this. There have been no e-mails and his 'nothing' phone calls make me sick."

Friday, May 4, 2001

Lance calls me at work. I had forgotten I had given him a tape by Neil Clark Warren titled *Finding the Love of Your Life*. Lance surprises me by telling me he has started listening to the tape. He mentions that Mr. Warren advises the listener to "find someone who is a lot like you."

Lance says to me, "I thought of you when I heard that. We are so much alike."

I am grateful for this much-needed lift. Lance is actually listening to my tape, and he is thinking about us.

He then tells me that he wants to travel to New York State for a visit and wants to meet my family. I can't believe it. We set a date for May 18, just two weeks away.

I ask him, "Do you want me to find you a hotel room, or do you want to stay with me?"

"I want to stay with you," Lance says.

My heart is beating with anticipation. Lance and I will be sharing a bed again. It won't be someone's lumpy mattress in a strange place, either. I can't wait for him to see my cute, cozy apartment.

I will cook up a batch of my special homemade spaghetti sauce and bake him a homemade apple pie. We will have a wonderful romantic dinner at my apartment when he arrives on Friday night. Of course there will be a bottle of wine and special dining music.

I will tell my family he is coming, and I will make reservations at a nice restaurant for Saturday night. We can all go out together and they can meet Lance.

I remember that Lance doesn't like the heat. He always has a fan going in his room, even when it's cool outside. The weather has been unseasonably hot. I decide to buy a new air conditioner for the kitchen. Since the kitchen is right off the living room, an air conditioner will cool off the entire apartment.

Monday, May 7, 2001

I purchase a new air conditioner. I drag Tony to my apartment, and we lug the heavy box inside. I am laughing hysterically as Tony and I try to lift the air conditioner into my kitchen window. He screws in all the bolts and secures it for me. He doesn't think it is funny, though; in fact he is livid.

"The only reason you bought this is because of Lance," he says, sounding disgusted.

"I have needed one anyways," I say, giggling like a teenager. I turn it on. The apartment is cool in a matter of minutes.

"Okay, gotta run," Tony says as he hurries out the door.

"Thanks, Tony," I say grinning like a Cheshire cat.

"Yeah, don't mention it," he says as he drives out.

I spend the next week preparing for Lance's arrival. I call our neighborhood Italian restaurant and make reservations for Saturday, May 19, at 6:00 p.m.

I contact my son, Jeff, and his wife, Marla. They would love to meet Lance and will join us at the restaurant Saturday night. My niece, Dawn, her husband, Tony, my sister, Lea, and her husband Dave will also come. Lance and I will pick up Marge. Marge knows more about Lance than anyone since I visit her every night.

I will make the spaghetti sauce on Thursday, the night before Lance's arrival on Friday. I will have a candlelight dinner with a bottle of wine.

I purchase a romantic CD to play during dinner. The ambience must be perfect.

Sunday, May 13, 2001

I will see Lance in just five days. I get his usual Sunday morning phone call.

"I can't wait to see you next weekend," I say.

"It just occurred to me, May 20 is the Sunday I go to the nursing home," Lance says.

My heart sinks. I don't respond.

"I don't mean I have to go," he says.

I sit silently, fuming. I know what is coming.

"Hello?" Lance says.

"I don't know how to respond to that," I say. "I am just listening to you."

"I have to refocus on some things. If I come the weekend after May 18, it will be Memorial weekend. This is my fault."

"I have contacted my family and made dinner reservations," I say. I am furious, and I do not intend to let him off the hook.

"I hear everything you are saying. You have gone to this trouble. I do believe I could get someone to substitute for me. I have taken off the nursing home before."

Lance waits for me to respond. I don't answer him.

I can tell Lance wants to change the plans. This does not set well with me. My family has put the date on their calendar, and reservations have been made.

"The nursing home ministry is important to me. I hate to miss it," Lance says.

Lance has already made up his mind. He says, "I value my words. When I say I am going to do something, I am a man of my word. I will definitely come the *following* weekend."

I don't answer. I am disappointed and angry. I am angry at myself as well as Lance. I know if I disagree with him, he will make me feel guilty.

"I can see you are in the process of processing that," he continues, trying to sound like he has it all together, and I don't.

"Let's see what God wants," he continues. "This is something you have to work through with God. Part of praying through is being sensitive to everyone and everything around us."

Yes, Lance, let's throw God into this! That makes me all the more wrong. Of course God would want him at the nursing home. Lance is being "sensitive" to what he wants. He even said he could get a substitute. Never mind me or my family.

My thoughts are interrupted when Lance says, "I am going to assume it will be Memorial Day, unless *you* say it will cause problems with your family…"

Now he is putting the decision on me. Lance is making this about me and not him.

"If you feel God wants you to change the plans, then go ahead. I will explain it to my family," I say, weakly.

I am not being honest with myself. I am angry and disappointed.

Why didn't Lance make sure May 18 was a date he could come? I am stuck. If I tell him not to go to the nursing home, I will feel responsible for keeping him from his "ministry."

"One extra week is good," Lance continues. "Every three weeks is probably the ideal time frame for us to see each other."

"Yep," I say. Lance is calling all the shots.

"I could see not canceling if we could not do another weekend. I am working with ya!" Lance says knowingly.

I don't answer.

"God is in control, and all is well!" Lance says, relieved.

All is not well. Lance is in control, not God. Lance always calls the shots "in the name of God."

"I can take a half day off on Friday, May 25, and come up that afternoon," Lance continues, trying to soften the blow. "We will have all day Saturday, and I will come back home on Sunday."

"That will be nice," I say. I don't mean it.

If Lance and I were maintaining the closeness we had just a few weeks ago, I would not have objected to the change in plans. This disappointment adds to my anxiety and insecurity about the relationship.

Lance is backing away, I know it! Why can't I just let him go?

CHAPTER 41

Lance's Visit to New York State

Thursday, May 17, 2001

Lance has decided to buy a new car. The transmission has gone on his present vehicle, which he has owned for about ten years.

"Last night I went to the Toyota dealer," Lance says to me during our early morning call. "I am leaning toward getting a smaller car."

"So, did you see anything you liked?" I ask.

"I test-drove some cars. The little ones aren't as stable as the bigger cars. I am confused, not knowing if I want to go big or small."

"Oh," I say, not knowing how I can help him.

"My wife brought up a good point," he says. "She mentioned that I want to be comfortable. When I ride in smaller cars, I am not as comfortable as I am in a larger car; that makes a big difference."

I wonder why his wife is involved in his getting a new car. Probably because she is his wife, and I am not? Obviously he has been discussing this with her.

Of course, I am not in the position to be talking to him about buying a new vehicle, because he is married to her and I am "the other woman."

The "search" for a new vehicle comprises the majority of our conversations for the next few days.

Wednesday, May 23, 2001

I get an evening telephone call from Lance. He has bought a brand-new 2002 Toyota Corolla. He is excited and describes it to me. It is red with beige interior, gold trim, and a spoiler to give it a trendy look.

I picture how handsome he will look in a brand-new vehicle. I want to be sitting in it next to him. For some reason I feel intimidated and envision him with another woman in the car. What's wrong with me?

"It is so nice to talk with you and have your support," he says. "It warms my heart to be able to call you and for you to share my joy. I wuv you, you sweet thing."

This is the first time Lance has said anything meaningful to me in weeks. I feel a much needed healing in my heart.

Lance will not be getting his new vehicle until next week. He will be making the trip to see me this Friday in a rented car. I will have to wait until "next time," whenever that is, to ride in his new vehicle. I will be seeing Lance in two days. I can't wait.

Friday, May 25, 2001

I wake up excited, my heart pounding. I will be seeing Lance today!

I spend the entire day cleaning the apartment and making my special Italian spaghetti sauce. My homemade apple pie is in the freezer. I will bake it early this afternoon so it will be fresh for our romantic dinner. I have a pink tablecloth, wine glasses, candles, and a centerpiece. A romantic CD will cap off a beautiful evening.

I am furious with Tony. He refuses to join us for dinner Saturday night. My family understood about my rescheduling the dinner with Lance. Tony won't even consider coming.

"I don't want to meet him, Lynne" he told me.

"Why, Tony?" I asked, feeling hurt and bewildered.

"I don't like him." Tony is adamant and has made up his mind. "I am not going to be a phony and meet him and pretend to like him."

"That is ridiculous, Tony. How do you know you don't like him if you haven't met him?"

"I know enough, now rest it!" Tony will not budge.

I hate it when Tony says, "Now rest it." I am livid over his lack of enthusiasm at something this important to me. What a fine friend he is. Well, I am not going to let my anger at Tony ruin my wonderful weekend with Lance.

I put the pie in the oven early afternoon. It smells wonderful and looks delicious sitting on the counter, still warm.

Lance pulls into the driveway at 4:00 p.m. I run out to meet him.

He gets out of the car, smiling. He looks so handsome. We hug and kiss in the parking lot. He feels so good to me. I hunger for his affection and love his arms around me.

I can't wait for him to see my cute apartment with its lacy curtains, pictures on the wall, and its homey, cozy atmosphere.

My two cats, Happy and Stubby are sitting on the bed in my small bedroom. I have several pillows on the bed; white and lavender; some floral. My white, lacy curtains and scones on the mirrors with purple candles in them make for a nice romantic ambience. I had purchased a small, Victorian, purple lamp for my nightstand to provide romantic lighting. There are also white, lacy curtains hanging across the closet door.

Lance and I walk into the apartment arms around each other. I take his overnight bag and place it in the bedroom. I smile while he looks around.

He studies the pictures on my living room walls. This is a good sign. Lance is interested in my friends and family. I show him pictures of my son, Jeff, in the air force, and Jane's wedding pictures. There are also pictures of my grandson, Brian, and a few of Tony and me.

Afterward, we sit together on my love seat. Lance puts his arms around me. He smells wonderful and feels so good.

"You know if we weren't Christians, I would carry you into the bedroom right now," he says. He then kisses me several times. His lips feel warm and sensual. I can't get enough of him.

Lance and I both want to have sex. There is a strong chemistry between us. I long for him to make love to me, but I know it would be a mistake.

An hour later, I start dinner. I heat up the spaghetti sauce, and arrange the table with a pink tablecloth, candles and a centerpiece. The water for the pasta is boiling. Lance sits on the love seat and turns on the television.

I lovingly make a salad for the two of us. It is an art to me. I tear the lettuce leaves just right, cut up the tomatoes, and slice the onions real thin. I sprinkle basil on the lettuce and pour on my homemade balsamic vinaigrette dressing.

The lights are dim, the CD is playing, and the candles are lit.

"Dinner is ready," I say proudly.

I can tell Lance loves the dinner. He comments on my fine cooking. After we eat, I sit on his lap, and we hug and kiss for a while. We will visit Marge after the kitchen is cleaned up.

Lance excuses himself from the table. He goes over to the love seat, sits down, and turns on the television again.

"I want to tell you up front, I do not help in the kitchen," he says.

"Oh," I say, surprised. "That's okay, I won't be long."

I hurriedly clear off the table, wash, dry, and put away the dishes. I also have to put the leftover food in the refrigerator. I sense Lance's impatience as I see him looking at his watch.

I think to myself, "If you were helping me I could have this done in half the time!"

I drive Lance to Marge's in my 1991 Toyota Tercel. It is a cute little red car with over a hundred and twenty thousand miles on it. I have always had used cars. There is no air conditioning, and smoke blows out of the tail pipe every time I start it up. I keep it clean on the inside. Its appearance hides the fact that it is an older used car. I am unable to afford a new one.

Lance is outgoing and gregarious at Marge's, to the point where I feel slightly embarrassed. Marge later tells me, "He is full of BS, isn't he?" She does like him, though.

After arriving back at my apartment, I eagerly hop into bed with Lance. No lumpy mattress this time; there are fresh sheets on the bed. Lance and I kiss passionately. I love being in his arms, and I happily fall asleep.

Saturday, May 26, 2001

Lance and I sleep in. I wake up, smiling, as I notice my cat, Happy, purring in Lance's face. He pets her.

I make breakfast in my pajamas while Lance showers. We have fun taking photos of each other in the apartment. Lance playfully pokes his head up from behind the head board on the bed. I snap a photo.

Later my sister, Lea stops by to meet him. She is unable to make it to dinner tonight because of a prior commitment. I think to myself that if Lance had come last week like originally planned, my sister and her husband could have made it.

Lea later e-mails me. She likes Lance and is happy for me.

We spend the afternoon watching *Seinfeld* reruns that he brought with him. I love snuggling with him.

Later that evening, we meet the family at Gance's, a landmark restaurant near my home.

Lance and I pick up Marge. We are the first to arrive at the restaurant. I order a glass of white zinfandel. Shortly after we sit down, my son, Jeff, and his wife, Marla, appear. I introduce them to Lance. The conversation is going smoothly. I am proud of Lance and pleased that he and my son are getting along.

My niece, Dawn, and her husband, Tony, are running late. I order another glass of wine. I wish there was bread on the table. I haven't eaten in six hours.

Dawn and Tony show up and explain that they had to wait for the babysitter. Dawn sits on the other side of me.

I feel woozy from the two drinks and excuse myself and go to the restroom. We finally order our dinner. I look forward to the bread and salad. I need to eat something.

Upon returning to my seat, I am surprised my salad has ranch dressing on it, since I had ordered Italian. I decide to eat it anyway, since I do like ranch.

I hungrily dive into the salad, taking a huge bite. I am starving. To my horror, I realize the dressing is Blu Cheese! I hate cheese and angrily spit it out.

"Who did this?" I ask.

Dawn and Lance are laughing hysterically at their prank. I don't share their sense of humor, and I use the "F" word to express my disdain. I am drunk on two and one half glasses of wine and an empty stomach. I am louder than I realize. A man at the next table yells at us to quiet down.

The rest of the evening is a fog. So much for my worrying what my family thinks of Lance and what he thinks of my family. I am acting like a total horse's ass. I barely eat anything, and I keep running into the ladies room to throw up.

I do not recall leaving the restaurant and driving Marge home. Since Jeff and Marla are coming to Marge's, Lance and I decide to go inside and visit. I excuse myself and use Marge's bathroom. I throw up and pass out on her bathroom floor.

Marla wakes me out of my stupor.

"Are you all right?" She is worried about me.

"I'm fine," I say. I ask Lance to take me home. I feel physically awful.

I can't wait to get home. I can hardly sit up. I fall into bed wearing a nightgown that I don't remember putting on.

I wake up in the middle of the night. Lance stirs.

"Are you wearing underwear?" he asks.

"Why?" I respond.

"When you came to bed, you said, 'I am not wearing underwear. Screw that!'"

I burst out laughing. "Oh Lance, I was drunk! I am so sorry. I feel like such an idiot."

Lance laughs, too. "Not a problem," he says.

I put on my underwear and go back to sleep.

The next morning, I wake up with a slight hangover. I feel guilty for my behavior the night before. I apologize to Lance.

"You kept your dignity, and I saw that," Lance says to me. He accepts my apology.

Lance and I spend Sunday at my apartment. I make him sandwiches for lunch. I had bought some fresh cold cuts from the neighborhood deli. I carefully layer the lettuce and tomatoes on the fresh Italian bread. Making a sandwich is also an art to me.

We go to the video store and rent the movie, *Miss Congeniality*. We enjoy snuggling on the couch while watching the movie.

Around 4:00 p.m., Lance looks at me and says, "Well, it's about that time."

This is the moment I am dreading. I hate seeing him go. I am sad already.

I pack up some sandwiches and a piece of my homemade apple pie for him to take with him on his drive home. I walk him to his car. He gives me a hug and a kiss, gets in the car, drives off, and happily waves.

I stand out front watching his car move farther and farther away. As it rounds the corner and disappears, I wonder if Lance is thinking about me.

CHAPTER 42

A Secret Revealed

I feel sad as I watch Lance's car turn the corner and disappear. I hop into my car and drive to Binghamton to meet Naomi. I had planned this previously, as I knew I would feel lonely after Lance's departure.

What I don't realize yet is that the lonliness I am experiencing is not because Lance has left. It is because Lance has not said anything meaningful to me in weeks.

While driving, I reflect on the weekend. It went well. Lance and I got along fine. He even understood my drinking behavior and was forgiving. He loved my cooking, and he liked my family. The chemistry between us was very strong.

So what could be wrong?

What is lacking between us is intimacy. I no longer feel close or connected to him. Also, I do not feel that our relationship is exclusive on his end. I suspect there are other women in the picture. I don't trust Lance.

I pull up in front of the video store in Binghamton. Naomi and I always meet here and then drive to a restaurant of our choosing. Naomi is waiting for me in her car. She smiles and motions for me to join her. I get in her car and start crying. Naomi hugs me.

"I miss him so much, Naomi," I say.

"I know it is hard for you to see him leave," she says. "Let's get us some comfort food, and we'll talk."

We go to the Park Diner, which is located on the Chenango River. The cup of hot, chicken-rice soup tastes wonderful and warms my heart and spirits. I tell Naomi about the weekend. I relate to her how foolish I feel about getting drunk.

Naomi surprises me with her response. She says, "I am glad he saw you like that, Lynne. He needs to see you as you. You cannot pretend to be perfect all the time, because you are not." Naomi is wise and aware of how I try to do everything right for Lance.

I recall saying to Tony a few weeks ago, "Lance must never see me upset. I must be perfect for him."

I have allowed myself to be taken in emotionally by this man, and I cannot let go. Lance, on the other hand, is happy as a clam, calling all the shots and in control of the relationship. I have given the control to him.

I feel much better after talking to Naomi. At least I don't feel guilty about getting drunk the night before.

Naomi drops me off at my car. I drive to Marge's. Marge tells me she was furious at the prank Lance and Dawn pulled with the bleu cheese on the salad.

"I told them you had an aversion to cheese," she said, "but it didn't do any good."

Marge is concerned that Lance is married. She says, "I didn't get the impression he was going to end his marriage any time soon."

"He wants to wait a year," I say, defending him. "He wants to make sure his wife is on her feet financially."

When I arrive home, there is a message on my answering machine from Lance telling me he has run into a hail storm just as he entered New Jersey.

He has also e-mailed me:

> *I am home sweetie, but I will tell you, THAT was one helluva ride! The hail storm I experienced 20 of the last 25 minutes home, was absolutely incredible. I could not get over how big the hail was and how hard and fast it was coming down on the car. I have NEVER experienced anything quite like that in my life. (I LOVED it, and glad it wasn't my new car!)*
>
> *Thank YOU again for a wonderful weekend. YOU made it very special for me. I just finished BOTH sandwiches. Will wait an hour or so, and then attack the pie.*
>
> *Talk to you soon!* [five smileys]
> *LYTPPK* [five smileys]
> *Lancecat* [five smileys]

The LYTPPK acronym has gotten old, is a good copout to avoid intimacy, and is meaningless to me. The words, "Love, Lance," would sound good to me.

His e-mail is nice, but I don't see "I miss you," or "I wish I didn't have to leave you," or "Can't wait to see you again."

Monday, May 28, 2001

The phone rings at 9:23 a.m. I know it is Lance. Today is Memorial Day, so I have slept in.

Lance and I talk for three hours this day. We talk about my drinking. Lance is understanding about my blunder on Saturday, a quality I do appreciate in him.

"We are progressing," Lance says. "We are encountering a lot of different situations, and we are going through them fine. The distance is good. It was really perfect. We have not gotten into sin, and we have handled our mistakes appropriately."

"Yes, I agree," I answer.

"Being with you kept me from committing real sin," he says. "There is such a drive in me to want the intimacy that I knew I could have with a woman. Now that I feel like it's there, I can relax. I don't have to go looking now."

Lance is finally talking about intimacy with me. I wish I was with him so I could touch him.

"I was horny as hell," he continues. "Sometimes I really miss you, I really do. I was only there two nights! I could feel it when I was leaving."

"I miss you, too, Lance," I say. I can't believe it. Lance actually misses me.

"I met you two weeks after I moved out of the house," Lance continues. "I am telling you, if I had not met you, I would be out sinning. God somehow brought a person into my life that I could love purely, whose mind is in the same place as God's. God could not have designed it any better."

"I feel the same way, Lance. I…"

"Let me just tell you this," Lance says, interrupting me. "I was at the point in my mind where I thought I would sin. I tempted fate. I had someone in this place, and I got naked."

I sit, stunned. He had someone in his apartment naked? When was this, I wonder? My mind goes back to April 15 when Lance changed overnight.

"I never told you," Lance said. "The person was from this area. It happened on the spot. I nixed that quickly. That was a major temptation. I played with danger with that one. I told her I wasn't going to go there. I crossed the line. I sinned."

"How did you feel afterwards?" I ask, feeling sick inside.

"Terrible," Lance says. "I went and did it again and felt better. I kept my limitations. I still did not commit fornication. I was that close; a fraction of an inch away. Not totally naked. I couldn't do it."

I am terrified to ask Lance when this event occurred, because I fear it was recent. If so, I don't want to hear it.

He continues, "She begged me over the Internet. 'Please, please, please, let me come over, I want you to have sex with me.'" Lance indicates the girl used the "F" word.

"How did you feel about a woman saying to you, 'I want you to have sex with me?'" I ask, shaking.

"There was another woman I met," Lance responds, ignoring my question. "She grabbed me by the crotch at a department store, she had me going. We did go back to her car and we touched."

"I must be pretty different to you," I respond in a rage. Now he is talking about a second woman.

"Yes, you are," Lance says. "I knew none of these women would ever be anything more. Regardless, I don't have that desire to go out and do it anymore. I am the master of my domain!" Lance says proudly.

"I am the master of my domain" is a reference to a *Seinfeld* episode which Lance and I have watched together. I remember it well. It has to do with masturbation. Is Lance now telling me he masturbates?

"I can't lie; it is something I do out of choice. This is my way of handling my own personal situation without hurting anyone."

He *is* referring to masturbation!

I suddenly realize Lance is talking about cyber sex on the Internet. It is instant-messaging women, talking dirty to them with an unknown identity, and masturbating at the computer. Lance considers this an alternative to having a girl naked in bed with him.

"This is the sin that I am allowing myself to do so that I don't commit a bigger sin," he says. "I feel at this point I am not tempted to bring anyone into this apartment; nor am I tempted to go out dating anyone else. This is my outlet. I have different identities on the Internet."

"How would you feel if *I* was doing that?" I ask him.

"If you did it, I would be shocked," Lance replies. "It is not within your scope."

"You are not ready to give this up, are you?" I ask.

"This is a choice," Lance says. "It has a strong hold on me. This is one of the things that keep me from going out and going to bars and trying to meet people or calling up someone."

Is this supposed to impress me? This is another time I should have terminated this relationship. Lance is telling me his relationship with me is not exclusive. He was naked with a girl in his bed, another girl grabbed his crotch in a department store, and now he tells me he is cyber-sexing on the Internet with strangers!

Why is he telling me this? Oh, that's right, he is being honest. Now that I know he did it he can go on his merry way with a clear conscience.

"I have had opportunities and backed down," Lance continues. "My conscience was too strong. We all have our weaknesses. In my mind, I don't use my own identity. My role is a totally different individual."

"But it is still you!" I reply. "God knows it's you!"

"There are certain characteristics that remain in me," he says.

"Lance, you are a womanizer!" I say. I am furious, bewildered, and hurt. I think to myself, "What a pig!"

"That is not my heart's desire, Lynne. It is really not me. It is an element that has become a part of my existence. It can change. This is not what I would call fun. It is something to do that fulfills a lack right now. I know that God is there."

God? Now he is throwing God into this?

"My rationale is, I don't know these people. Lynne, I don't think there is anything in my life I can't tell you the truth about. When you are relating to a woman, you should be able to feel you can tell her the truth."

Lance is saying this to appease himself. Now that he has been "honest" with me, he can continue his sin and not feel guilty.

"You have the freedom to ask me whatever you want. I feel close to you that I was able to tell you. This is an intimate part of me. I am being a character. It is not really me."

Lance is so good at justifying his wrong behavior. And how nice of him to "allow" me the freedom to ask him whatever I want! He does not know the meaning of intimacy.

"The kind of horny I get with you is different. When I am around you I don't feel I need Viagra. I feel this doesn't affect the way I feel about you".

Is that statement supposed to make me feel better?

"I feel very fortunate and blessed, and I give God the glory to see how we can be so *honest* and real and work everything out so peacefully," Lance says to me. "I am not meeting anybody; I am not going out with anybody."

No, Lance is just jacking off at his computer with strange women!

Before Lance hangs up, he says, "We have had a good conversation today! Being able to share these things with you helps me to love you more. I love you."

We hang up. I sit there, holding the phone and feeling like an idiot.

It is amazing how a woman can convince herself there is a reason to hang onto a relationship. I rationalized he was sexually frustrated and needed to be doing this.

I still have not come to my senses. Deep down, I know in my heart that Lance does not desire an exclusive relationship with me. Lance would like for me to open a door for him to end the relationship. I have no intention of making it easy for him.

Why am I willing to set myself up for more pain?

CHAPTER 43

Vacation Plans

Tuesday, May 29, 2001

I wake up, distraught over Lance's and my conversation from the day before. During his usual early morning phone call, the conversation is chit-chat. I can tell he does not take issue with anything we discussed yesterday. I feel differently, but I remain silent.

Lance is going to Karen's apartment today to give her another computer, since hers is not working. He is also excited about picking up his new car at the dealer's this week.

"You have a nice day. I will be in touch with you," he says. "Love you."

Wednesday, May 30, 2001

"I didn't sleep too well," Lance says in our early-morning conversation. "Happy anniversary!"

I realize it is the thirtieth of the month. We had met on the Internet, September 30. We have known each other eight months.

Lance talks nonstop about his new car. He is picking it up today.

"When I talk to you, I know you are with me. You make me feel very good about everything," Lance says to me.

I wonder if he cyber-sexed on the Internet last night.

Friday, June 8, 2001

Lance suggests we go on vacation together. This gives me a much-needed lift.

We decide to go to Lancaster, Pennsylvania. Lancaster is located in the heart of the Pennsylvania Dutch Country and inhabited by the Mennonites. It is famous for its history, museums, tours, and fine home cooking. The Mennonites still use a horse and buggy for transportation.

"It would be nice to drive with someone in my new car," he says. "I don't know how we would do it. Perhaps you could meet me somewhere in the middle."

I cannot believe Lance is expecting me to drive my 1991 Tercel by myself. It has over a hundred thousand miles on it and no air conditioning. In addition, it blows smoke out the tail pipe every time I start it.

"There is a place called The Tabernacle, Lance says. "They do a film presentation. I have seen it several times. It is very nice. You would enjoy it. There are several nice restaurants. We could spend a couple days and one or two nights there."

I tell Lance my sister has been to Lancaster several times and has brochures and information. I will stop by her house and borrow her brochures in the next couple of days.

Lancaster is less than two hours from where Lance lives. It is a four-hour drive from where I live.

We set a date for Saturday, June 30.

"If we stay two or three nights that will keep the expenses down" Lance says. "If your sister has been there, she will be excited for you and can come up with some ideas of things for us to do. Find out what you can, and we will talk about what we want to do."

Sunday, June 10, 2001

I write to Lance, letting him know the rates of the Harvest Drive Motel, which is out in the middle of a huge cornfield. I tell him all about a map my sister gave me, with other hotels and information on sightseeing. I send the e-mail at 11:30 a.m. I cannot wait to hear back from him.

Nine hours later, at 9:41 p.m., Lance responds. He writes:

Thank you sweetie! I will talk to you tomorrow morning!

I record in my journal: "Got a patronizing e-mail from Lance nine hours after e-mailing him about going to Lancaster."

Monday, June 11, 2001

Lance calls me early morning before going to work. We talk about our trip. He is agreeable to the idea of me making the plans, since I have all the brochures. I tell him about the various shows they have at night. We decide we will definitely go to the tabernacle.

We then discuss how we are going to travel.

"You are four hours away," Lance says. "You would have a long ride by yourself. We could meet some where in between. I know there's a place near the turnpike."

I am livid. I cannot believe he expects me to drive my used 1991 Toyota with no air conditioning on a trip even if it is only a couple of hours.

"Why don't you come and get me?" I say boldly.

Lance gasps. Then there is a long pause. I sit, doodling. I can tell he is shocked that I would make such a suggestion.

"Four hours to your place?" he says. "And four hours back? That is a lot of driving. I would have to do it twice. Ugh! And then I would have to drive all the way to Lancaster."

I don't answer.

"In my mind, you would have two hours of driving," he continues. "We would meet somewhere and go. You could park your car, and that would be all the driving you would have to do."

"If you can think of a place, let me know," I say, fuming.

"I would have to look at a map," he says.

"My car has two hundred thousand miles on it!" I say, not backing down. "It blows smoke out the back. In addition, it has no air conditioning. I don't know if it would be safe for me to drive it that far."

"It would be a terrible hardship on you, and I wouldn't want you to go through that," Lance says, finally starting to get it. "But it is a vacation, and I would be doing all this driving…"

"I know, that really sucks," I respond. "But you could drive here and spend the night and we could get a fresh start in the morning."

"I am not opposed to the idea," Lance says. "But if you could handle two hours by yourself, we could find a place two hours away."

I do not answer.

"We would end up coming back to your place another four hours," Lance says, sounding full of anxiety. "By the time it's time to go back to New Jersey, it will be sixteen hours of driving for me."

"You have a brand-new car," I say. I am not backing down this time. Lance is not even thinking of my safety, welfare, or the thought of us traveling together. All he has on his mind is how much *he* will have to drive.

Lance is silent again. "It is not the worst situation, but to me, it is not practical. I would rather think of a way we could minimize the drive, especially since it is a vacation. Still, it wouldn't be the worst thing."

I cannot stand the thought of having to drive alone in a car that may not be safe. I use my car to drive locally and have always rented a car to travel.

"I will do that," Lance says. "I will put myself out for anybody I care about, so it's not a problem. We will be together, and that will be fun. I will come and get you."

Lance finally gets it.

"Call the tabernacle and get the info. Find out if they still have a tabernacle tour. Ask what motels are nearby. Find out where Sights and Sounds are," Lance says.

"Okay, I will," I say, feeling relieved that Lance will be picking me up.

"I totally trust you with the plans," he says. "Look over the map and decide what you want to do."

"I will let you know," I say, getting excited again.

"I will come to your place Monday night, July 2, and stay over," Lance says, his wheels turning. "Then we will drive to Lancaster Tuesday morning, stay overnight Tuesday and Wednesday, and come back to your apartment on Thursday. I will spend the night with you and go home on Friday. That is July 4 weekend."

"Sounds good," I say.

"Okay, Lynnie cat," he says.

We hang up.

I am glad we have a plan.

CHAPTER 44

Lance's Problems on the Job

Saturday, June 16, 2001

I receive Lance's Saturday-morning phone call. We talk for two hours, mostly about his job situation. He informs me that several changes have been made. His department has merged into a larger group. Consultants from another company have been called in to help with the process.

Lance has been asked to work with a consultant who I will call Marcia.

Lance and Marcia do not click, mostly due to Lance's impatience at explaining things to people. He continually expects people to understand and grasp instructions the first time.

Thursday, June 21, 2001

Lance e-mails me late afternoon, informing me he has received a "written warning" regarding his job. He states he is being "unfairly judged" and needs to write a rebuttal by the following Monday. He is not overly concerned. However, he is not taking the warning lightly, either.

Lance asks me to assist him with his rebuttal letter. I tell him I will. He wants me to look over his response and give him my opinion before he sends it.

The written warning addresses three issues with Lance:
-Attitude
-Interpersonal Skills
-Working Hours

The warning states Lance "yelled" at the female consultant and became very impatient with her during an hour of one-on-one training. In addition, he rudely pointed to his watch during an interview and said it was time to leave.

Monday, June 25, 2001

Lance forwards his response to me, which addresses the three issues in the memo.

It is hard for Lance to admit he is wrong. I fail to see this as another flag regarding his personality. I am one hundred percent supportive of him and the position he is taking regarding the warning.

I read Lance's response to the written warning. He is being defensive. I gently and tactfully tell him so. I spend all morning revising his letter while at work.

I send him my revision around noon.

Lance e-mails me and says:

> *I think your suggestions were excellent and I incorporated all of the changes. I appreciate your input and the tact, care and trust for me that you communicated. Thank you, thank you, thank you! Here it is again.*

He attaches the four-page response with my suggested changes and revisions to his e-mail for me to look over.

I tell him it looks good and to send it on.

I am terrified that Lance will lose his job.

CHAPTER 45

Vacation in Lancaster with Lance

Monday, July 2, 2001

There has been no response to Lance's rebuttal letter at work, so he has assumed all is well. Now he can relax and not worry about his job during our vacation time together.

I have spent weeks preparing for this trip. I have the map and directions ready to take with us. I have also made all the reservations.

We will be staying at the Harvest Drive Motel, which is located in the middle of a cornfield with a beautiful view surrounding it. We have reservations at the Dutch Apple Dinner Theatre tomorrow night. We will enjoy a wonderful buffet dinner, and afterwards see *The Wizard of Oz* which will be performed on stage. I was able to get us a front seat near the stage.

Lance will be arriving at my apartment around 6:30 p.m. this evening. We will leave for Lancaster early tomorrow morning.

I recall Lance complaining several times about Karen "always having to go to the bathroom." This concerns me, since I have a strong addiction to caffeine. My first cup of coffee in the morning is a necessity. Since coffee is a diuretic, I am sure I will have to make a couple bathroom stops during our drive.

I decide to forgo the coffee and wait until we arrive in Lancaster. That way, I will not have to ask Lance to make any stops for me on the way there. The trip is a four-hour drive, so I should be all right.

I spend the day with last-minute packing and preparations. Lance knocks on my door at 6:10 p.m. I am thrilled to see him.

We walk outside. He proudly shows me his brand-new 2002 Toyota Corolla. It is a beautiful rose color with beige-cloth interior. There is a spoiler on the back, giving it a trendy appearance. I envy Lance. I have longed for a new car for years. I am not able to afford a new vehicle at this time.

I order chicken wings from the neighborhood deli. After eating, we visit Marge. We are getting along wonderfully, and my heart is full. I love being with Lance. I look forward to a wonderful week with him.

We go to bed after watching a *Seinfeld* video he brought with him. We hug and kiss and fall asleep in each others arms.

Tuesday, July 3, 2001

Lance and I are up at 6:00 a.m. I make sandwiches and put them in a cooler, along with two bottles of Diet Coke. As planned, I do not drink any coffee. We are on the road at 8:30 a.m.

Lance informs me he has the "conversation" planned for the trip. He is going to tell me about his job history and how he has evolved to the present. Of course, Lance has his job on his mind. The written warning was received only a week ago.

Lance begins his story of his first employment. He gives me a detailed description of his job at the Port Authority of New York and New Jersey, which he held for nine years. I do not realize at this time the Port Authority was housed in the Twin Towers of the World Trade Center. I picture him being on Forty-second Street in Manhattan.

Lance calls himself the "scapegoat" at his regular job when things were not going as his boss desired. As he continues talking, the back of my shoulders start to hurt. I realize I am not feeling well. My head starts to throb.

"I got downsized out of my job," Lance says, not noticing me massaging my shoulders to get rid of the excruciating pain. My stomach starts to feel nauseous.

Suddenly it hits me. I am having withdrawal symptoms because I did not have my morning coffee! My plan has backfired. If I don't have my "caffeine fix," I get ill. I had forgotten this since I always make a pot of coffee the minute I get up.

Lance is on a roll with his job-history story. He continues, "During this time off from a permanent position, God allowed me to go to Canada, where I spent a week in renewal services and began to get encouraged again. Then, just before Thanksgiving, God got me a temp job at the New Jersey Hospital Association. This job did wonders for my self-esteem as a professional accountant. Unfortunately, this job lasted only four months and, I was jobless for another three months."

Oh my God, I have to throw up! I grab a bottle of Diet Coke. Diet Coke has caffeine in it. Maybe I can save myself. I start guzzling down the Coke, hoping and praying Lance does not notice I am horribly sick. He doesn't. He is too busy talking about his job experiences and himself.

"The following July, I got a temporary job at a Cellular One office, and by the end of November they made me a permanent employee," Lance says, totally oblivious to my drinking the Diet Coke and trying not to hurl.

Maybe if I burp, I'll feel better. I feel terrible. How am I ever going to make it through the day? I can't imagine sitting through the show at the Dutch Apple Theatre tonight, either. This is awful.

"Lance!" I yell. "Stop the car! I have to throw up!" I can't stand it another minute. Lance stops the car with a bewildered look on his face. I dash out of the car and run over to a ditch. I can't stop vomiting.

This is great. I accomplished my mission of not having to stop for me to go to the bathroom. I had to puke instead. Way to go, Lynne!

"Are you all right?" Lance seems genuinely concerned as I roll myself back into the car after hurling nonstop for at least a full minute.

"Yes, thank you. But I need to get to a gas station right away to buy some crackers. I need to get something into my stomach."

I had forgotten I do not travel well on an empty stomach, especially if I haven't had my morning coffee.

"Of course I will be glad to stop," Lance says. "I feel so terrible for you." Lance means it, and he has no idea what lead up to this minute.

Fortunately, we find a gas station within minutes. I have some crackers and a can of cold Diet Coke. I am out of the woods, thank God, and I start feeling normal again. I also get myself a cup of coffee. So much for my "plan" of "not having to make any stops." Surprisingly, Lance is lovely about it all and feels bad for me.

Why didn't I just have coffee at home and not worry about annoying Lance? This is not his fault, it's mine. Am I so insecure and unsure of myself that I can't be me? Will I ever learn?

Lance continues his rendition of his job history during the remainder of the drive. He is still concerned about his present job, but feels the rebuttal memo, which I helped him write, was accepted. He has to stay on his toes, though and conform to the conditions set forth by his supervisors in order to avoid any further problems.

We arrive in Lancaster around 12:30 p.m. The Harvest Drive Motel is located in the heart of Pennsylvania Dutch country and is surrounded by miles of Amish farmland. Horses and buggies are still used as transportation by the area's Amish. There is an adjoining restaurant on the other side of the parking lot, which is noted for its home cooking and wonderful buffets. A gazebo to the right of the complex adds a romantic touch to the scenery.

After taking our bags to our room, we walk around outside. The sun is shining and feels like a warm blanket. I take a picture of Lance in the cornfield. We ask a tourist to take a picture of us sitting together in the gazebo. How romantic this is. I am so thankful to be feeling better.

We return to our room. "I have to freshen up," I say to Lance as I head to the bathroom.

"I have a surprise for you when you come out," Lance says.

When I come out of the bathroom, I see he has replaced the light bulb in the lamp on the dresser with a green bulb, giving the room a romantic ambience. He has also closed the blinds and lit a candle. He turns on a tape with some romantic songs he's recorded for our time together.

We lie down together and take a nap in each others arms. I feel his caring and wonder why I ever doubted the relationship.

That evening we go to the Dutch Apple Theatre and enjoy a wonderful buffet dinner. We have a table up front next to the stage. There is an elderly couple seated with us. They are pleasant. The conversation flows smoothly. I am surprised when Lance suggests going fishing with the man. I wonder why he would do that, since this is our vacation. I am glad the man politely turns him down.

The show starts. It is *The Wizard of Oz*. The color, music, and performance is spectacular. Lance holds my hand or has his arm around me the entire time.

Wednesday, July 4, 2001

We enjoy a delicious breakfast buffet at the Harvest Drive Restaurant.

Afterwards, we go to the tabernacle reproduction at the Mennonite Information Center. It is an illustration of the ceremonies recorded in the Old Testament and the story surrounding the tabernacle the Israelites carried with them on their exodus to the Promised Land. Lance has his arm around me during the entire demonstration. I love his attentiveness.

We then go to a nearby mall. Lance likes the bargain places and shops for hours for himself. He buys several shirts. I help him pick out clothes. He is having trouble finding shoes. He spots a nice vase he thinks his wife, Karen, would like, and pays one dollar for it.

I tell Lance I would like to go to the Kitchen Kettle Village. They have nice crafts, there along with homemade baked goods, jams, and jellies. They close at 4:00 p.m. We continue shopping for clothes for him. I notice it is after 3:00 p.m.

"The Kitchen Kettle Village closes at 4:00," I say to Lance.

"Well, 45 minutes should be long enough, right?" he says, sounding a little "short."

"I guess," I answer, feeling annoyed. I wonder why we can spend three hours shopping for Lance, and I get only forty-five minutes to do what I want.

We make it to the village around 3:25 p.m. I feel rushed, but browse as best I can. I buy a couple jars of jam to take back with me.

That night we go to Miller's Smorgasbord. I had made the reservations a few weeks ago. All the food in Lancaster is delicious. I wear a pretty orange sundress. Afterward, we attend the fireworks in Lititz. It is raining. The weather is wonderfully warm. Lance and I playfully skip down the street with our umbrellas.

On the way back to the hotel, Lance plays an Enya tape. It is a romantic moment. He has removed the sun roof off his car. A gentle breeze flows on us. I stand up and shout, my head going up through the open roof. The sky is black; the stars are beautiful. I am having a wonderful time. I never want this week to end.

Thursday, July 5, 2001

I record in my journal: "We had lovey dovey this morning. No sex, just hugging and kissing. Wonderful chemistry."

I love Lance's touch; I love holding his hand; I love Lance! We enjoy the breakfast buffet. We check out of the motel. We will spend the day here and start back home tonight.

Again we shop. Lance still can't find the right shoes. We finally find two pairs. He buys them, along with a pair of khaki pants. I buy a shoo-fly pie for Tony, a hot plate to give to my friend, Diane, and some more jelly.

Subtle Deception

At 1:00 p.m. we go to the Living Waters Sight and Sound Theatre. I had ordered the tickets weeks ago. We attend a dynamic show called *Abraham and Sarah*. We are only three rows back.

The show is moving. There is no program with the names of the cast. They prefer being anonymous. They are performing for God's glory. The spirit is truly alive in this place.

At halftime, I have to go to the bathroom. I stay seated. The entire trip I have been careful to not use the bathroom too much, as it annoys Lance. I cannot wait until the show is over so I can use the bathroom.

After the show, we grab a sandwich and start back home. I feel sad. Our trip is coming to an end.

Lance has the conversation planned for the return trip home! "This time I am going to tell you about how I have evolved sexually," he says.

I sit, stunned, as Lance begins to tell me of his sexual escapades. Why do I need to know this?

After describing his sexual escapades with women, he reverts back to when he was a boy.

He tells me he was molested by a man who was a friend of the family. This saddens me. I sit, horrified, as he reveals to me he is attracted to men as a *result* of his being molested!

"I really don't want to get involved with a man," he explains. "It's all about the sex. I would just as soon put a paper bag over their head and just have the sex."

Is Lance bisexual? I am in a trance. I do not respond to him.

He then says "I wanted you to know this about me in the event we end up getting married."

On the positive side, Lance cares enough to share with me his job history and his sexuality. On the negative side, he is not even remotely aware of what I am feeling inside.

Did I hear him mention marriage? I am totally confused; a feeling I am used to in this relationship.

"I have to ask God every day to keep me from putting an ad out asking for a man," Lance says.

"Lance, are you gay?" I ask.

"No, I am not gay," he answers. "It's an urge I feel overtaking me at times. I love women and want to be with one special woman."

"One special woman?" I think to myself. What about *me*?

"I cannot believe what I am hearing!" I say. Lance keeps right on talking, ignoring my comment.

"Now you know all about me," he says. "I feel closer to you now."

I suppose that is a good thing; the fact he "feels closer to me?"

We arrive at my apartment at 11:00 p.m. I give Marge a call to let her know we are home safe. I take a hot bath and hop into bed. Lance puts his arms around me. He is fast asleep in five minutes. I lay there, wide awake.

CHAPTER 46

Dark Zone

Friday, July 6, 2001

I am awake early. I did not sleep well. Lance snored all night. It amazes me how he can sleep soundly and behave so nonchalantly after sharing major issues with me that could have a significant impact on our "relationship."

While lying next to him, I think about the time we have spent together the last few days. It was a wonderful time. Lance was attentive and affectionate. So what is bothering me?

Lance did not once tell me that he was having a wonderful time, nor did he *say* anything intimate. The words "I love you" have not been spoken by him in weeks.

Lance is proud of his "honesty." Surely he would tell me if he no longer had feelings for me, wouldn't he? And he *did* "mention" marriage to me. Isn't that why he shared his innermost secrets with me on the drive to and from Lancaster?

I continue pondering. Why is everything always about Lance? What about me? The whole trip was about Lance; *his* job, *his* sexuality. During our week together, we mostly shopped; for *him*. The shows and tours had been prearranged by me for *our* enjoyment.

My main concern is our conversation from last night. Is Lance bisexual? He can't possibly be gay; he loves women too much. I recall the ridiculous Solomon letter from months ago.

Why would Lance tell me he is attracted to men? To what purpose? Also, is he still having cyber sex on the Internet with women? It occurs to me he could be doing it with men, also.

Lance wakes up, turns over, and smiles at me. He dashes to the bathroom to brush his teeth and use mouthwash. We both do that in the morning. I smile at him as he hops back into bed and grabs me. We snuggle under the covers, giggling, hugging, and kissing. I hate the thought of him leaving today. I love his touch.

We spend the morning watching *Seinfeld* videos. Afterward, we sit down and "settle up" the cost of our trip. Everything, including gas, hotel, shows, and food is split in half. I give Lance cash I had saved up for the trip.

Early that afternoon we go to Kmart, Home Depot, and the Dollar Store. Lance still needs some things.

He snaps at me when I show him a left turn at the last minute into a parking lot. "Why didn't you say so?" he snaps.

I sit silent, in a rage, feeling hurt and humiliated. I don't like being snapped at.

"I'm sorry I snapped at you," he says. I don't answer.

Lance will be leaving soon. I don't want to argue. I want to be sure he leaves on a good note.

We return to my apartment. Lance says, "Well, it's time."

I hand him some sandwiches that I had packed for him to take on his trip back to New Jersey. He grabs his suitcase and duffle bag.

"Please, God, have him say he will miss me. Have him say something meaningful," I pray.

"I'll e-mail you when I get home," Lance says, getting into his car. He smiles, beeps his horn, and drives away.

I stand, frozen, in the driveway. Did we not just spend a week together?

I record in my journal: "He never said he misses me, or that he can't wait to see me. He never says he loves me. I am very angry at him for messing with my feelings. He never should have said those intimate things to me months ago. He told me he was in love with me. I am heartsick. I miss him so much."

In a daze I drive to the credit union. Later, I visit Marge. Upon returning home, I check my e-mail. Lance has arrived home safely. He writes:

Hello Sweetie! I had a real easy wonderful ride home with delicious sandwiches, potato chips, sugar cookies and coke! (thank YOU again!) [smiley]

It only took me about 3 hours and 15 minutes. No traffic at all. It got warmer as soon as I got to Southern Pennsylvania. When I left, the outside temperature was 70. It got as low as 67 degrees on Interstate 81 but it was 78 degrees in Southern Pennsylvania and New Jersey. The sky was mostly clear too. It is a shame the weather out by you isn't as nice, but it was nice and even nicer being with you.

Talk to you tomorrow morning [smileys]
LYTPPK [smileys]
Lancecat

I stare at the e-mail. That's it; no substance, no depth, no "I miss you?" Most of the letter was about traffic and the weather! How patronizing can he be? Who cares about the weather? The weather is something people talk about when they are trying to find something to talk about.

I go to bed, wondering why I am staying in this relationship. I already know why. I am in too deep. I am afraid to confront Lance about his feelings, because I know what the answer will be.

Saturday, July 7, 2001

I wake up, feeling lonely, empty, and depressed. This is not how I should be feeling after spending a week with my boyfriend.

I miss Lance terribly. If Lance missed me, it would be bearable; but he doesn't.

I get his patronizing Saturday-morning call.

"Beautiful here, cool, fans are blowing in my apartment. Peaches, [his new cat] snuggled with me all night between my legs."

"Nice," I say.

"I completely unpacked when I got home. I had such a relaxing time away. Easy ride back."

He pauses. I don't speak.

"It was certainly nice to have Lynniecat with me. Very compatible, good time we had together, seeing all those things, everything was wonderful."

Lance brings up snapping at me the day before. He had sensed that I was upset.

"I was crabby," he says. "It was a momentary frustration. I probably felt it for a second. I can understand; you hate feeling stupid and you hate that you were made to feel that way. It is about how you feel about yourself."

How I feel about myself? It is how he made me feel! Lance is putting his "wisdom" hat back on now, and telling me my feelings were appropriate. He is also being my psychologist.

"You behaved right by being still," Lance says approvingly. "That could have been the beginning of a fight. We will be tested by God. My compulsion, my frustration, my impatience are all a part of my nature."

I am glad I "behaved right!" Who the hell does Lance think he is, an authority on behavior?

Lance and I talk almost three hours. I hang up, feeling empty. Even though we communicated at length about our feelings and emotions, but not towards each other, I feel something is missing. I know what is missing!

I long for Lance to tell me he loves me, he misses me, and he cannot wait to see me again. Isn't that the way people "in love" talk to each other?

I go to our local bookstore. Maybe if I read a book and have a cappuccino, I'll feel better.

I grab a book to read, self-help, of course. I then buy a large raspberry cappuccino and head for a table. As I put the drink down, it lands partly on the book and partly on the table, spilling all over the place. I am in tears as I see the hot foam landing on the cloth chair and liquid pouring all over a brand-new book that I only intended to read; not to mention the huge puddle on the table!

This is the last straw for me. I completely lose it. I hurriedly find some napkins and clean up the table as best as I can. I purchase the ruined book, since I know it cannot be sold to anyone in its condition. I dart out the door and head for my car. I am sobbing as I drive to Marge's. Why can't I get it together? I calm down and fake it when I visit with Marge. I am too ashamed to tell anyone my fears.

Sunday, July 8, 2001

I record in my journal:

> *The depression continues. I am livid all day. Lance called. Nothing conversation. He doesn't have a clue that I am totally grief-stricken with his being gone and how much I miss him. Tony and I met for*

coffee, and I told him about Lance possibly being bisexual. He found it amusing. No support whatsoever. I feel so alone.

The entire week has similar journal entries. Lance's calls continue to be patronizing. I feel trapped within myself. I am scared; scared to stay in the relationship, and terrified to end it.

Lance is saying by his actions, "I love you, but I am not *in love* with you." To hear him speak those words to me would be unbearable.

It will not be long before my worst fears are realized.

CHAPTER 47

Lance Gets Fired

I am scattered during the entire month of July. While Tony jokes about my "bi-sexual" boyfriend, I continue to feel anxious and bewildered over Lance's mixed signals. The only bright spot this month is that Lance is planning to visit me the first weekend of August. We will be going to Cooperstown, NY for the annual Baseball Hall of Fame weekend.

Tuesday, July 24, 2001

The "Written Warning" Lance received at work a few weeks ago has resurfaced. Because of this, Lance has decided to apply for another position with the Human Resources Department in his company.

Wednesday, August 1, 2001

Jack, the vice president of the company has called a meeting in his office today regarding Lance's request for another position. He had previously asked Lance to give him a list of personal references.

Sayid, Lance's boss and Arnold, Sayid's supervisor, are also present at this meeting.

Jack informs Lance that none of the people on his list of references had anything good to say about him. An argument ensues between Lance and Arnold. Lance gets angry and touches Arnold's arm during the confrontation. Arnold yells, "Don't touch me!"

Lance raises his arm and says "I would like to touch you and…"

This results in an immediate harassment charge. Lance is fired on the spot and walked out of the building.

Lance is distraught and admits he behaved inappropriately.

I know it is over for Lance. His behavior was unacceptable. Lance's personal relations at work are not good, not to mention the fact that even his references did not speak well of him. This has me concerned.

I want to be a comfort and an encouragement to him, but there is nothing I can say or do.

Lance will be visiting me this weekend. Hopefully, the diversion will be good for him.

Lance will have to start looking for another job. He has learned a hard lesson. It is too bad I haven't yet.

CHAPTER 48

Trip to Cooperstown

Thursday, August 2, 2001

I take the day off to prepare for Lance's visit this weekend. I shampoo the carpet, dust, and vacuum. I put new slipcovers on my loveseat. My apartment looks great.

Lance calls me around 10:00 a.m.

He is traumatized by the sudden, unexpected change in his life this past week. One day, he was working; the next day, he was out of a job.

"I allowed the job to beat me," he says to me on the phone. "I let the job wear me down. I can't do that."

"You will be okay," I say, trying to be encouraging. I know there is nothing I can say to make him feel better. All I can do is be supportive.

"You also made me think I could relocate, if necessary."

I sit up like a prairie dog. Relocate? Is Lance thinking of moving here to be with me? A tremendous surge of hope flows through me; a feeling I have not had in weeks.

"I do have a lot of options. I will start my search."

Lance is ready to start looking for another job immediately.

He will be coming tomorrow to spend the weekend with me. The trip will be good for him, and it will take his mind off the horrible events of this past week. I will do all I can to make sure he has a wonderful, relaxing weekend.

"I am scared to death to tell my wife," Lance says. "She will say God judged me for abandoning her. I am so used to the guilt."

"God is not judging you," I reply.

"Your words, your nourishment, give me strength and motivation to fight and do the right thing," Lance says affectionately. "I mean it out of my heart. It makes a difference to know someone understands."

"God is on your side," I say. I want so badly to make it better for him.

"The deck was stacked against me. There was nothing I could have done. That was the final straw."

"God did not cause this," I say. "It will all work out."

I wish I could believe my words.

Friday, August 3, 2001

I wake up, excited. Lance will be arriving here this afternoon. I look forward to our going to the Baseball Hall of Fame Weekend in Cooperstown tomorrow.

Lance gives me a quick call before leaving. "I will leave around noon," he says. "I am going to bring some discs with songs on them to download onto your computer. I don't know how much space you have."

I don't know what he is talking about. I have a radio and a CD player. I don't need to have music downloaded onto my computer.

6:30 p.m.

Lance pulls into my driveway. He looks great in his blue shirt, and he smells so clean.

He is hungry and enjoys the tomato/hamburger casserole I prepared, along with fresh rolls from the bakery and tossed salad with my special, homemade, balsamic-vinaigrette dressing.

After dinner, Lance sits at my computer and starts downloading several songs from numerous CDs that he had brought with him. I have no idea why he is doing this. I did not ask him to.

I clear the table, wash the dishes, and clean up the kitchen. Lance does not offer to help.

Two hours later, Lance is still downloading songs onto my computer. I start to feel irritated.

I was hoping we would visit Marge. It is almost 9:30 p.m. I know Marge is anticipating a visit from us. I don't even want these songs. He has hundreds of songs on his computer, but that doesn't mean I want them on mine.

Around 10:00 p.m., I say, "I think Marge is hoping to see you tonight."

"It's too late," Lance says. He continues downloading the songs.

I call Marge and tell her we will not be over. "Lance is tired," I say. "We will stop by tomorrow when we return from Cooperstown."

"Okay," Marge says. "Have a nice night." I know she is disappointed. I am furious, but I don't say anything. Not only is Lance engrossed in doing something I don't want, he is not spending any quality time with me. I sit next to him after cleaning the kitchen. What else can I do?

Finally, around 11:00 p.m., he is done, thank heavens. I now have a zillion unwanted songs downloaded on my computer. I know I will never listen to them.

We watch a *Seinfeld* tape and go to bed. We hug and kiss, which makes my waiting worthwhile.

Saturday, August 4, 2001

Lance and I pack some sandwiches and head for Cooperstown around 8:00 a.m. This time I have enough sense to drink a cup of coffee before leaving. Lance looks sharp in his silk, yellow, short-sleeved shirt. I love his new car and am envious. I wish I had a new car.

I think to myself about what a catch he is. He looks so sharp and handsome in his new vehicle. I long to be a major part of Lance's life.

One hour later we arrive on the outskirts of Cooperstown. There are crowds of baseball fans lined up to take a trolley into town. The atmosphere is one of excitement and nostalgia. We park the car and board the trolley.

There are banners and baseballs signs and memorabilia lining the quaint streets. The shops are open with displays out front. I am thrilled for Lance. He loves baseball and is an avid Yankee fan. It does my heart good to see him enjoying himself.

Ernie Banks, Whitey Ford, Hank Aaron, and several other famous players are there in person, signing autographs on baseballs, calendars, and bats. The price for the autographs is quite high, but well worth it to Lance. He purchases a huge ball as a memento and asks Whitey Ford and Hank Aaron to sign it. I am able to take some photos of him with the players.

Lance purchases old baseball cards, a cap, and some pins from past games. The karma is wonderful. Baseball is in the air all over the streets and hundreds of fans are milling around.

We walk down the street to the notorious Doubleday Field, which was built in 1939. Two major leagues play here every summer. There are no individual seats, just benches with backs. We take pictures and grab a hot dog.

We then go to the national Baseball Hall of Fame Museum. It is a shrine to baseball's greatest players. We explore the lists from twenty to thirty years ago and enjoy browsing the artifacts where souvenirs, engraved with signatures of famous players are sold.

The romantic part of the day is a walk to nearby Otsego Lake. We sit on the shore together for almost an hour. Lance asks me if I have ever been to Hawaii. I tell him no.

"How does a honeymoon in Hawaii sound?" Lance asks.

"Yes, I would love that!" My heart is beating a mile a minute. I look out at the water. I love listening to the waves lapping against the docks. Lance and I are sitting back-to-back on the stone ledge. The sun is shining on the water. A warm breeze is blowing. This is a magical moment.

On the way home, Lance and I admire the scenery. The mountains are a luscious green. The cornfields are high, and can be seen for miles. The sky is bright blue. The sun is just starting to set.

"You should see it here in the fall," I say. The foliage is gorgeous on the mountains."

"Let's see it together this year," Lance says. "I will come back for that."

"Great!" I say. "Around the second or third week of October is when the leaves are the prettiest."

We stop at Marge's before going to my apartment. Lance shows her the huge baseball he bought and the autographs he obtained. I feel wonderful about our day together.

Lance has not mentioned losing his job. Hopefully, his time with me is providing him a much-needed lift.

Later, after a hot bubble bath, I climb into bed next to Lance and fall into his arms. We kiss for over an hour, and he holds me. I feel like a starved puppy at a banquet.

Sunday, August 5, 2001

I cook bacon and eggs for breakfast. Lance and I stay in all day, hugging, snuggling, and watching videos. I love being with him. Later, we order Chinese takeout and drop off our photos from yesterday at a nearby pharmacy. Since Lance will not be working tomorrow, he has decided to stay until Monday. I have taken the day off to be with him.

Monday, August 6, 2001

Lance and I sleep in. We spend an hour snuggling in bed. We watch some *Seinfeld* videos and then go shopping. Lance thinks I should set up a deeper litter box for my cats, Happy and Stubby. He buys me a large litter box and a huge container of litter and fills it to the brim. It is the crystals that clump. I cannot get over the difference it makes. I can see the clean up is much easier for me, and the cats love it.

We watch an intense movie called *Life is Beautiful*. I start to feel sad. Lance will be leaving soon.

"What time do you have to go to work tomorrow?" Lance asks.

"8:30 a.m.," I answer.

"Why don't I stay over tonight and get up with you and leave when you go to work?" Lance says.

I am thrilled. Lance is not leaving today. He actually *wants* to spend more time with me!

"I would love that!" I say.

We eat leftover food from the Chinese place and then visit Marge. I am happy Lance will be with me for another twelve hours.

Tuesday, August 7, 2001

Lance and I get up together. He packs his things while I get ready for work. He loves the dress I am wearing. He is turned on, and he tells me so. I love it.

"Why don't I leave my shirt here?" he says. "I will get it the next time I visit you."

"Of course," I say. "I will wash it and iron it for you." Lance leaves behind the yellow silk shirt he wore to Cooperstown. I love that shirt, and I love the thought of having it with me after he leaves.

Lance holds and kisses me. I can tell he has an erection. There is nothing I can do to help him.

He hugs me and says goodbye. I am not upset like I was a month ago. Surely Lance loves me. He mentioned a honeymoon when we were in Cooperstown, and he stayed an extra day.

I meet Tony at work for coffee about a half-hour later and tell him all about my weekend. Tony patiently listens and tries to act interested.

I go back to my desk and send Lance a "Welcome Home" e-mail.

Hi Sweetie,

What a wonderful weekend we had. I always think it couldn't be any better than the last time, and it always is! I loved watching you enjoy yourself in Cooperstown, because when Lancecat is happy, that makes Lynniecat happy!

Hope you had a great and relaxing trip home. Just wanted to greet you and say hello and love you to pieces, Pussykot! [smileys]

Lynniecat [smileys]

Lance writes back to me at 11:29 a.m.

Thank you! And I too had a great time and I'll say it again too, you made everything we did special! And thank you for making me feel right at home, and for the sandwiches and the food and drink and all the love that went in it! It was very relaxing for me. The ride home was easy and pleasant. Thank YOU again for everything. Talk to you later PK!. LYTPPK [smileys], *Lancecat*

I feel good again at least for a few hours. Lance does not call or e-mail me the rest of the day.

I take his yellow shirt to bed with me. Lance's scent is on it. I fall asleep hugging it and wishing it was him.

My doubts start to return.

CHAPTER 49

Nightmare Visit in New Jersey

Lance spends the month of August looking for jobs, mostly on the Internet. He is able to download applications and contact human resources people and set up interviews.

In the meantime, I am busy firming up plans for a visit to New Jersey early September. I will rent a car and drive to my daughter Jane's on Friday, September 7. I will spend the evening with her and my grandson, Brian. Lance will pick me up at Jane's on Saturday, and we will drive to Lancaster, Pennsylvania, to see the show *Noah* which is advertised as being spectacular.

Lance wants us to have dinner at the Harvest Drive Motel, the place where we stayed in July. I suggest we spend the night there. He politely declines. I feel he is hedging.

August 25, 2001

Lance gets two job offers this day. He accepts an offer from Zone Telecom in Cherry Hill, New Jersey. It is about a half-hour drive, but they offer him a substantial salary. He will be starting his new job on Monday, September 10.

I am pleased and impressed that Lance has found another job so quickly. I purchase a bottle of wine and buy him a congratulatory card. I will give it to him when I visit him in a couple of weeks.

Friday, September 7, 2001

Lance has a fender-bender with his new vehicle earlier this week. It will be tied up in the shop. This changes our plans. Lance will not be picking me up at Jane's tomorrow. Instead, I will drive to his house from Jane's, and we will use my rental car to travel to Lancaster.

Lance says, "I will pay for everything, including the car rental, since I will also be using the car." I appreciate and accept his generous offer.

I start out early this day on my drive to New Jersey. I do not like the car I am renting. The windows are automatic, which is confusing for me. The turnpike and the tolls make me nervous, and I fear getting lost, even though I have driven there before to see my daughter and Brian. I always have to have the directions in front of me when making this trip.

I arrive at Jane's late afternoon. Lance calls me and gives me directions to his house, which is about fifteen minutes away. I will drive there in the morning.

I spend a pleasant evening with Jane, her husband, Paul and Brian. Jane later reads over the directions Lance has given me to his house.

"Mom, I don't understand these directions," Jane says. "They are on the back roads, and you could get lost. I know an easier way."

Jane calls Lance and discusses the route with him. He argues that his way is fine. He says to her, "I know your mom can do it."

Saturday, September 8, 2001

Jane insists on taking me to Lance's apartment this day. She is worried that I may get lost. I follow her to his apartment, relieved I don't have to try and find it myself. Lance's directions are confusing to me. We arrive at his apartment around 10:00 a.m.

Lance is furious at Jane for interfering and openly displays his disdain to her.

"Your mom was perfectly capable of finding her way here," Lance says to her in an annoyed tone.

"Are you going to drive her back to my house tonight?" Jane asks. I can tell she does not like Lance.

"I am not sure yet," Lance responds.

"I don't want her driving home alone in the dark on those back roads," Jane retorts. "I don't want her getting lost late at night!"

"She is a big girl, and I have confidence in her that she can do it!" Lance snaps back.

"Mom, call me if you need me," Jane says. She hops in her car and drives away.

At least Jane is concerned about my safety and welfare. I wonder if Lance is.

I go into Lance's apartment. He mentions how nice I look in my tan, flowered dress and light-beige jacket.

"Jane does not have to worry I am not going to be considerate of you," Lance says. "We may end up having a confrontation." It is clear he is upset with her.

"She cared about my safety and did not want me to get lost," I say.

Lance does not answer. Already, I have an uncomfortable feeling about the weekend ahead of me. For starters, my daughter seems to care about me more than Lance does.

I give him the wine and the congratulatory card. He smiles and thanks me.

I am glad Lance will be driving from this point on. We arrive in Lancaster about an hour later. Lance buys us a pretzel at Auntie Anne's. "This is our lunch," he says.

The *Noah* show is good, but not half as spectacular as I had hoped. Lance puts his arm around me and gives me a kiss. This is the only affection I will have from him this weekend. We later shop (for him) and eat dinner at the Harvest Drive Motel. Somehow it is not the same as in July. I can feel the difference.

I cannot wait to get back to Lance's apartment and have some "alone" time with him.

We arrive at his place just before dark. "Duck!" Lance says as we drive by his wife's complex. I put my head down, feeling like a fool.

Lance opens the bottle of wine I had bought. We sit on the couch and watch *Seinfeld* tapes. He puts his arm around me, and I snuggle close to him. He does not kiss me. There is no closeness or intimacy this night.

Lance is worried about the hard drive on his computer. "I will have to try and fix that tomorrow," he says.

At 11:00 p.m., Lance says he is tired and will drive me back to Jane's. He will keep the car and pick me up in the morning for breakfast.

Why does Lance want to end the evening so early? We are always up past midnight when we are together. Why can't I stay with him? We are adults. I am tired and just want to lie down and be in his arms.

I feel empty on the quiet ride home. I can sense Lance has no desire to be with me.

"See you tomorrow," he says as he drops me off at Jane's. He pulls out of the driveway before I am in the house.

I lay awake all night, feeling despondent and lonely.

Sunday, September 9, 2001

I enjoy spending time with Brian before Lance picks me up at 11:15 a.m. I say goodbye to Jane and Brian, as I will be driving home later from Lance's apartment.

We drive to Perkins Pancake House, which is close to Lance's home.

"Now we may run into people that know Karen and me," he says, cautiously. "I don't want them thinking you are my girlfriend. I don't want my wife to know I am dating."

We get out of the car. I reach for his hand as we approach the restaurant.

"Don't touch me!" Lance snaps. "Someone might see us!"

I quickly pull my hand back like a child who accidentally touched a hot stove. I am livid!

I can hardly eat my pancakes while Lance continually gazes around, scared to death that someone he knows will spot us. There is little conversation. I am appalled he doesn't notice how upset I am.

We drive back to his apartment. The energy between us is terrible. "I have to get that hard drive fixed on my computer," Lance says. "It has me nuts!"

"Duck!" Lance says again as we drive by Karen's complex.

"Screw you," I think to myself. I sit up, straight as six o'clock. Lance sighs and acts annoyed. I don't care.

Lance's roommate, Roy, is at the apartment. I say hello to him. He smiles and says, "How are you?"

"Fine," I lie.

Lance and I go into his room. Disheartened, I sit on the couch and pet the cat. I get out a sheet of paper and try to figure out the price of the car rental. I hope Lance will sit with me for a few minutes. Not so; he is already at the computer working on his hard drive.

"My printer software is not working," Lance says, sounding upset. "It doesn't read consistently. Now it is telling me my printer is not connected. This is terrible; it's really, really terrible!"

What is terrible is I am sitting in his room, feeling ignored. Why can't he wait until I leave before working on his computer?

Lance goes into the hallway and talks to Roy about the hard drive. I sit alone, feeling like an idiot and out of place. He comes back in. He never once comes over to me or shows me any attentiveness.

"I guess I'll get going," I say.

"Okay," Lance says. "Do you know how to get out of here?"

"I think so."

Lance rapidly explains to me how to get out of the complex to Route 1 North, which will take me to the Pennsylvania Turnpike.

He steps outside the door with me. He is in his bare feet. "I can't walk you to the car," he says.

"That's all right," I say, thinking to myself, "Why don't you put on your damn shoes, you bastard?"

Lance doesn't even say goodbye. He is back inside the apartment before I drive out of the complex. I am in tears as I drive past the Quakerbridge Mall, trying to find my way to Route 1 North. It is hard enough for me to find my way around in a strange place, let alone doing it while I am upset.

Suddenly, I run into a tollbooth. I panic. Nobody mentioned a tollbooth to me in the directions. I am lost!

I have no choice and nowhere to go. I cannot turn around. I pay the toll and keep driving. I see signs for Philadelphia. I don't want to go to Philadelphia! Damn you, Lance, I don't know where I am!

I call Jane. It never occurs to me to call Lance. I am crying hysterically. I can hardly talk.

"Mom, where are you?" Jane asks.

I pull over to the side of the road and start reading the signs to her.

"Mom, you are fine," Jane says. "You are going the right way. Just keep going. Just keep following the signs and stay on Route 1."

"Thank you, honey," I say. "I'll call you when I get home."

I am relieved, but sobbing as I drive. My cell phone rings. It's Lance.

"Just wanted to see how you are doing," Lance says.

"I just panicked," I answer. "I ran into a toll and thought I was lost." I can't believe he doesn't notice I've been crying.

"We drove through that toll yesterday, don't you remember?" Lance says, sounding critical. "You *always* have to pay a toll when you leave New Jersey."

"I don't remember," I say, furious.

"Well, hon, I will catch you later. Drive careful," Lance says and hangs up.

"How the hell am I supposed to remember where we drove yesterday," I scream out loud while driving. "How the hell am I supposed to know you *ALWAYS have to pay a toll when you leave New Jersey,* you inconsiderate, pompous bastard?"

I am crying so hard I can hardly drive. I am in a rage! How dare he treat me this way? How dare he tell me not to touch him! How dare he ignore me when I have driven all this way to see him! And then he tells me to duck so his wife doesn't see me? He can go straight to hell!

I pull into a rest stop about an hour later and try to get myself together. My cell phone rings again. It is Lance. I can tell he knows he was rude to me at his apartment. He patronizes me and tries to make me believe he cares about my safety. I know better.

Why didn't I let him have it when he called? I should have screamed at him. He damn well deserved it.

I arrive home safely, three hours later, after crying most of the way. I am an emotional wreck. What a horrible weekend.

I unpack, take a hot bath, and visit Marge. I have three glasses of wine.

I scream at Marge and her friend Nellie, who is there. I say at least five times, "How the hell am I supposed to know you *ALWAYS* pay a toll when you leave New Jersey! No one ever told me that!"

Marge and Nellie look at each other. They have unconditional love for me in my manic state.

Lance calls me later. "I should have waited until you left before I fixed the computer," he says. I can tell he feels bad about his rudeness.

"I agree with you, you could have waited," I say coldly. We chat a little while longer. Lance hangs up, knowing he has done his Godly duty: he has apologized.

I know my relationship with Lance is over.

What I don't know is that I will never see him again.

CHAPTER 50

September 11, 2001

Monday, September 10, 2001

I am still furious with Lance for his complacency and inattentiveness to me over the weekend. That is the last thing on Lance's mind, though. Today is the first day at his new job.

He sends me an e-mail informing me of his work address so I can e-mail him there.

He calls me this evening and briefly tells me about his day.

"Basically, I am going to be doing a lot of spreadsheets. I know that stuff. My new boss took me out to lunch today," Lance says happily. He is totally clueless about his inappropriate behavior toward me over the weekend.

After we hang up, I wonder if I should call him back. I never call Lance. Somehow, over the past few months, he has relayed to me, without ever saying it, that he does not like women calling him. Lance has to be in control.

However, I am not at peace. I need to address his rudeness to me yesterday. After all, Lance appreciates "honesty." I have felt tormented since my return home, and I am still upset.

I dial Lance's number. He is surprised to hear my voice.

I tell him I was offended and hurt when he snapped at me at the restaurant and told me not to touch him.

"We could have eaten some where else farther away," I say. "That way, you would not have had to worry about running into someone who knew you."

"I can see why it was a difficult situation for you," Lance says apologetically. "I understand perfectly how you felt and I am sorry. Next time I see you I will use better judgment." We discuss the situation at length, and Lance reiterates that he will make sure it does not happen again.

I do not feel better after we hang up. I sense no true remorse or regret from him. Lance is a smooth talker, and he uses eloquent language when confronted. He tries to come off as having much wisdom. He mentions at least twice that I may have "overreacted a little," but he does "understand."

Tuesday, September 11, 2001

I have a brief conversation with Lance before going to work. He has to be at his new place of employment at 8:00 a.m. "Have a wonderful day," he says. Neither of us knows that today will be one of the worst days in history.

7:54 a.m.

Lance sends me a short e-mail.

> *Just a quickie hello. Hope your day goes well. TTYL* [talk to you later]. *LYTPPK* [smileys].

I don't answer his e-mail. My heart is not in it.

8:50 a.m.

I am screening cases and chatting with my coworkers, Maureen, Pam, Jennifer, and Debbie. Debbie has a radio on at her desk.

Suddenly, Debbie yells out, "A plane just went into the World Trade Center! They think it's a terrorist attack!"

I run over to Tony's unit. "Did you hear about a plane crashing into the World Trade Center?"

"No, I didn't," Tony says.

Within minutes, everyone in our building is congregating into the conference room, where there is a television set. We all watch in shock as the next scene unfolds. It is like watching a horror movie.

We gasp as we see another plane, a Boeing 767, crash into the South Tower at 9:03 a.m. I run back to my desk and e-mail my cousin, Patti, who lives and works in New York City. She e-mails me back to let me know she is all right. I can tell she is in a state of trauma. She tells me the whole city has shut down.

My son, Jeff, calls to make sure I am not in the city this day. He knows I travel there often. He is relieved I am at work and okay.

I return to the conference room and am shocked to hear that a third plane has crashed into the Pentagon!

I need to talk to Lance. I run back to my desk and send him an e-mail.

This is awful. I am praying for the city and our country. My cousin is in New York City and sent me an e-mail. I know you are praying, too. Just heard the Pentagon got hit, too. Love you, Lynnie

Lance writes back:

The second tower went down too. This is the most surreal horrific thing I have ever been alive for. I am leaving for home now. They are sending everybody home from my company. LYTTPK Lancecat [with a smiley!?]

At noon, the regional administrator announces that Governor Pataki has ordered all state agencies to close. My coworkers and I are relieved to be sent home for the rest of the day. I run a couple of errands. The streets make it seem like a ghost town. The few people I see are in shock and are conversing about the terrible events that have transpired. By that time, a fourth plane has crashed in a field in Somerset, Pennsylvania.

I think to myself how traumatized Lance must be. He is only about forty-five minutes away from the city.

I go home and turn on the television set on for updates. I stare at the screen, which continues to show a huge cloud of black smoke coming out of the towers. My heart aches for the hundreds of people trapped in the towers with no escape, not to mention the people killed on the planes.

1:25 p.m.

The phone rings. It is Lance. I can't wait to talk to him.

"God is in control," Lance says, sounding surprisingly calm.

Before I can answer, he says, "This guy I work with is so nice. I made a suggestion today, and he did just what I suggested."

I can't believe Lance is talking about his job. He doesn't even mention the attacks.

"I've been watching television," I answer.

"They are blaming these attacks on a Saudi-born guerilla; a leader named Osama bin Laden," Lance says. "He's a Saudi millionaire and Islamic militant. He is believed to be in exile in Afghanistan."

"Really?" I say. This is the first time I hear the name Osama bin Laden, a name that will become a household word for years to come.

"Yes, there's no question of who did it. This has been planned for quite awhile; otherwise they never could have pulled it off."

I am trembling. "I wish you were here with me," I say.

"I know what I want to do," Lance replies. "I want to go out and get myself lunch. I will catch you later."

"All right," I answer.

"Have a good day," Lance says and hangs up.

"Have a good day?" "Have a good day?" Weren't hundreds of innocent people just killed? Is our country not in an uproar? How could anyone have a good day today?

I long to hear Lance say to me, "I wish we could be together now, holding each other and comforting each other in this time of crisis." I also wonder why he seems so unconcerned about today's event.

Is Lance being complacent, or am I overreacting?

I spend the rest of the day watching television. Later, I visit Marge.

I do not hear from Lance the rest of the day.

Wednesday, September 12, 2001

Lance calls me briefly before going to work.

"Got my cable modem working," he says. From what I can see, there are three basic problems. The scanner doesn't work, the printer doesn't work, and the CD burner is inconsistent."

"Hmmm," I answer. I have no idea what he is talking about.

"Oh, and my car is almost ready," he continues. "I may try and get off early so I can pick it up before they close."

It seems like weeks since I was with Lance in New Jersey, driving that horrible rental car. The tormenting, upsetting weekend in New Jersey was only three days ago. I had forgotten Lance's new car was at the shop having body work done.

All right, hon, I will catch you later!" Lance says. "Have a good day."

"You, too," I say.

I record in my journal this day: "The world has stopped. Total television and radio coverage twenty-four hours a day. Thousands of people killed. I cannot remember what I did today."

I feel bad for my cousin, Patti. Today is her birthday, and she is in the city. I am unable to reach her by phone, as all circuits are busy.

Tony reminds me he has an audition in New York City at Columbia University *tomorrow, September 13!* I had forgotten all about it! I had previously promised him I would go with him by bus to the audition!

"I am sure it will be postponed," I say to Tony. He will call and find out.

A few minutes later, Tony returns to my desk. "They are still having the audition," he says. "My dream is to perform in New York City. I don't want to pass up this opportunity."

I call the bus station. The buses *will* be running tomorrow. Port Authority has been shut down for two days.

Tony and I decide to make the trip. My sister and family, as well as Tony's family, are concerned and worried about Tony and me traveling to the city only two days after a terrorist attack.

Thursday, September 13, 2001

I talk to Lance briefly before going to work. I tell him I will be making the trip to New York City.

"It will be a phenomenal sight for you when you enter the city," he says, sounding totally unconcerned about my making the trip.

I tell Lance I will send him an e-mail with my itinerary for the day. I want someone close to me to know where I am.

I e-mail Lance around 7:00 a.m. I tell him we will be taking the 8:40 a.m. bus and hope to return before 10:00 p.m. I write:

> Due to the circumstances in New York City, I want someone to know where I am.
>
> Tony's audition is at 3:15 p.m. at the Horace Mann Auditorium at the Teachers College at Columbia University, 2960 Broadway, on the corner of 120th Street.

I give him Tony's cell phone number. He knows my cell number. I sign the e-mail with the usual "LYTP."

Lance is the only person who has my itinerary.

On the long, shaky ride, Tony and I think about nothing else but the terrorist attacks. We are extremely nervous. There are only eight other passengers on the bus besides us.

As we enter the city, we see a huge cloud of black smoke over to the right of the Empire State Building. A helicopter hovers over the clouds. I record in my journal: "tons of smoke, can see the damage."

As we enter Lincoln Tunnel, there are several flags proclaiming the city's patriotic-but-broken spirit. There are only two other vehicles in the tunnel.

We arrive at Port Authority on the upper level. As we enter the building, a policeman suddenly appears. "Leave the building immediately!" he shouts. People are scurrying and running wildly in every direction. Tony and I don't know how to get out. All we can think of is that the building is going to blow up any second!

We run as fast as we can, following the small groups of people. Policemen are everywhere, pointing and shouting. We go down a couple of escalators and are relieved to be on the ground floor. All we can think of is "get out of here!"

I spot the door to Eighth Avenue. "Run, Tony, come on!" I grab his hand, and we tear outside. People are running down the street. "Let's get as far away as we can!" I say.

We run for about three blocks and finally stop and catch our breath. People are on their cell phones saying, "I'm okay!" The unknown is terrifying!

I call my sister, Lea, in Binghamton, on my cell phone. She informs me that Port Authority had just had a bomb scare. She is relieved to know I am all right and is glad I called. She was worried.

Later that day, a policeman informs Tony and me that there have been over thirty bomb scares in the city this day.

"Oh my God," I think to myself. I have to call Lance and let him know I am all right. He has my itinerary and knows my bus has arrived around this time. He will be worried.

I dial Lance's number at work. He answers.

"Hi, hon!" I say, still trying to catch my breath.

"Hi," Lance answers, sounding bewildered. I immediately sense that he is wondering what I want.

"I just want you to know I am okay," I say.

Lance pauses. "Oh, all right."

"Haven't you been listening to the news?" I ask.

"No, I haven't heard anything," Lance says, sounding distracted.

"There was a bomb scare at Port Authority. We were there," I say. "I was terrified. We are on our way to the audition now. Our cell phones will be on if you want to call."

"What are the phone numbers?" Lance asks.

What are the numbers?

He has my itinerary. He knows my cell number. Suddenly it occurs to me, Lance did not even bring my itinerary with him to work! He can't even remember my cell phone number!

I give him Tony's cell phone number and say goodbye. I am furious.

I am in a rage as Tony and I hurry down Broadway, looking for a cab.

"He doesn't even give a damn that I am in New York City today," I scream at Tony. "I gave him our itinerary because I thought we could be in potential danger! I gave him times and places we would be, so that someone would know where we were! I should have given the information to my sister!"

"I know," Tony says. "Come on, hon, let's get some lunch."

Tony and I take a cab and have lunch at a pub near the Horace Mann Theatre. There are several TV sets on the walls updating the customers on the dreadful events of two days ago. The atmosphere in the city this day is fear, bewilderment, and chaos. People's faces look sad and drawn.

Tony looks at me. Tears are streaming down my face.

"I can't believe him, Tony! He didn't even care where I was, the bastard! He was so complacent and distracted. He does not give a damn about me at all. He is so self-centered!"

"Lynne, I have been telling you that for months," Tony says gently. "Get rid of him." Tony is a good friend and hangs in there with me. I am grateful for him.

"I am turning off my cell phone," I say angrily. "He can go to hell! I don't care if he calls or not!"

Tony turns his cell phone off, too.

I know Tony is right. Damn that Lance! If he is so frigging *honest*, then he can break up with me! I am not going to make it easy for him. I know it is only a matter of time. Knowing this does not dismiss the fact that I am heartbroken.

Tony's audition is right on time at 3:15 p.m. As we walk out of the Horace Mann Auditorium, a cab pulls up! "Divine order," I say, grateful that God loves me, even though Lance doesn't give a damn about me.

When we arrive at Port Authority, we discover two bus runs were canceled during the afternoon. Our bus is right on time, another divine coincidence.

Tony and I talk on the bus. He tells me he was terrified, thinking maybe the building was going to blow up when we arrived earlier. "My heart was racing so fast, and I felt sick to my stomach," he says. "You don't have time to think, you don't have time to process it, you just move. You just try to get away."

"We have much to be thankful for, Tony," I say.

"Thank you for making the trip with me," he says.

"Thank you for putting up with me," I say.

"It's not easy, honey," he says. We both laugh. I close my eyes and thank God for our safety and my many blessings. We are both relieved when the bus pulls safely into the station in Binghamton.

Upon arriving home I check my e-mail. Lance has answered my e-mail from this morning giving him my plans and my itinerary.

He writes, "Please e-mail me when you get home." [smiley is added].

I don't e-mail him. He can take his e-mail and inappropriate smiley's's and go straight to hell.

CHAPTER 51

Empty Conversations

Thursday, September 13, 2001
9:44 p.m.

I get ready for bed after a long exhausting day in New York City. I am still furious at Lance for his complacency today and not caring about my safety and welfare.

The telephone rings. It is Lance.

"I tried yours and Tony's cell phone numbers," he says.

"We turned our cell phones off," I say coldly.

"Um, how did Tony do on his audition?"

Again, I tell Lance about the bomb scare at Port Authority.

"Oh my God," Lance says. "I had no idea you went through that! You could have called me!"

"I *did call you!*"

"I didn't realize you had just been through hell."

"I was wondering why you didn't seem concerned."

"I figured you were safe. Wow, if I had heard about it, I would have freaked out. I had no idea what you went through. I got the impression you were giving me information."

"What an idiot," I think furiously to myself! Why did he think I even called him? As usual Lance is trying to smooth over his lack of caring and concern.

"I *was* giving you information," I say, coldly. "I was shook up and needed to talk to you!"

"If you had just told me what you had been through, I would have stopped everything I was doing. Oh my God, one more reason not to live in New York," Lance says, shifting the blame onto me as usual.

"I did tell you," I say, not backing down. Lance is again making me the wrong person in this scenario.

Lance and I talk a few minutes and say goodnight. I wonder why he even called.

It doesn't matter to me at this point how Lance feels. It was today I needed him. His words are nothing more than appeasing and patronizing. If he truly cared, I would have felt it from him earlier.

Saturday, September 15, 2001

The leaves on the trees are starting to change color. I recall Lance promising a visit around the peak period so we can enjoy the scenery together.

"Fall weather is coming," Lance says to me during our Saturday-morning conversation.

"How are the leaves?"

"They are just starting to change," I say. "I will keep you posted."

Lance talks at length about his new job. They are allowing him to take his work home. He is anxious to get started on a work project and tells me he will talk to me tomorrow.

Lance also takes two days off from work this week. One day, he has a cyst removed from his shoulder. The other day is Rosh Hashanah, a Jewish holiday. I wonder how he is able to do this, since he just started a new job.

The day he has the cyst removed, he calls me four times, as it is painful for him. Of course I am attentive and supportive.

I have other things on my mind, though. My car is not working right. I am frustrated and cannot afford another used car.

Saturday, September 22, 2001

I am distracted from Lance's and my conversation this morning. While he talks about his job, his surgery this past week, and his cat, I worry about my vehicle which needs a new part and is not running well.

After we hang up, I drive to our local Saturn dealer. I look at some 2002 vehicles. I think to myself how I would love to own one. Two days later, I fill out an application.

The next day, the salesman calls me. "When would you like to pick up your new car?" he says. I am ecstatic. I have a brand-new, 2002 Saturn!

After work, I pick up a Burgundy 2002 Saturn with black interior. It also has a CD player in it!

I am so happy I could almost cry. After years of struggling and paying cash for used cars, I finally have a beautiful new vehicle.

Thursday, September 27, 2001

I tell Lance about the car. He is happy for me and shares my joy. He says, "This is the beginning of your restoration." This is the one statement in our relationship Lance has made that I agree with.

"I can't wait for you to see it," I say, excitedly.

"How are the leaves?" he asks.

"They are real pretty, Lance."

"Well, I have been quite busy at work and haven't had much time for a social life. I don't know how much time I can take off."

I recall he has taken two days off already, one for the cyst, the other for the Jewish holiday. I say nothing.

My new car provides me with a much-needed lift and distracts me from thinking about how my relationship with Lance has deteriorated.

Sunday, September 30, 2001

Today is our one-year anniversary. I responded to Lance's ad on September 30, 2000.

I recall how my heart skipped a beat when I received Lance's response. I also think about his first kiss, the romantic times in New York City, the wedding in Roslyn, New York, and the recent trip to Cooperstown.

I know the magic is gone. I want so much for it to be the way it was.

I receive Lance's Sunday call. He talks about his job. He does not mention today's date. I finally say to him, "Do you know what today is?"

"Oh man," he says, "I forgot. Happy anniversary."

"I thought I would remind you I exist," I say, trying to maintain a sense of humor while feeling empty inside.

"I am not sure at what point it would hit me," Lance says. "It has been a nice year."

He then says, "I can't wait to have my first ride in your new car. It must be so demeaning to be living the way you are living, especially at your age."

"What do you mean by that?" I ask. What is he talking about? I love my cute, clean and cozy apartment with the frilly curtains. It is certainly much nicer than Lance's shabby place!

"Well, I guess it is nice for one person," Lance replies in his usual patronizing tone. "I just noticed your love seat was ripped up a little from the cats scratching on it. You had it covered with a throw."

I am furious! I think to myself about how proud I was to show him my apartment and all the effort I put into making it look nice for him. I even bought an air conditioner for his comfort!

Sensing my silence, Lance again says, "anyway, I sure am looking forward to you giving me a ride in your new car."

"When are you coming?" I ask, feeling angry and disheartened at his cruel remark.

"I have the nursing home ministry coming up soon," Lance says, hedging. "Also, I am so bogged down here at work."

"The leaves are the nicest about the second week of October," I say.

"I will keep that in mind," Lance says.

I have hopes we will get together soon. I tell myself he needs more time. He still has to get a divorce.

It is amazing how your heart can play tricks on you while your head tells you to find a way to terminate a relationship that is no longer progressing.

Tuesday, October 2, 2001

Lance has cut the phone calls down to once a day. His e-mails are impersonal, few, and scattered.

Tony is amused. He asks me, "So what did you and Lance talk about this morning?"

"The weather and the Yankees," I respond.

"Oh, that's close and personal!" Tony laughs. "I can tell he is crazy about you!"

I am not laughing.

Sunday, October 7, 2001

"How are the leaves?" Lance asks as he ends his early-morning call.

"About half-and-half," I answer. By now, I am annoyed. The peak period for the fall foliage is about a week away.

Lance does not respond to my statement. Instead, he says he has to go. I hang up feeling despondent, a familiar feeling these days.

11:30 a.m.

I am surprised to hear from Lance. We had already talked today.

"My wife Karen has found out I am seeing you," Lance says in a panicky voice. "Remember Jacob and Rose's wedding? They sent the thank you note to Karen's apartment which is my old address and said in the note, 'Dear Lance and Lynne.' Now she knows all about you!"

I have no idea what to say to Lance. He continues, "She wanted to know if I was seeing you before I left her. I had to explain. I reminded her she knew I had an ad out on AOL."

"I am sorry she knows, Lance," I say. "She is probably hurt."

"We are both going our own ways," Lance says. "She started in on me, Lynne. I am the adulterer. All those years I lived with her, I never pursued anyone. I was committed to her."

"She is in shock," I say. "You were separated when we started seeing each other."

"I cannot reason with her. She is hurt," Lance continues. "With you, I am not looking any further down the road. What will be will be. I feel bad for her that she cannot enjoy the fact that I do care about her and love her and want her to get her life back on track."

The reality hits me like a ton of bricks. I have been dating a married man. What was I thinking? And did I hear him correctly? Did he not just say to me, "I am not looking for anything further down the road?"

Lance's worst fears have taken place. All these months, he has kept me hidden from his wife. Now she knows Lance is seeing me. He feels awful. I feel awful.

"I needed to tell you," Lance says. "I needed to talk, and I needed to tell you."

We hang up. I think to myself, "What is it that is still connecting Lance to Karen? What is it that he needs from her that makes him stay married to her?"

Lance is sorry he got found out. I am sorry I am even in the picture.

It will not be for long, though. My biggest fear is just around the corner.

CHAPTER 52

The Breakup

October is my favorite month of the year. I love the feel of the crisp, cool air as summer subtly changes into autumn, and the leaves begin to gradually change color.

I keep thinking about Lance's promise to visit me and enjoy the fall foliage together.

Autumn also gives me a sense of loneliness. The leaves falling off the trees remind me of loss and change. The summer's sunshine and warmth are transitioning into coolness. Leaves are changing color, dropping, and dying. In a few weeks, the trees will appear lonely and barren with coldness all around.

This matches my state of mind. I have started the desensitizing process, mentally and emotionally, regarding my feelings for Lance.

Our relationship has turned into a farce. There is no substance or depth in our conversations for weeks. I wonder why he even calls. The dialogue between us is boring. As usual, it is all about him; his job, his wife, his ministry at the nursing home, and his cat.

Thursday, October 11, 2001

Lance's promise to visit me to see the fall colors is brought up in our morning conversation. He is considering coming this weekend, which is two days away.

"It is not one hundred percent out of the question for this weekend," Lance says. "If I come, though, I might be distracted like I was the weekend you were in New Jersey. There might be a lot of things regarding my job, you know what I am saying…"

No, I don't know what he is saying. I certainly remember how distracted he was, though, when I saw him last. Is that what he is saying?

What I am hearing is another excuse as to why he will not be coming. I am smart enough to know that, if he truly cared about me, his job would not be distracting him from our time together.

"I am not going to hassle you," I say, feeling disappointed, again.

"If there was a choice between this weekend and the twenty-eighth of October, you would probably prefer the twenty-eighth, since it is your birthday," Lance says. "Next weekend I have the nursing home ministry. Let's play it by ear."

"The leaves will be gone by the twenty-eighth," I say. "Right now is the peak period."

"If you don't get an e-mail by 6:00 p.m. tonight, I will be coming up tomorrow."

"Okay," I say. "Don't pressure yourself."

I am not one bit surprised when Lance e-mails me this evening.

> *Hi Hon, as you have assumed by now, I have decided not to push it, and instead stay home this weekend. Hopefully in two weeks, for your birthday, things will cool down a bit and coming out won't be a stress factor. Talk to you tomorrow morning!*
> *LYTPPK* [smileys added]
> *Lancecat* [smileys]

Visiting me is a "stress factor"?
I do not answer his e-mail.

Friday, October 12, 2001

Lance calls me early this morning. He is surprised I did not answer his patronizing e-mail from the night before.

"I sent an e-mail," he says. "I am used to always getting some kind of response."

"There was nothing for me to say." My voice is cold.

"It is not like you, to not e-mail me back."

"I am sad you cannot make it. It was important to me we see the leaves together."

"At least *you'll* see the leaves," Lance says unfeelingly.

"It is not about that!" I snap. "It was about you and me seeing them together!"

"I was joking!" Lance answers, sounding surprised.

"Well you told me to communicate my true feelings to you. That is what I'm doing."

"That I understand," Lance says in an attempt to appease me. "Anyway, how was your day yesterday?"

Lance changes the subject and goes on to his favorite topic: him! He tells me about an incident that occurred at his workplace yesterday.

Before he hangs up, he says, "If I don't get to see the leaves in a couple weeks, there will be your birthday. That will make it real special. I realize it will be six to seven weeks since I have seen you."

This is the longest Lance and I have gone without seeing each other since we became involved.

I rant and rave to Tony at work. "This is the second time he has canceled on me. What a crock of shit this is, Tony. I can't believe all these excuses! He just doesn't want to come."

"Is the light finally starting to go on, honey?" Tony asks.

Thursday, October 18, 2001

Lance has definitely committed to visiting me the weekend of October 28, which is my birthday. There is a ray of hope in my heart, knowing I will be seeing him again. I am excited about driving him around in my new vehicle, which has been a positive force in my life the last few weeks.

The terrorist's attacks of September 11 are still weighing heavily on everyone's mind. This week, there is a scare over anthrax being sent in the mail. One of the post offices that found a letter containing this deadly poison is located in New Jersey, not far from where Lance lives.

"Yes, it is terrible about all that has happened," Lance says to me in our morning conversation today. "I keep thinking about when I worked at the World Trade Center."

"You worked at the World Trade Center?" I ask.

"Oh, yes," Lance says nonchalantly. "I worked for three years in one tower on the sixty-eighth floor and nine years in the other tower on the sixty-ninth floor."

I cannot believe what I am hearing. Why didn't Lance mention this during the attacks? If it were me, I would have been worried and traumatized, knowing I used to work there. I would have been concerned about my former coworkers. Lance has a twelve-year history with the World Trade Center and never once expressed concern for any individual during the attacks.

I record in my journal this week: "I cannot get over Lance's complacency."

Friday, October 19, 2001

Lance gives me a quick call before work. I talk about my aerobics class. It occurs to me, in all the months I have known him and have taught aerobics, he has never once shown an interest.

"So what's on tap for this weekend?" Lance asks.

"Nothing planned," I say. "Just some cleaning." I don't tell him I am going to be busy preparing for his visit in a week.

"Anyway, I got to get going here," he says. "Have a good one."

"You, too, dear," I say.

Later at work, my phone rings. It is a brief hello from Lance. He says, "I will catch you later."

I hang up, not knowing it will be the last time I will ever talk to him again.

After work, I hurry home. I will spend the weekend preparing for Lance's visit next Friday. I take a hot bubble bath, put on my aerobic clothes, and have a bite to eat. I am ready to work out for a half-hour and then watch television. I decide to check my e-mail first.

I am surprised to see an e-mail from Lance, since we have been communicating mostly by telephone for months. The title of the e-mail, written today at 4:34 p.m. is "Us." He writes:

> *Dear Lynne,*
>
> *It's been a little over a year now that we have been communicating, and I can't imagine how difficult it would have been for me during this year if it were not for you. You have been the brightest spot in my life, a help to me in so many ways and truly a great friend. I do love you very much, but as I have said before, not 'in love.' And that is the problem, Lynne, after a year of having a relationship with you, I am still not in love with you. The magic that I thought was there is really not there. I think you have sensed it, but I think you were hoping it would not come down to this. I think the beginning was infatuation*

and it has grown into a wonderful friendship, but truthfully, that is all I believe it can ever be.

Maybe the infatuation was partly due to the fact that our relationship was a 'rebound' relation for me. You are really nothing like my wife and actually very much like me, and I do feel we are compatible in so many ways. But as I have said before, there has to be five elements to the intimate relationship, physical, mental, spiritual and then there has to be the 'in love' factor and there has to be the practical. It is really not all there for me and I am really sorry for you that it is not, because I think we both really hoped it would be. I hope that after you have processed this, you will still want to stay in touch with me and be friends. I really want that. It will take time to get used to the change, but I hope you will adjust and get comfortable with me as just a friend.

The last four weeks or so, I have begun to really face the facts of my true feelings. I realize that I really want to start looking again for another woman to date and it is only fair to you that I tell you the truth, now that I believe our relationship cannot go any further than a good 'friendship.'

I didn't know if I should tell you this in person, over the phone, or in an e-mail. I chose e-mail, because it will give you a chance to process this before you have to talk to me on the phone or see me in person. I think e-mail is the easiest for you to handle and you can e-mail me back after you have had some time to yourself. I also decided to send this on a Friday so you have the weekend to think about it before having to go back to work. I am glad you don't have anything major planned for this weekend.

Although I know this has to come as a shock to you at this time, you are probably not completely surprised. I am sure you have sensed at some level that there has been a lack of intensity in my feelings. It was just a matter of time before I could understand them completely myself so that I could communicate them to you in an honest loving way. I hope you are not upset with me for telling you this, this way, but I really tried to prayerfully and thoughtfully do this in a way that will minimize the pain.

I am sure you know that I think the world of you as a person, and I could go on and on as to how much you mean to me as a friend. I've enjoyed all the time we have spent together and I still want to get together occasionally, just not as often. You have a beautiful heart, and I love you dearly! But as it has been disappointing for me that the feelings didn't grow beyond friendship, I am sure it is also disappointing for you. I want to see other women and it is only fair to you that I am honest and up front with you. I am sorry, but honesty does prevail, and honesty doesn't always get us what we want, but as I have said before, in the end, you end up with something better. And that applies to both of us, Lynne. By telling you the truth, I know I risk losing you as a friend, because I understand that it could be too painful for you to be just friends after it seemed we were moving to something more serious in the relationship. I sincerely hope that won't be the case because I do not know where I could find a better friend.

I won't call you until we have communicated for a while by e-mail. I think that is best. I care for you very much and don't want to lose you as a friend. I hope you believe that and feel the same way about our friendship and hopefully, I will hear from you soon.

Love,
Lance

I stare at my computer, feeling paralyzed; a deer, looking at headlights.

CHAPTER 53

Cruel Kindness

I sit, frozen at my computer, staring at Lance's "Dear John" letter. As I begin to process his words, I realize he has been planning this breakup for weeks, even down to the time he sent the e-mail. He knows I arrive home from work every day at 4:30 p.m. The e-mail was sent at 4:43 p.m.

When he asked me this morning, "So what's on tap for this weekend?"; it was a setup. He even said in his heart-wrenching epistle, "I am glad you don't have anything major planned for this weekend."

He had no intention of visiting me to see the fall foliage. He has been stalling and trying to come up with a way to end the relationship.

I call Tony while printing out the e-mail. I am in tears. I read Lance's letter to him. Tony thinks it is awful, and he is supportive and caring. He lives forty miles away, so there is nothing more he can do, but he tells me he is available and to call him if I need to talk some more.

I need to get out of the house. I call Naomi. She drops everything and meets me for coffee. I do not remember anything she says to me this night.

In his e-mail, Lance refers to me as a "friend" twelve times, which is the most painful word a woman can hear from a man she is in love with. Twice he says he wants to start looking for another woman to date. Why does he have to say that?

Lance is correct in saying he is sure I am not surprised. But how can you be "not" surprised and shocked at the same time?

It is like knowing someone with a terminal disease will be dying soon, but death, when it comes, is still a shock. Lance's and my relationship has been terminal for months with a couple of remissions here and there. I have been holding on, waiting for a miracle cure that never came.

God, how I hate him for his patronizing, self-centered, gentle, "Let me down easy," contrived, plotted, appeasing letter! What a narcissistic prick!

He wants to give me "time to process his e-mail?" And then "adjust to being only friends?" Should I feel honored to be included in Lance's long list of female friends?

Saturday, October 20, 2001

I wake up after a night with little sleep. I notice the telephone does not ring this morning. I will no longer be getting a Saturday-morning telephone call from Lance. What is there to miss, though? Our conversations have been fruitless for weeks.

I forward his e-mail to my sister, Lea. She is heartsick and thinks his e-mail is cruel.

"He has met someone," she says. "Also, I think it is odd he never told you he worked at the World Trade Center after the terrorists attacks. Something is not right."

Lea drives me to the mall to get me out of the house. I mechanically browse the shops, feeling like a zombie.

Lea is wonderful and encouraging. She says to me, "You can go on with your life. You have a new car and a new attitude now."

Later, I visit Marge and tell her the news. She is sad for me. Tony calls me several times this day to make sure I am doing all right.

"It will be hard for you," Tony says. "Do not answer his e-mail. I wouldn't give him the time of day. He has to live with himself. He has no courage or character, or he would have talked to you in person."

"I do not want to write to him," I say. "I want absolutely nothing to do with him."

"He wants your permission to break up," Tony says. "Have no communication with him at all. You don't ever have to see him or talk to him again!"

My only comfort is knowing I never have to see him or talk to him again.

Sunday, October 20, 2001

I awake, feeling heartsick and lonely. All I can "process" is the fact that he is a rat who lead me on for months. Lance would give me just enough crumbs to keep me going. I am to blame for this. I should have ended the relationship long ago. Why couldn't I?

Because of fear of rejection and of hearing the words: "I don't love you, but let's be friends." The word friend is the "f" word in a relationship. No one wants to be "just friends" with someone they are in love with.

I make a pot of coffee and check my e-mail.

I am shocked to see an e-mail from Lance sent at 10:00 this morning. The title of the e-mail is "Hello." He writes:

> *Lynnie I miss you. I have been thinking about you a lot. I imagine you in tears and lost for words. This is the longest time in a very long time that we haven't communicated by phone. I am sorry I had to do this. I felt it was the only honest thing I could do at this point. You haven't done ANYTHING to bring this about, and I am honored to have you as my friend. I hope I will hear from you soon. I truly care for you and wish "I" could comfort you, but I know I can't, and I am really very sorry. Have you spoken to Lea? I have been thinking about e-mailing her, but I don't want to make things worse. I am quietly suffering too, knowing you must be.*
>
> *LYTPPK* [with a smiley]
> *Lancecat* [with a smiley]

He signs his e-mail "love you to pieces, Lancecat?" He even adds a smiley! How unfeeling can he be? There is no more Lynniecat or Lancecat! This unfeeling gesture confirms to me that his LYTPPK and smilies have been meaningless and "friendship based" for months.

Apparently, Lance is surprised I haven't e-mailed him back. I have no intention of doing so. The fact that it bothers him provides me with a tad of comfort, even though it is all ego on his part.

Tuesday, October 23, 2001

Four days have passed since the breakup. I feel like it's been years.

I record in my journal, "I hate Lance for hurting me." I am functioning at work and in my daily life, but I feel sick and lonely inside. It will take me a while to heal."

I am surprised to hear from Lance again this evening. He sends me an e-mail with the title "I miss you." He writes:

> Lynnie, it has been four days and I still haven't heard from you. Are you okay? Don't you think we should talk either on the phone or by e-mail? You must know I care for you very much. Did you tell Lea and Tony? It hurts me too that I can't speak to you, but I want to give you whatever time you need. It would be nice to just hear a few words from you. I miss you!
>
> LYTPPK [smiley added]
> Lancecat [smiley added]

What's with this guy? How can he be so cruel to *continue* the LYTPPK's, the "Lancecats" and the smilies when we are no longer a couple? Is he *that* clueless and insensitive?

I conclude that he is.

I ignore this e-mail. Lance is only thinking of himself. I have nothing to say to him, and I never want to be his friend. He has plenty of female friends.

Wednesday, October 24, 2001

I record in my journal: "I wish I had never bothered with Lance after that stupid Solomon letter a year ago. He can have all his women. I hate him."

This evening Lance has the audacity to send me an online joke! He writes:

> This it TOO funny! I had to send it to you! Enjoy! Lance

I cannot believe this. Does he think he can make me laugh?

Thursday, October 25, 2001

I am surprised to get *another* e-mail from Lance. Why can't he leave me alone? It's over. I am out of his life. His e-mails torture me. I don't want to hear from him any more.

I am shocked when I read the contents! He writes:

Lynnie, are you okay? You have a birthday this weekend and I am supposed to come up there. Don't you think you should say SOME-THING to me? We have always been able to communicate before. I haven't stopped being honest with you and being kind to you and caring for you. Can't you at least after a whole week say something to me?

Lance

I can't believe what I am reading. Lance still thinks he is coming to see me for my birthday! And he has the nerve to say he is being *kind* and *caring*?

Suddenly I realize his strategy. Lance planned to break up with me a week before my birthday, make the trip as planned and patronize me, now on a "friendship" basis. He might even throw in some hugs and kisses. His goal is to make himself feel good by being my "friend," continue the friendship, and then return to New Jersey and see other women. Of course he will continue to correspond with me by e-mail as a "friend only." And he will "see me occasionally, just not as often as before."

This does not fly with me at all. I am infuriated. I call Naomi. I scream at her, "What is he thinking, Naomi? I can't believe this. I cannot believe he has the audacity to think he can visit me this weekend!"

"I can't believe he has the balls to say that, Lynne," Naomi says. "I can't believe my ears. That letter sucked."

"What should I do, Naomi?" I ask crying.

"Do nothing, do nothing! Let *him* process this. It is cruel what he is doing, Lynne. I am telling you, this man is not well."

"I don't want to see him," I say, still in tears.

"He had all those months to say something meaningful to you, and he was masturbating off the Internet," Naomi says. "You are too good for that. Rejecting him is the most loving thing you can do. It will turn his history upside down."

"Yes, Naomi," I say. "That is the answer. I am too good for him. He cannot stand the fact there is one woman who wants *nothing* to do with him!"

"Don't worry about his needs. This is about you, Lynne. For once, let it be about you. This is your day of dignity."

Naomi always calms me down and makes me feel better. She is a wonderful friend. I ignore Lance's e-mail.

Friday, October 26, 2001

My birthday is two days away. I record in my journal, "I am at peace not responding to Lance's e-mail. It is less painful not having to see him or talk to him."

The girls in my department at work bring in a cake and some cards for my birthday. I am grateful for wonderful friends and nice coworkers.

Saturday, October 27, 2001

This day is ruined for me by an e-mail from Lance sent at 9:36 a.m. The title of the e-mail is "I guess I won't see you this weekend." He writes:

> *Well, I kept this weekend open for you Lynnie, but your silence tells me I am not coming. Sorry it has to be this way. The alternative would have been me not sending you the "Us" e-mail, and then coming up this weekend and me finding myself in a position where I would have to be honest with my feelings. I don't think that would have been good for you, especially on your birthday.*
>
> *I think about you a lot because you ARE a dear friend to me, but I guess that doesn't cut it much for now. I hope you are able to have a Happy Birthday tomorrow, although I imagine it will be tough. If at some time you can get over this, for your birthday, I would love to take you out to dinner and give you a present I have wanted to give you for a very long time. You deserve it!*
>
> *There are many decent men out there, Lynnie, so don't be like my wife and give up on having a relationship. The way I have treated you in our relationship is the way you deserve to be treated, and should have been treated by men all your life. You probably feel somewhat like I am patronizing you, but I am not. I am trying hard to console you, and affirm you, which is something I have done as long as we have known one another.*
>
> *I really don't know what to say any more because you have thought better to remain silent. I hope that will change soon. I am sure a part of you feels angry at me, and I think another part of you may think you should have no reason to be, but it IS perfectly normal emotionally to feel angry and hurt, so I do validate those feelings. I just don't know how to make it any better for you except to give you time and space now.*
>
> *And I know there are feelings of rejection you must have also, but please know, although I validate those feelings too, I have NOT*

rejected you in any way as a person. I just don't think what I believe I am capable of having in a relationship with a woman is there or can ever be there with us. In many ways I always sort of suspected it at some level, but there was just so much good about you, and we are so much alike, that I hoped things would progress. It doesn't mean you are any less of a person because things didn't for me.

I even think it was a rebound relationship for you somewhat. You DID say you didn't want a relationship and you DID soon find yourself in one. It just happened and neither of us did anything wrong. And I believe we are both better people because of it. I feel I am, and I definitely believe YOU are!

Our relationship was a positive step in the right direction ordained by God for both of us. We have both healed in many ways. And hopefully after some time and space, you will come around to believe that too, and hopefully be able to relate to me as a special friend. You will ALWAYS be special to me! ALWAYS! And I do love you to pieces! Lancecat [with a smiley!]

I sit, frozen at the computer, and burst into tears.

CHAPTER 54

Struggling to Let Go

Lance has ruined the day before my birthday. I am relieved to know he will not be attempting a visit, as I cannot stand the thought of looking at him.

I can't believe Lance thinks he "treated me the way I deserved to be treated." His complacency towards me during my last visit to New Jersey and his inattentiveness to me the last few months have bordered on being emotionally abusive.

I later meet Naomi. She always takes me out to dinner for my birthday. I have allowed Lance to ruin my time and my birthday celebration with her. She is a wonderful, caring friend. She understands my state of mind. I talk of nothing else but Lance and how much I am hurting.

I show her Lance's cruel e-mail written this morning.

"You know what?" Naomi says. "I think it is time to send Lance a response. We're going to wrap this up!"

"Oh, Naomi, if you help me do this, it will be your birthday present to me," I say gratefully and in tears. I wonder how she puts up with me.

We drive to my apartment and sit down at the computer. Together we compose a rough draft. Tomorrow, on my birthday, I am going to send Lance a letter.

"I'll call you tomorrow and read you the finished response," I say to Naomi. I thank her a dozen times for her friendship and help.

"You just have a great birthday, girl!" Naomi says.

Sunday, October 28, 2001

I wake up feeling sad on my birthday. I decide not to put a damper on it.

I have a great day, considering the pain I am in. Shirley, my friend and aerobics buddy, takes me out to breakfast. She knows about my relationship with Lance. She remembers the wedding in Roslyn months ago, and how happy I was back then. She is shocked and saddened when I tell her it is over.

Later, my son, Jeff, and his wife, Marla, come over for a visit with a card and gift. It is humiliating for me to have to tell my family it is over with Lance. I simply say it did not work out. Marla e-mails me later, telling me she is so sorry and hopes I will be all right.

After Jeff and Marla leave, I go over my rough draft e-mail to Lance. I call Naomi. We read it over and make a few corrections. I tell her I am terrified to send it.

"This is a gift you are giving yourself for your birthday," Naomi says. "This letter is saying 'I am not interested in a friendship with you.'"

I visit Marge this evening. I am grateful for my friends and for having a nice birthday.

Upon returning home, I sit at the computer. I am ready to write to Lance.

Lance has sent me an online birthday card. Should I open it? My vulnerability gets the best of me. I click on the link.

As the card pops up, it is accompanied by beautiful, romantic music. The message on the card reads, "Love is a gift from heart to heart. You are a wonderful person and I am so glad you're a part of my life. I hope you know how much I love and care for you."

I feel like throwing up. A card like this would have met the world to me six months ago. Now it is crumbs and is condescending.

Lance adds a personal note: "My greatest wish for you would be for you to find happiness and joy on your birthday and in the days, weeks, months and years ahead of you. I am sorry we couldn't be together on your special day but my heart is with you. I love you to pieces Pussykot."

I cannot stand his "love you to pieces" at the end of his patronizing e-mails. It adds to the cruelty and affirms to me that those words were meaningless during the last few months when I thought we were in a serious relationship.

I feel myself weakening and getting upset. He is only appeasing me. As usual, I call Naomi for help.

"That card was very inappropriate. I don't even understand why you opened it," Naomi says, reprimanding me. "Send that e-mail now!"

"Okay, Naomi, thanks."

I hang up the phone and bring up Lance's e-mail titled, "I guess I won't see you this weekend." I hit the reply button, making it the title of my response. I eliminate the salutation ("Dear Lance") and I write:

> *I am getting the impression from your e-mails this week that you are misinterpreting my silence.*
>
> *The reason I have been silent is because there was nothing for me to say to you after your initial e-mail.*
>
> *If you want to date other women, that's your business, but there is something wrong with a married man who dates other women, and as I have found out, it is just as wrong for a woman to date a man who is married to someone else. As far as a friendship between you and me, I am not interested in that kind of a relationship.*
>
> *What is clear to me now, Lance, is being with you has made me realize what I do not want in a man. You have a lot of good qualities, but the kind of man that I want to end up with is one who is honest with himself, with God, and with others. I desire stability and exclusiveness in a relationship, and I revere a person with these qualities. I am not a person who wants to have any kind of competition.*
>
> *My birthday was not a tough day for me - it was a celebration. I had fun.*
>
> *I sincerely hope you will come to terms with who you really are, so it doesn't ruin every friendship and relationship you have down the road. Lynne*

I stare at my letter. I am terrified to hit the send button. What will he think? He will probably get defensive and challenge everything I said.

Why do I care how he feels? I have lost him anyway. Trembling, I hit the send button. I turn off the computer and go to bed.

Monday, October 29, 2001

I wake up early. I am afraid to check my e-mails. I know Lance has sent me a response. He is not the type of person who is going to accept my letter without a comeback.

Naomi had said to me, "You will get more e-mails from him. He will water down this whole thing."

How right she is.

I bravely log on to AOL. An e-mail pops up from Lance, titled, "Your e-mail to me." It is over two pages long.

> *Dear Lynne, A very well articulated e-mail, but some incorrect assessments, and a little cold and unlike the Lynne I have come to know.*

Lance's entire e-mail is defensive. He picks apart my response to him, line by line.

Regarding my telling him it was wrong for me to date a married man, he says:

> *Maybe I should have just not dated anyone, being that I am LEGALLY married. Is that how YOU live your life Lynne, ALWAYS doing the LEGAL thing? Sorry Lynne, but you know as well as I do, that God ordained our friendship, and it was just meant to be only friends, and that is what I have been to you and you to me.*

I cannot believe this. Did Lance not sweet talk me for six months, tell me he was "in love" with me and mention marriage more than once? And now he is saying we were meant to be only friends? He continues:

> *Here is what really upset me. You said 'being with you has made me realize what I do not want in a man. You have a lot of good qualities but the kind of man I want to end up with is one who is honest with himself, with God and others…'*
>
> *So what I gather here Lynne, is that you are saying I am NOT a man who is honest with himself, with God and others?*
>
> *And YOU always are? Tell me ONE way I have not been that way. Have any of us arrived? Or are we all in the process? Sorry again Lynne, that statement is very self-righteous on your part.*

I knew that line would upset him. What an ego-buster. I actually told him that being with him has made me realize what I do not want in a man. I am telling the truth here. He does not like it.

I feel a tad of satisfaction knowing I have ruffled his feathers. He continues:

> *What I sense Lynne, is anger from you. I sense someone who is not being completely honest with herself!*

Just like Lance to blame-shift and not be able to take being told the truth. How dishonest can he be? He adds:

> *YOU are hurt and you feel rejected and you are not facing it completely, but instead have resorted to shifting the fault to me, instead of just accepting the facts.*
>
> *I think you were doing better by remaining silent, because at least THAT was honest. And frankly rather than saying what you have in this e-mail you would have been better just e-mailing a brief response saying something like 'I am okay, all things considered, I would rather just not communicate at all for awhile.' THAT would have been honest Lynne, but to try and say I HAVE NOT been honest with God, others or myself is wrong and unfair. You will have to tell me now EXACTLY what you mean, or you owe me an apology.*

Lance's letter confirms to me how self-centered and egotistical he is. Is he giving me orders now to tell him "exactly" what I mean? I will not apologize to Lance for my honesty.

He is also upset about my stating, "I desire stability and exclusiveness in a relationship. I am not a person that wants to have any kind of competition." He writes:

> *And what makes you think I am any different? I am NOT looking to do the 'Solomon' thing, Lynne! I want exclusiveness in a relationship and I am not looking to put any woman I date into any kind of competition. Shame on you Lynne! You know me better than that.*

I think to myself, really? Yes, Lance I know you very well now, more than ever. You are a narcissistic bastard! Lance finishes by saying:

> *I value you and love you as a person and want you as a friend. If you can't handle that emotionally, I can understand but please*

don't turn this into a flaw in my character and integrity. I am not angry with you and know you are hurting. I am sorry I cannot be the one to comfort you. I have a lot to offer a woman, but just because I cannot be her lifetime exclusive partner doesn't mean we can't have a friendship.

He caps this e-mail off with a blockbuster ending. He writes:

I am really glad you were able to celebrate your birthday and have fun!
Lance

Lance's ego is bruised hearing my birthday was not a tough day for me, because of him.

I feel sick inside after reading his cruel words. I truly was in love with Lance.

I cannot turn off my feelings overnight. I start to cry, again. I am heartbroken. It has only been a week since Lance's letter, and the wounds are still fresh. I am not up to hearing him reiterate over and over that he does not love me and wants me as *only* a friend.

I forward Lance's response to Naomi. Later that evening, I talk with her on the telephone.

"I wish I had not e-mailed him," I say to Naomi. "His e-mail made me feel like crap."

"Your e-mail was great," Naomi says. "It was done in a right spirit and with clarity."

"I hope I don't hear from him again," I say.

"Oh, no way have you heard the last of him," Naomi says. "He has lost a good friend. You stated clearly you do not want a friendship with him."

Naomi is correct. The next day, Lance writes me again. The title of this e-mail is, "More comments on your e-mail." He writes:

Why Lynne? Why are you not interested in a friendship with me? What have I done to ruin our friendship? How have I NOT been a good friend to you? Tell me Lynne. The only thing I found wrong about us as a couple is that all that needs to be right in that type of relationship for me was and is not there. That puts you in the same category as every other woman I have ever known.

> *However, as for somebody that I enjoy being with, and that I have fun with, and love and care for as a friend, you are at the top of the list. NUMBER ONE!*

What a bastard! His e-mails are jabbing at my heart. Doesn't he get it? Any woman who is truly in love with a man is not going to be his buddy suddenly. And why tell me he has put me in a "category" with "every other woman he has ever known"? He continues:

> *I HONORED you Lynne, in our friendship/relationship and YOU honored me and we were good friends to each other, which I believe in time should be rekindled. I understand perfectly if that is hard for you to emotionally do. I think your feelings for me did become more than friends and I thought for a while that mine were going there too.*

I cannot believe him! He *thinks* my feelings for him were more than a friendship?

He is minimizing what we had for the last year and basically calling our relationship a friendship. He is denying the fact he called me his girlfriend on the Internet, slept with me, told me he loved me and dated me for a year.

He ends his patronizing epistle with:

> *Anyway, I still think about you and am concerned about your happiness. I was really glad to hear you had a good birthday. I am looking forward to the time when we can talk again on the phone, but to be considerate of your feelings, I am just waiting for the right time. When you feel up to it, share some more of your thoughts with me by e-mail. Please try not to let your emotions get in the way of your judgments. I care for you very much. Lance*

It will be a cold day in hell before I will ever talk to him again.

CHAPTER 55

Empowerment and Enlightenment

Friday, November 2, 2001

Two weeks have passed since I received Lance's "Dear John" letter. Today, he sends me a brief note:

I am thinking of calling you tomorrow. Is that going to be a problem?

I don't answer. He does not call.

Tuesday, November 6, 2001

I record in my journal: "I truly despise Lance. He looks down on me as if he has all this knowledge. I cannot stand his condescending attitude."

Sunday, November 18, 2001

Lance is back on the scene again almost two weeks later. I get an e-mail from him, titled "Hello." He writes:

Hi Lynne,
   I haven't heard from you in a long while and was wondering how you were doing? I am trying to give you time to process all that has transpired and wish we could still be friends. You must know my heart, Lynnie, I never wanted to hurt you. I just did not know

> myself as well as I had thought or hoped I did. I tried to take things slowly and one step at a time, but maybe I just steered us further into a relationship faster that I should have. I am sorry if I did, really! It was definitely NOT my intention.

How right he is. It was *him* who told me he was 'in love' with me in March. It was *him* who said "our relationship," *not* "friendship," had to be cherished, nourished, and flourished.

Then he suddenly cooled off overnight in April. I blame myself, not him, for allowing the relationship to continue. He adds:

> It has been a month now since I sent you the 'us' e-mail. I was hoping you would have come around a little faster to at least be pen pals with me.

"Pen pals"? I don't believe him. I am sure he has several female "pen pals" already. He concludes his e-mail with:

> For your information, I taught healing in the nursing home today, I love my job, and I am not seeing anybody in particular, just keeping the female relationships at the friendship level. Hope you are doing okay and looking forward to the holiday season.
> Lance [smiley added]

Lance's letters and his stinking smileys only add to my pain and slow the healing process. It infuriates me how he denies ever being "in love" with me. If he is so *honest*, he could at least admit he lead me to believe we had a romantic relationship.

"Delete his e-mails! Don't even read them!" Tony says to me.

Tony is right. Every time an e-mail from Lance pops up, I know it will upset me. However, I am not strong enough to keep myself from opening it. I know Lance thinks I will come around and eventually be friends with him.

Wednesday, December 26, 2001

I have not heard from Lance, except for a short greeting on Thanksgiving three weeks ago. It is a one-liner wishing my family and me a Happy Thanksgiving.

Today I receive a lengthy greeting titled "Hope you had a Merry Christmas and Happy New Year"

This cruel e-mail opens up a fresh wound. He writes:

> *I am sorry you have chosen this route to cut off communication with me. It has been over three months already and really, we only knew each other for a year.*

I can't believe what I am reading. "Only a year?" This was a year out of my life that I dedicated to him.

> *I would always welcome you as a friend but I guess YOU must have fallen "in love" with me, which makes "just" friendship very hard for you. Hasn't enough time passed?*
>
> *Also, I have a sense that a part of you thinks that if I am not with you at all for a period of time, I will come around and realize what I could have had. The problem with that is Lynne, I DO know what I could have had, and as much as there were many things I loved and want in a relationship that were there with us, it wasn't "in love" with you, and that never happened and I believe WOULD NOT and CANNOT happen.*

I burst into tears. He continues:

> *It is really a shame, though, that we cannot still continue a friendship, we had so many special moments together. It sort of diminishes their value by cutting off the friendship like this.*
>
> *Why don't you just try writing e-mails to me again for awhile as a pen pal, not every day but just here and there?*

Lance asks about my family. He also tells me about his Christmas with his cousins. He states it was one of his best Christmases he has had in a long time.

He ends with:

> *Well, share whatever you'd like. I hope to hear from you some time. I am interested. I care for you.*
> *Always,*
> *Lance*

He adds a P.S. on his unfeeling e-mail:

> *PS: Could you please mail me back my yellow silk shirt and a copy of the prints of the last pictures you took of us and the cats? Thanks!*

The yellow-silk shirt Lance had left with me after his visit in August is still hanging on the back of my bedroom door, washed, and ironed.

I recall what a nice time we had in Cooperstown that weekend and how he had mentioned a honeymoon in Hawaii while we sat at the lake. It had been a wonderful, romantic time. It was that weekend that he had promised to come back to see the fall foliage.

I cannot believe he is asking for a copy of the "last pictures" I took of him! That visit to New Jersey was horrendous.

I had forgotten I took some pictures of him and his cats while being ignored at his apartment. He does not know I threw them out in a hurtful rage right after he broke off the relationship.

Monday, December 31, 2001-New Year's Eve

I recall the New Year's Eve blow-up from a year ago and how upset I was. Ironically, Lance sends me an intimidating e-mail one year later on the exact same day.

The title of his e-mail is in bold, solid caps. It says: "I DON'T APPRECIATE YOU NOT READING MY E-MAILS." I am puzzled by this.

It must be that Lance thinks I haven't read his e-mail since I have not mailed the shirt back to him.

He writes:

> *I have requests of you. You have my shirt and pictures of mine. It would be nice to get them back, and MAYBE even hear from you! Hope you have a HAPPY NEW YEAR! Lance*

I fold up the yellow silk shirt. I place it in a large bubbled envelope and send it to him "Return receipt requested."

On January 9, 2002, I receive an e-mail titled "The Shirt and the Pictures." He writes:

> *Hi Lynne,*
> *Thanks for the shirt. It looks great. You did a nice ironing job. But Lynne, I really want those pictures you took of the cat too, actually a set of all the pictures would be nice, but at least the ones you took of me and the cats, would really be nice to have.*

He does not care about any pictures of him and me; just himself and the cats.

Also, he cannot believe I will not correspond with him. He continues:

> *Why are you being so stubborn about talking to me? It isn't making me feel better about you at all, in fact it is causing me to lose some respect for you, and the longer you choose to be silent now with me the less I feel fond for you.*
> *It has been almost three months and we only went out for a year.*
> *The more I am apart from you, the more I realize that our going out was something I needed at the time and I think I was someone you needed at the time. WE had a wonderful friendship only I was wrong thinking there was something romantic between us or that there could be. I was infatuated Lynne, very infatuated.*
> *I am sorry. Why can't you forgive me for making an innocent mistake?*

I cannot believe he is minimizing our relationship and calling his behavior and mixed signals the last few months an "innocent mistake."

What he doesn't get is that I want *nothing* to do with him. And does he expect me to care that he is "less fond of me?"

He ends his e-mail with:

> *I want to move on, but I feel we do not have proper closure. Either we should remain as friends or you should be honest with about why we can't be.*
> *Please at least send me the pics. Thanks, Lance*

I realize Lance still has power over me.

Tony screams at me. "Block him, Lynne, so he cannot e-mail you any more!"

What keeps me wanting to hear from him when his e-mails emphasize we can never be more than "just friends"? Why can't I let go?

I know it is over. I have to stop reading his e-mails.

I get one more e-mail from him before the end of 2001. He states:

> *Isn't it about time you stopped this little game of silence and acted like the friends we supposedly were? I am starting NOT to appreciate it!*
>
> *I ALWAYS respected you and treated you decently, you cannot deny that, but now I do not feel like I am being respected in return. Enough is enough, don't you think?*

I do not respond. Lance did not treat me "decently" the last time I saw him.

Saturday, February 2, 2002

I have not heard from Lance for a few weeks.

Tony and I are on a train from New York State to Florida. We arrive in Fort Lauderdale this day.

Tony will be joining his brother and going on a cruise for a week. I will be staying at a hotel on the beach by myself. I need this getaway.

I have several days to walk along the shore, sit in the sun, read, journal, and browse the gift shops.

I discover who my best friend is; me! I love the solitude.

It suddenly occurs to me I have not thought about Lance for five days! My focus is changing.

Saturday, February 9, 2002

It is early evening. I stand on the beach, looking at the ocean. The sunset casts a pink-orange reflection on the waves. A few seagulls hover over the water.

What is different?

I no longer feel lonely and empty. I sense not only calmness, but also a feeling of strength. The saying "time heals" is very true. I have had time to process my feelings for Lance, along with my behavior.

I realize I was also at fault during my one-year courtship with Lance.

I wonder how I could have been so blind. Perhaps I was weak in hanging on so long. That was all I knew then. My heart was in the right place, and I allowed it to override my common sense.

I know now that my life does not have to be hard unless I choose to make it that way. I am no longer embarrassed. I am empowered and enlightened.

Thursday, February 14, 2002 - Valentine's Day

I return home from my Florida trip.

I check my e-mail. Lance has sent me an online valentine. It is a "Friendship card."

He includes a personal message written in the center of a heart. He writes:

> *Get over it Lynne and let's be friends! It's been four months! I am sure life must be good for you in the post Lancecat era.*
>
> *You know my wife has totally forgiven me for everything I have done and is being real sweet to me. She and I are good friends now. It would be nice if you would be my friend too!*
>
> *I hope you have met someone. I would be happy for you. Lance*

His wife is now his friend. I think to myself "how nice."

I go into the privacy setting on my computer and block Lance's screen name. From now on, any e-mails he sends me will be returned to him stating he has been blocked.

I realize the error of my ways. I reclaim my life, and I no longer need Lance to interfere. God has been with me all along. He understands my shortcomings and mistakes. This horrific journey has finally come to an end, and I am able to find peace.

Lance can't hurt me any more because he no longer exists. It is now time for me.

EPILOGUE

There is such a fine line between love and hate. The raw pain one feels from being dumped by the love of his or her life can cause hatred, anger, bitterness, and resentment. Yet, we are still in love with our rejecter. How twisted is this?

Like a moth to the flame, I hovered around Lance, hoping to connect with him. Ultimately, in the end, I got burned.

Lance told tell me he was in love with me six months into the relationship. I believed him. Then in his "Dear John" letter he said he was never "in love" with me.

I chose to torture myself for months by staying in the relationship. I was afraid to ask Lance about his feelings, because I knew my worst fears would be realized if I did. It wasn't until after the breakup that I came to terms with Lance's true character.

When you lose respect for someone, you cannot love them any more. I have no respect for Lance.

In August of 2003, almost two years after I blocked Lance from writing to me on the Internet, he sent me two lengthy letters using another screen name.

He stated he did not understand why we could not be friends, especially since so much time had passed. He reiterated, though, that it could never be more than a "friendship," but he wanted me to know I was "special."

I did not answer either of these letters.

Lance does not like the fact that there is one woman on this earth who wants nothing to do with him. He thought I would "come around" some day and be his friend.

He also contacted me on my birthday in 2004, exactly three years after the "Dear John" letter stating he still wished we could be friends, although he is sorry it "can't be more."

He is so narcisisstic that he fears I will think his contacting me means he wants to resume the relationship.

When he did not hear back from me in 2004, he e-mailed my sister, Lea, asking her if she could let him know why I was not responding to his e-mails. Lea did not answer his letter.

To date, I have had no contact with Lance.

Lance still occasionally sends me cute little holiday forwards and spiritual messages. He sends these e-mails to me as an "undisclosed recipient," meaning he does not want me to see other women on his mailing list.

Lance likes the thrill of the chase. Once the challenge is gone, he starts looking for someone else.

My message for anyone searching the Internet for that "special someone" is to be very cautious.

If you give your heart and soul to a person and sense you are not getting back what you are contributing to the relationship, you need to evaluate the situation. Please don't hang on and let it drag the way I did. Time is precious.

What I learned from this experience is how much we rationalize what we do in life to satisfy our hunger. Never settle for crumbs in a relationship. We are all worth more than that.

You don't get stronger and then face things. You face things and then get stronger. I should have faced the fact that Lance wanted out of the relationship months before it ended.

It is important that intimacy be expressed in a relationship. People like Lance avoid intimacy. He wants to string women on, because it makes him feel powerful. This man cannot love. He is incapable of loving anyone except himself.

I believe by cutting Lance off from all contact, I showed him what honesty really is. I did this for myself. By *not* communicating with him, I took my power back and kept my dignity.

We want the truth to reign. The truth is I cannot be connected to a person who lacks character.

Lance's cruel e-mails after the breakup were disguised as caring and only added to my pain and made it harder for me to heal. I should not have opened them, but at the time, I was not strong enough.

Lance is not a fictional character. He is presently on the Internet. He has several ads under different screen names and on different sites. Beware, Lance is a predator!

Lance will never change. He will always perpetuate the same pattern and will never stay with one woman. He "needs" to have many women in his life to feed his low self-esteem. He is indeed a "Solomon." He does not want just "one woman."

Ladies, be careful. You do not want to fall in love with this man.

ABOUT THE AUTHOR

Lynne Epstein is passionate about encouraging empowerment in women by sharing her experiences in writing. She has published two articles. She also served as an editorial assistant for film book author Tony Villecco on the release of his book "Silent Stars Speak" which was published by McFarland & Company in 2001. She was formerly employed by the NYS Department of Disability Determinations full time before leaving her employment in 2003 to move to another state.

She has now returned to her home state of New York and is pursuing a career in writing. She is a certified aerobics instructor. She is also a theatre student at Broome Community College, Binghamton, NY and has taken numerous acting courses and performed in several plays. She loves to travel, her two favorite places being New York City (it's magical) and Florida (loves beaches and palm trees).

When she is not writing or doing aerobics she loves to travel with her husband, Larry. She also enjoys reading, the movies and feeding the birds and critters who reside outside her kitchen window. **Visit her online at** LyEpstein@aol.com.

Printed in the United States
85751LV00004B/1-99/A